SOUL EATER

1

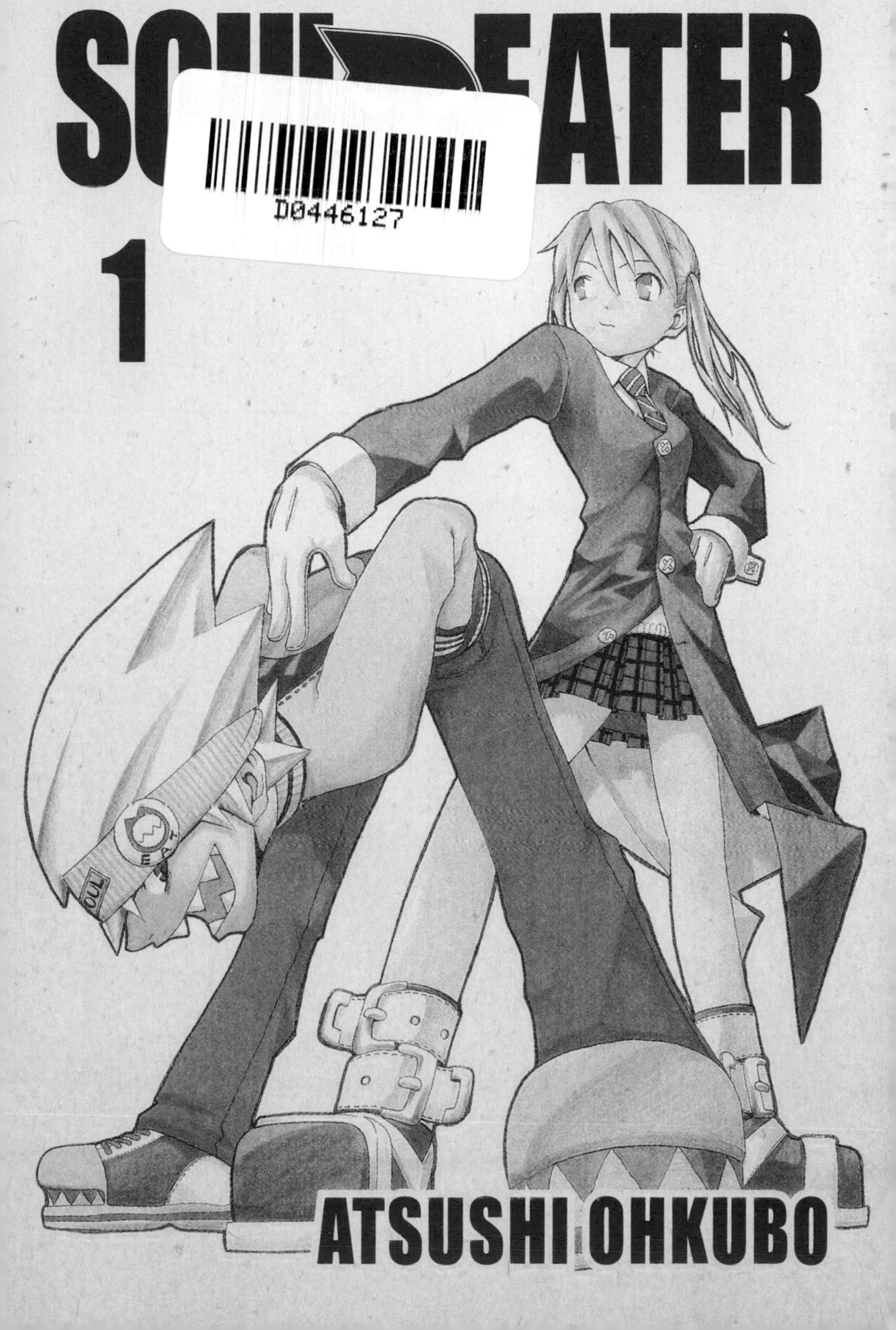

ATSUSHI OHKUBO

SOUL EATER

vol. 1
by ATSUSHI OHKUBO

Listen to the Beat of the SOUL

CONTENTS

PROLOGUE 1: SOUL EATER

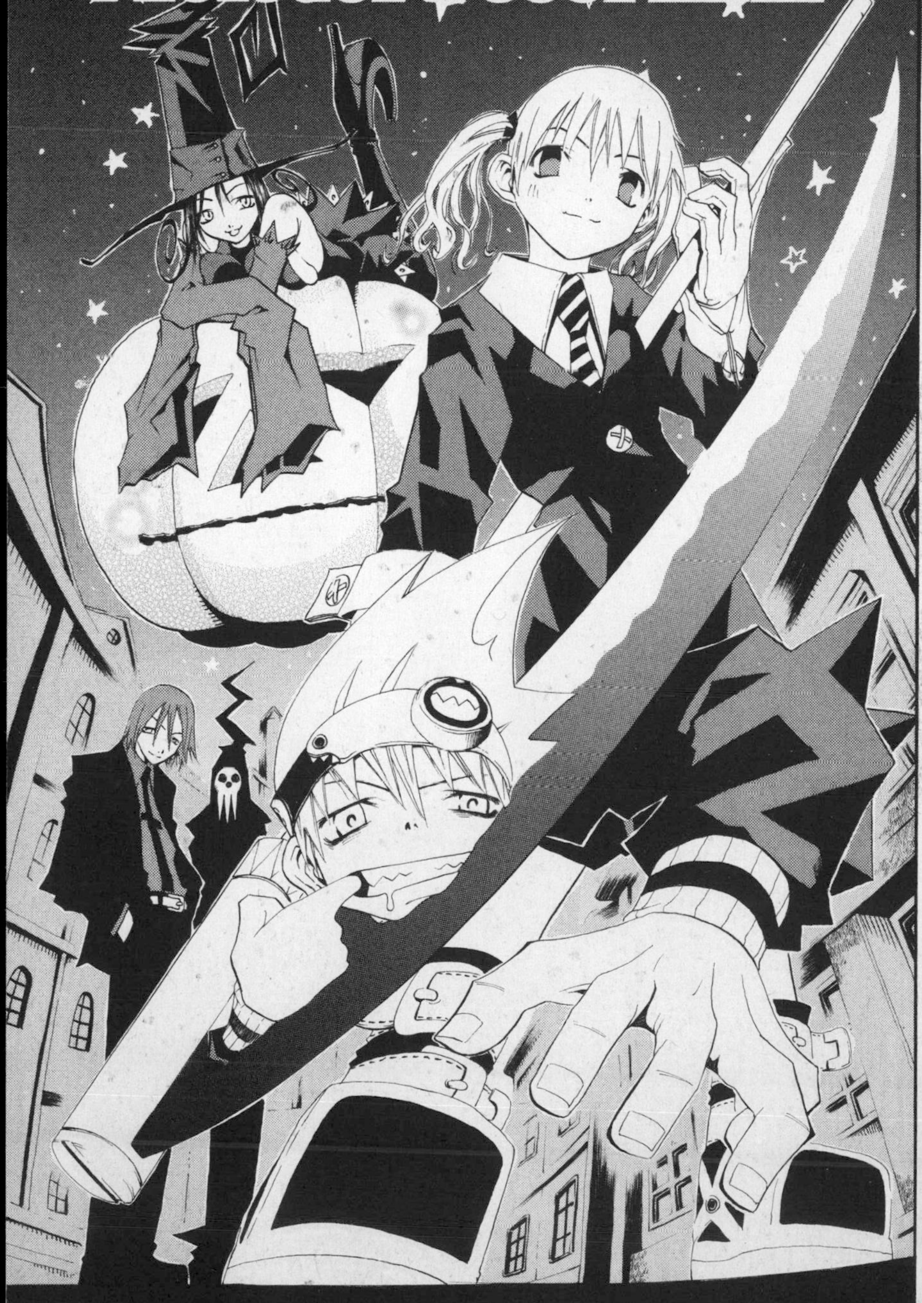

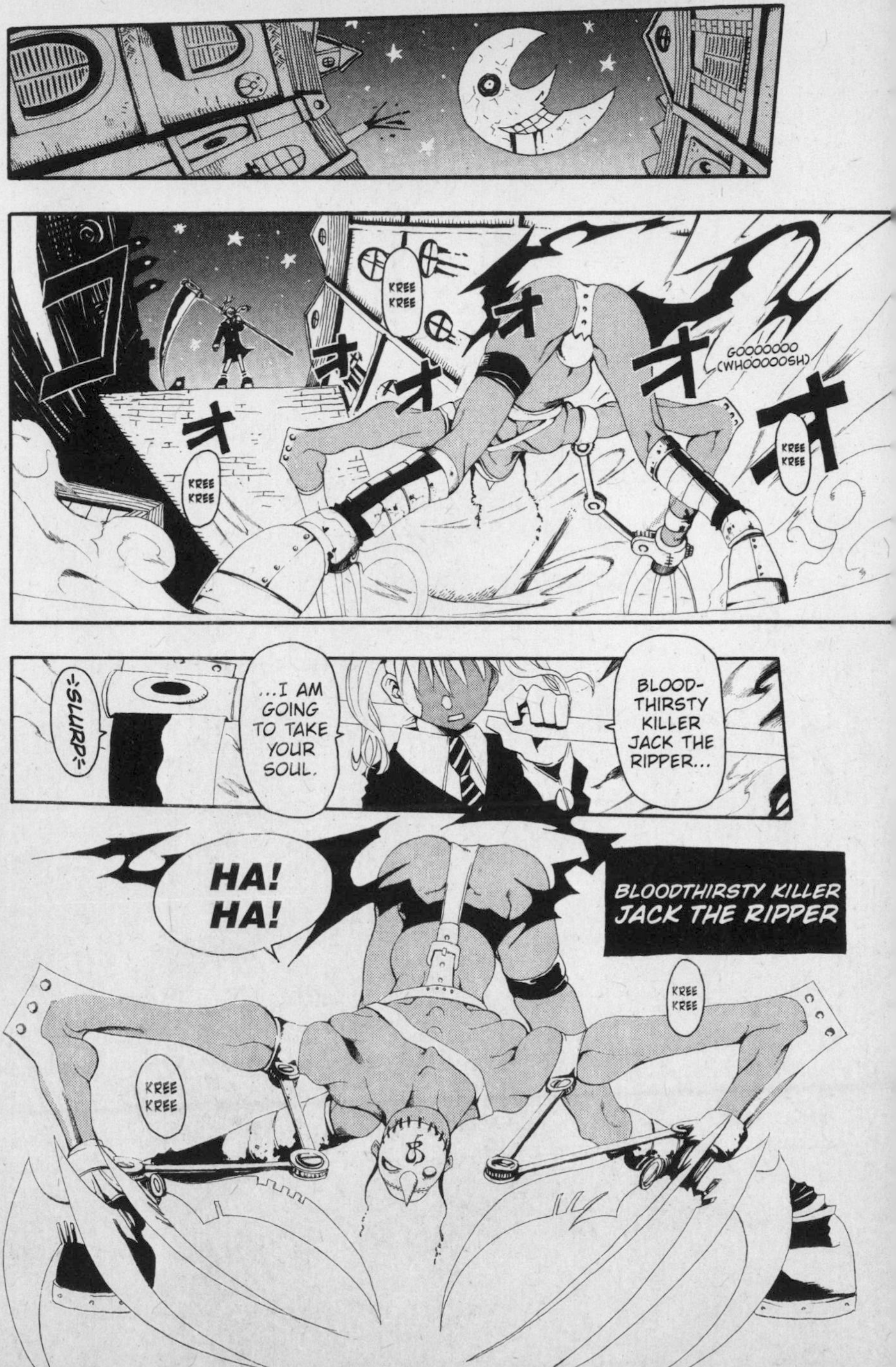
GOOOOOOO (WHOOOOOSH)
KREE KREE
KREE KREE
KREE KREE
BLOOD-THIRSTY KILLER JACK THE RIPPER...
...I AM GOING TO TAKE YOUR SOUL.
SLURP
BLOODTHIRSTY KILLER JACK THE RIPPER
KREE KREE
HA! HA!
KREE KREE

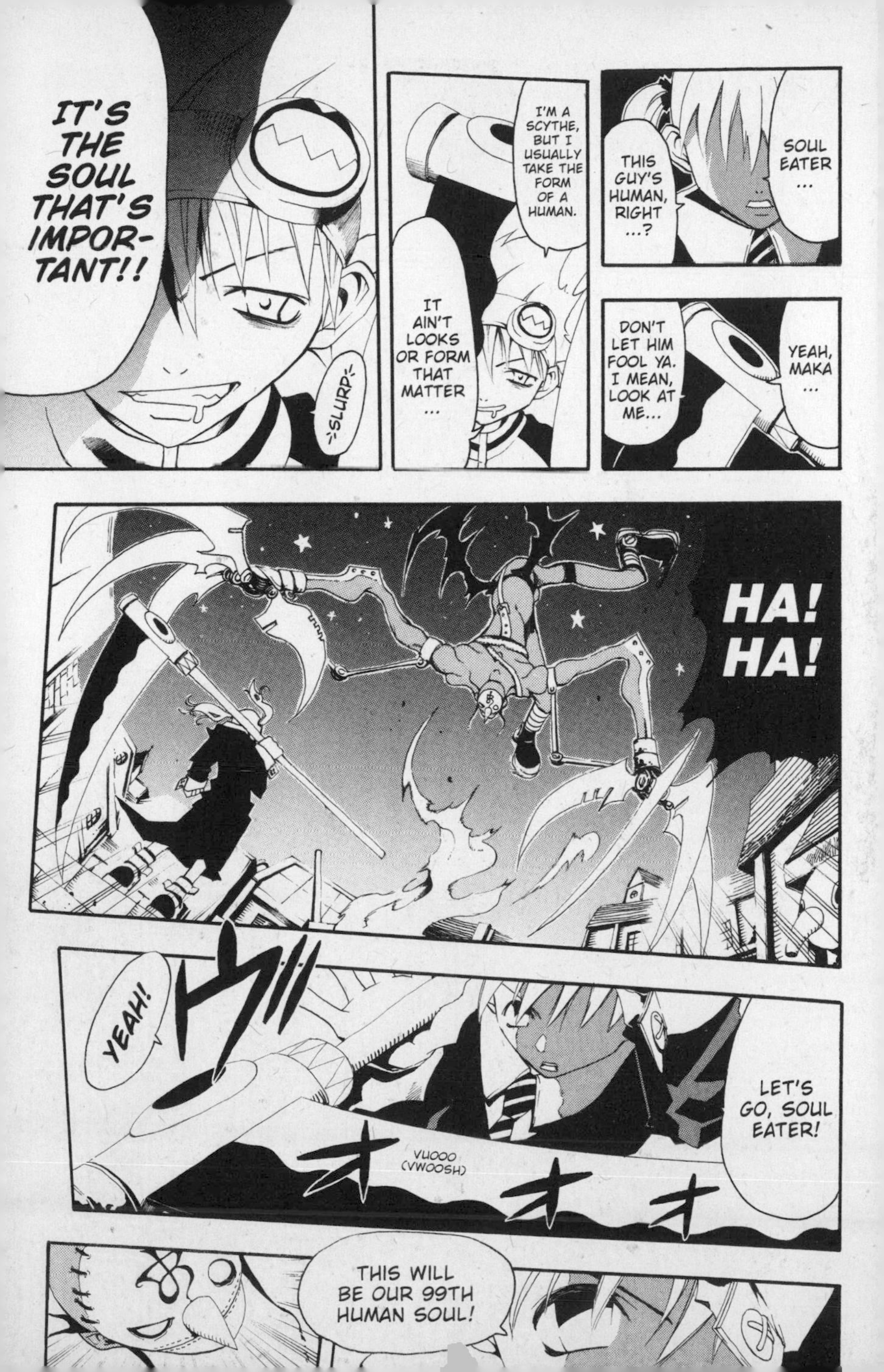
SOUL EATER ...
THIS GUY'S HUMAN, RIGHT ...?
YEAH, MAKA ...
DON'T LET HIM FOOL YA. I MEAN, LOOK AT ME...
I'M A SCYTHE, BUT I USUALLY TAKE THE FORM OF A HUMAN.
IT AIN'T LOOKS OR FORM THAT MATTER ...
IT'S THE SOUL THAT'S IMPORTANT!!
SLURP
HA! HA!
LET'S GO, SOUL EATER!
VUOOO (VWOOSH)
YEAH!
THIS WILL BE OUR 99TH HUMAN SOUL!

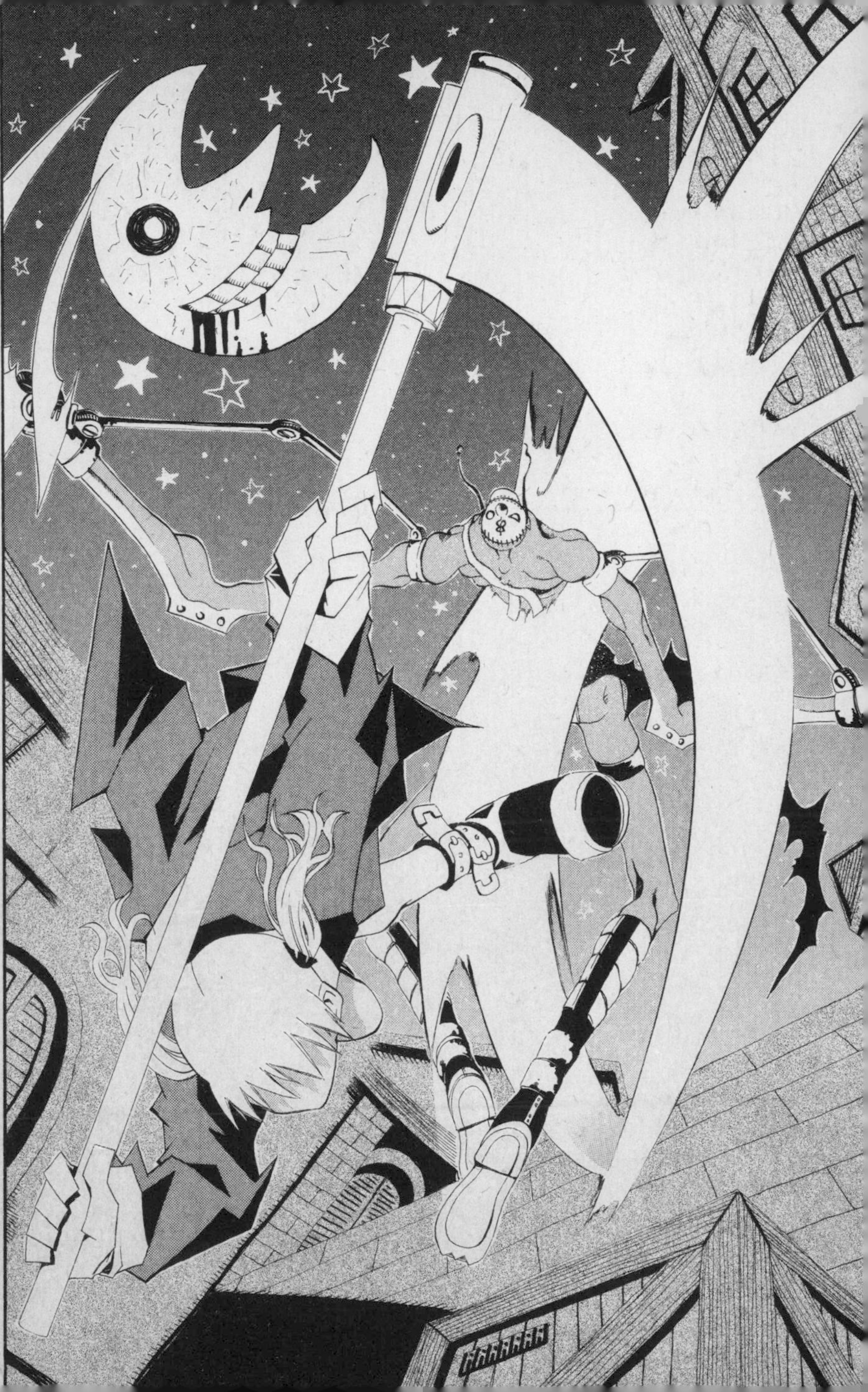

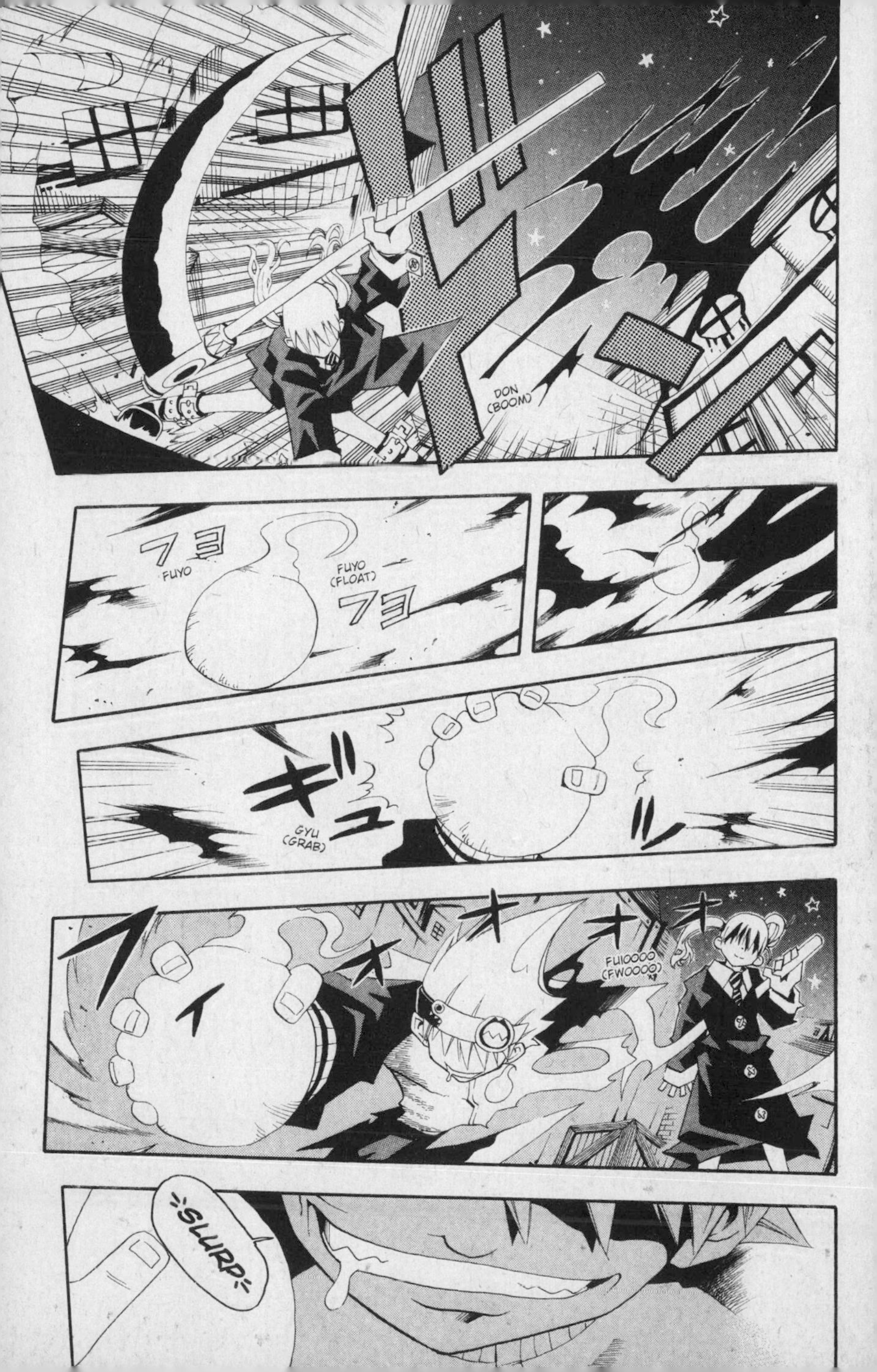
DON
(BOOM)
FUYO
(FLOAT)
FUYO
GYU
(GRAB)
FUIOOOO
(FWOOOO)
SLURP

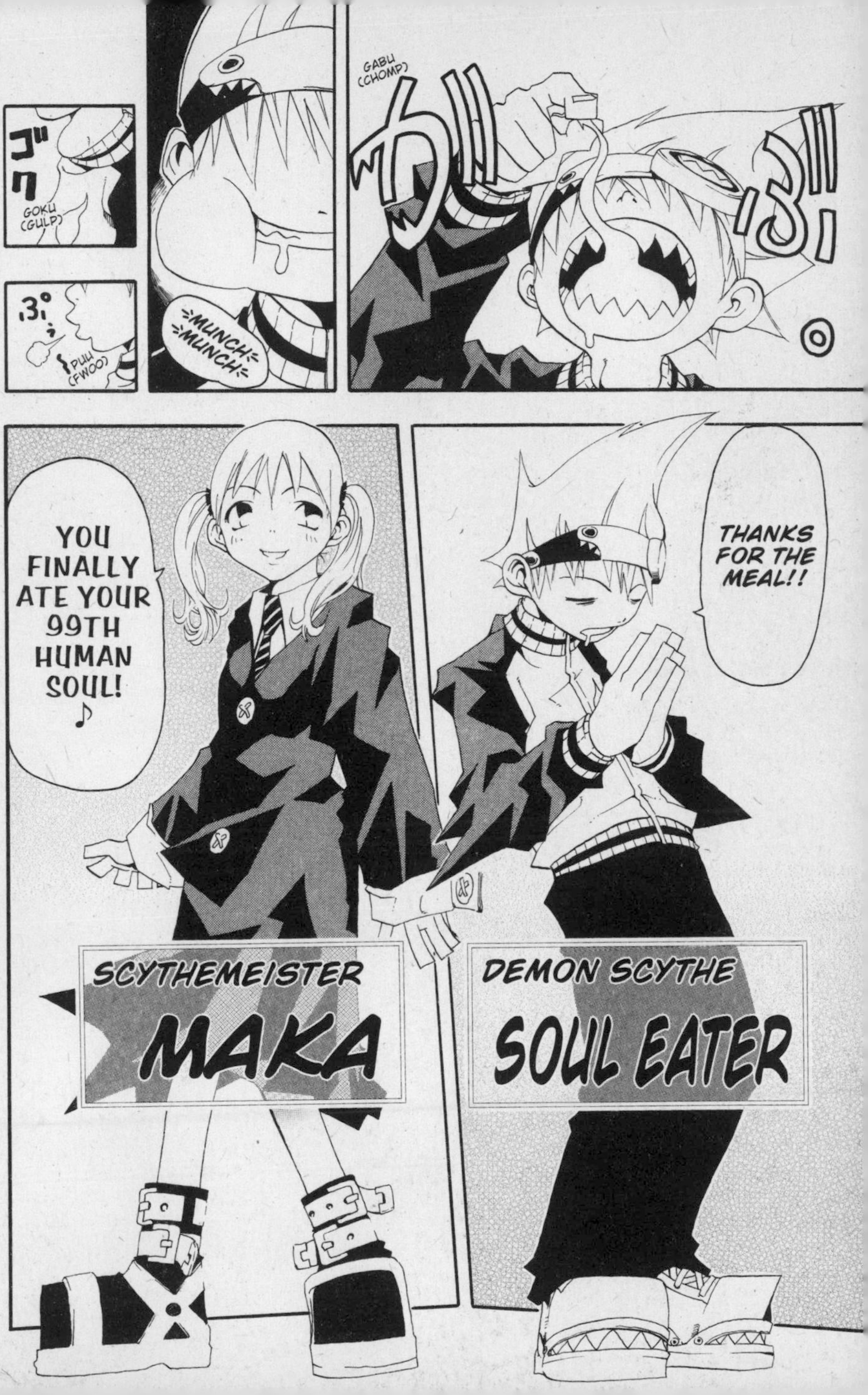

GABU (CHOMP)
MUNCH MUNCH
ゴク
GOKU (GULP)
PUU (FWOO)
THANKS FOR THE MEAL!!
DEMON SCYTHE
SOUL EATER
YOU FINALLY ATE YOUR 99TH HUMAN SOUL! ♪
SCYTHEMEISTER
MAKA

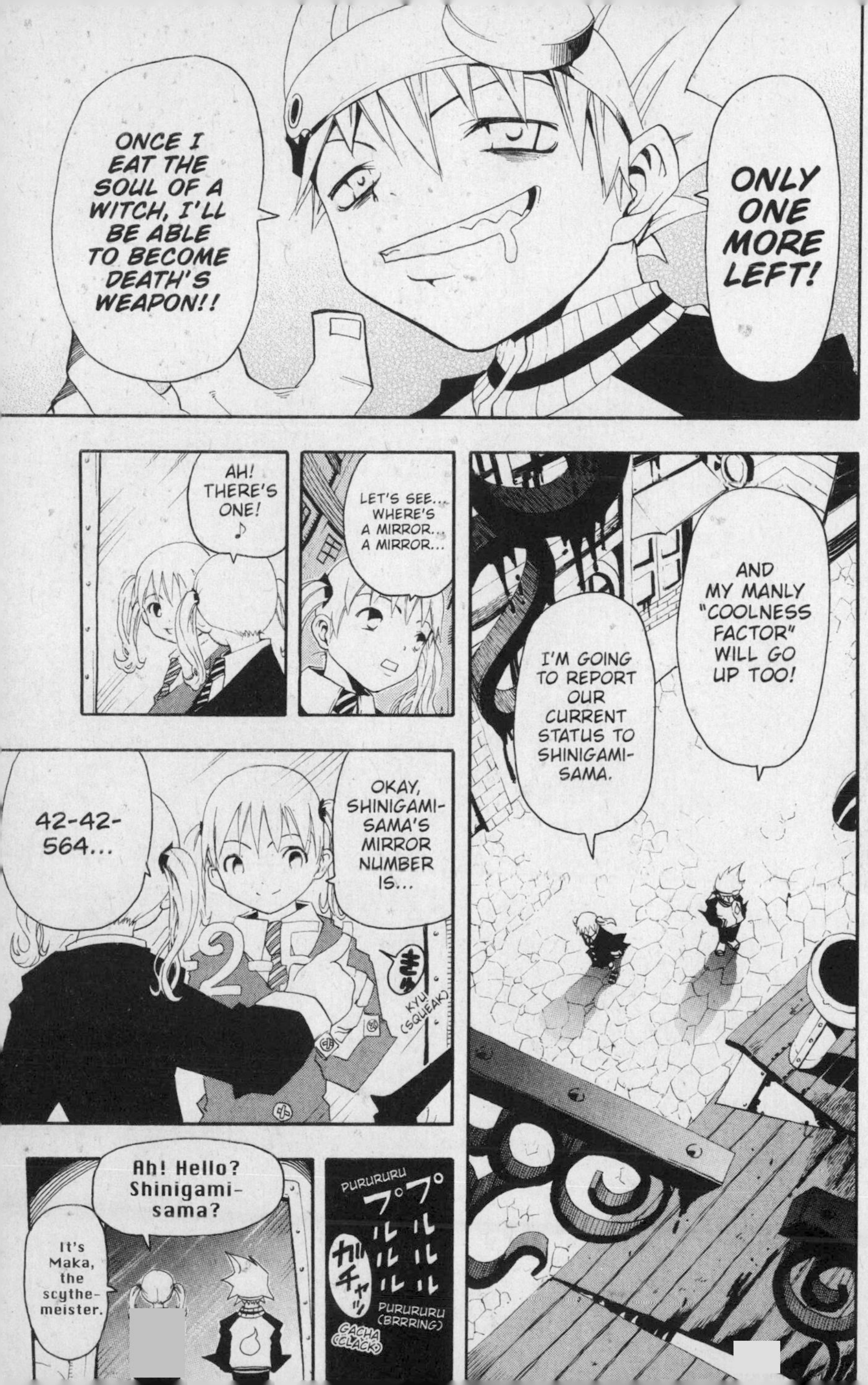
ONLY ONE MORE LEFT!
ONCE I EAT THE SOUL OF A WITCH, I'LL BE ABLE TO BECOME DEATH'S WEAPON!!
AND MY MANLY "COOLNESS FACTOR" WILL GO UP TOO!
I'M GOING TO REPORT OUR CURRENT STATUS TO SHINIGAMI-SAMA.
LET'S SEE... WHERE'S A MIRROR... A MIRROR...
AH! THERE'S ONE! ♪
OKAY, SHINIGAMI-SAMA'S MIRROR NUMBER IS...
きゅ
KYU (SQUEAK)
42-42-564...
プルルル
PURURURU
プルルル
PURURURU (BRRRING)
ガチャッ
GACHA (CLACK)
Ah! Hello? Shinigami-sama?
It's Maka, the scythe-meister.

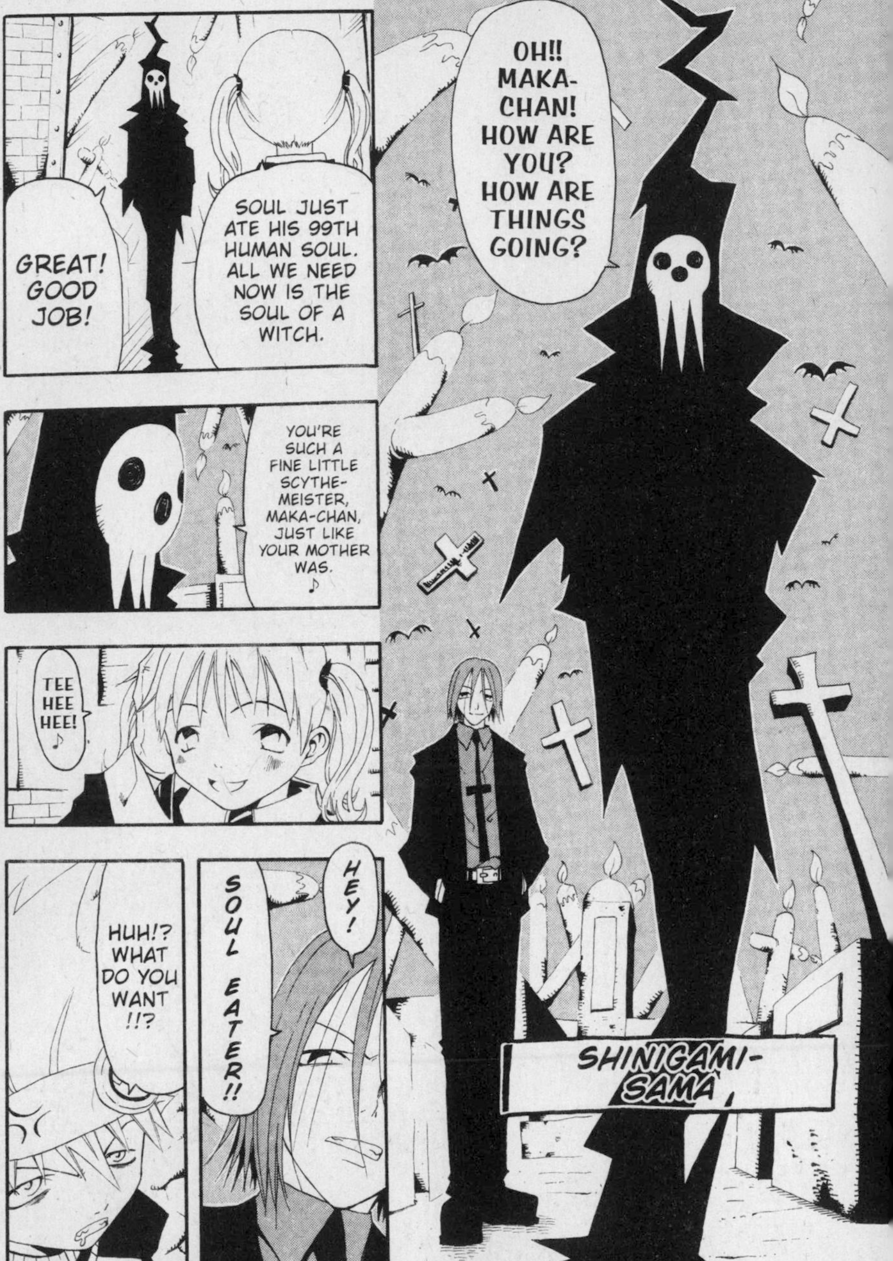
OH!! MAKA-CHAN! HOW ARE YOU? HOW ARE THINGS GOING?
SHINIGAMI-SAMA
SOUL JUST ATE HIS 99TH HUMAN SOUL. ALL WE NEED NOW IS THE SOUL OF A WITCH.
GREAT! GOOD JOB!
YOU'RE SUCH A FINE LITTLE SCYTHE-MEISTER, MAKA-CHAN, JUST LIKE YOUR MOTHER WAS. ♪
TEE HEE HEE! ♪
HEY!
SOUL EATER!!
HUH!? WHAT DO YOU WANT!!?

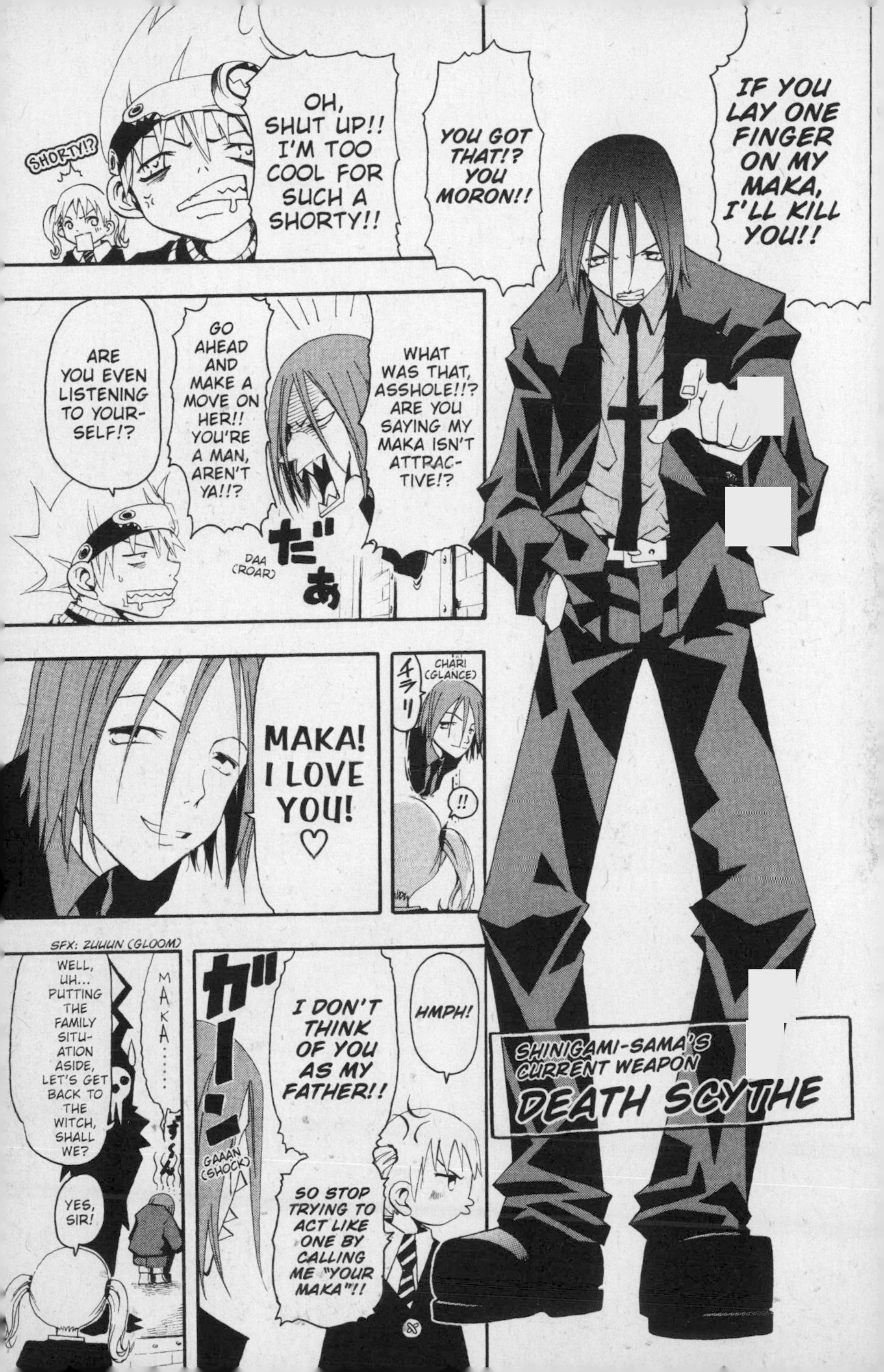
IF YOU LAY ONE FINGER ON MY MAKA, I'LL KILL YOU!!
SHINIGAMI-SAMA'S CURRENT WEAPON
DEATH SCYTHE
YOU GOT THAT!? YOU MORON!!
OH, SHUT UP!! I'M TOO COOL FOR SUCH A SHORTY!!
SHORTY!?
WHAT WAS THAT, ASSHOLE!!? ARE YOU SAYING MY MAKA ISN'T ATTRAC-TIVE!?
だあ
DAA (ROAR)
GO AHEAD AND MAKE A MOVE ON HER!! YOU'RE A MAN, AREN'T YA!!?
ARE YOU EVEN LISTENING TO YOUR-SELF!?
CHARI (GLANCE)
!!
MAKA! I LOVE YOU! ♡
HMPH!
I DON'T THINK OF YOU AS MY FATHER!!
GAAAN (SHOCK)
SO STOP TRYING TO ACT LIKE ONE BY CALLING ME "YOUR MAKA"!!
SFX: ZUUUN (GLOOM)
MAKA......
WELL, UH... PUTTING THE FAMILY SITU-ATION ASIDE, LET'S GET BACK TO THE WITCH, SHALL WE?
YES, SIR!

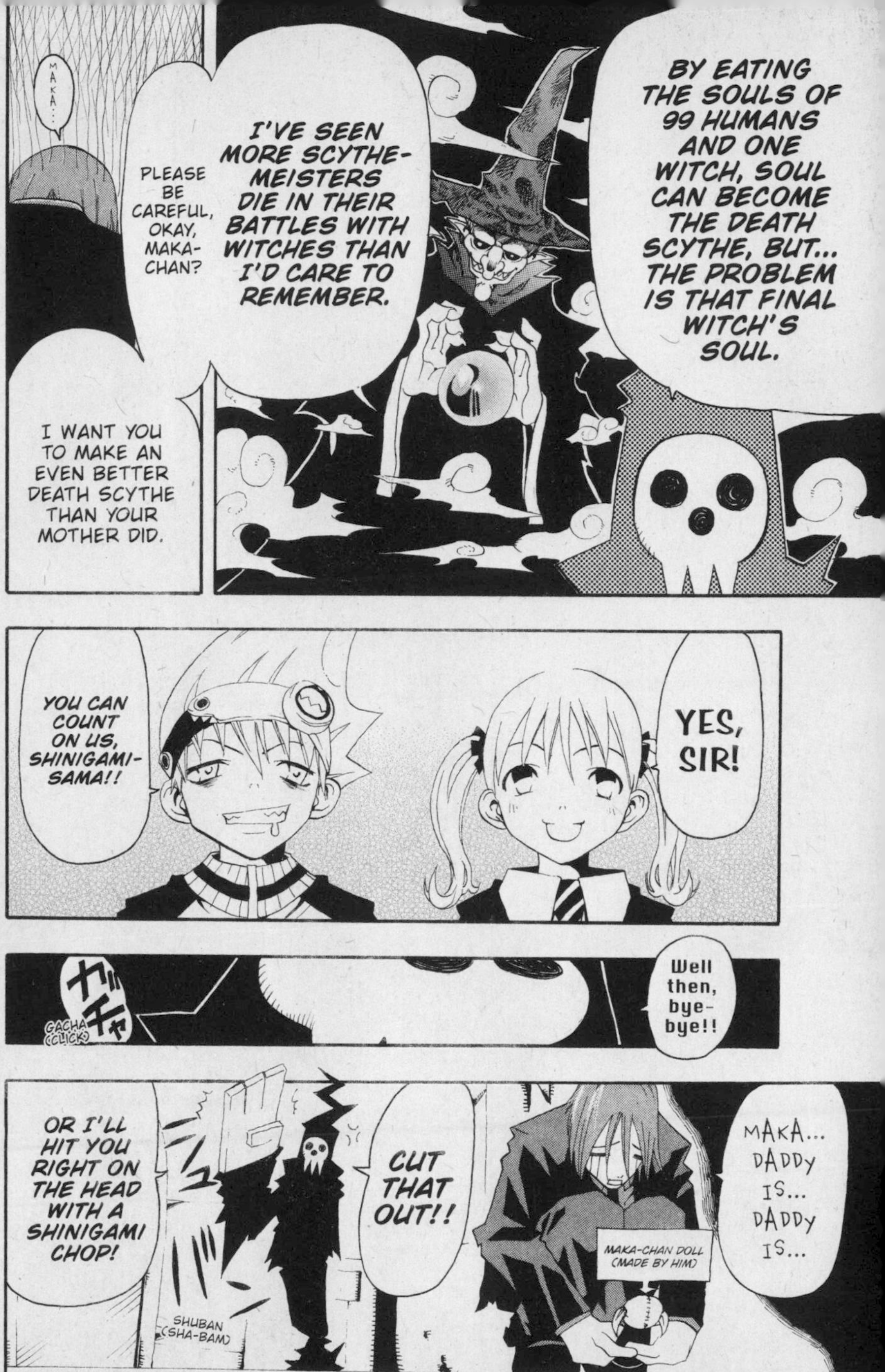
BY EATING THE SOULS OF 99 HUMANS AND ONE WITCH, SOUL CAN BECOME THE DEATH SCYTHE, BUT... THE PROBLEM IS THAT FINAL WITCH'S SOUL.
I'VE SEEN MORE SCYTHE-MEISTERS DIE IN THEIR BATTLES WITH WITCHES THAN I'D CARE TO REMEMBER.
PLEASE BE CAREFUL, OKAY, MAKA-CHAN?
MAKA...
I WANT YOU TO MAKE AN EVEN BETTER DEATH SCYTHE THAN YOUR MOTHER DID.
YES, SIR!
YOU CAN COUNT ON US, SHINIGAMI-SAMA!!
Well then, bye-bye!!
カチャ
GACHA (CLICK)
MAKA... DADDY IS... DADDY IS...
MAKA-CHAN DOLL (MADE BY HIM)
CUT THAT OUT!!
OR I'LL HIT YOU RIGHT ON THE HEAD WITH A SHINIGAMI CHOP!
SHUBAN (SHA-BAM)

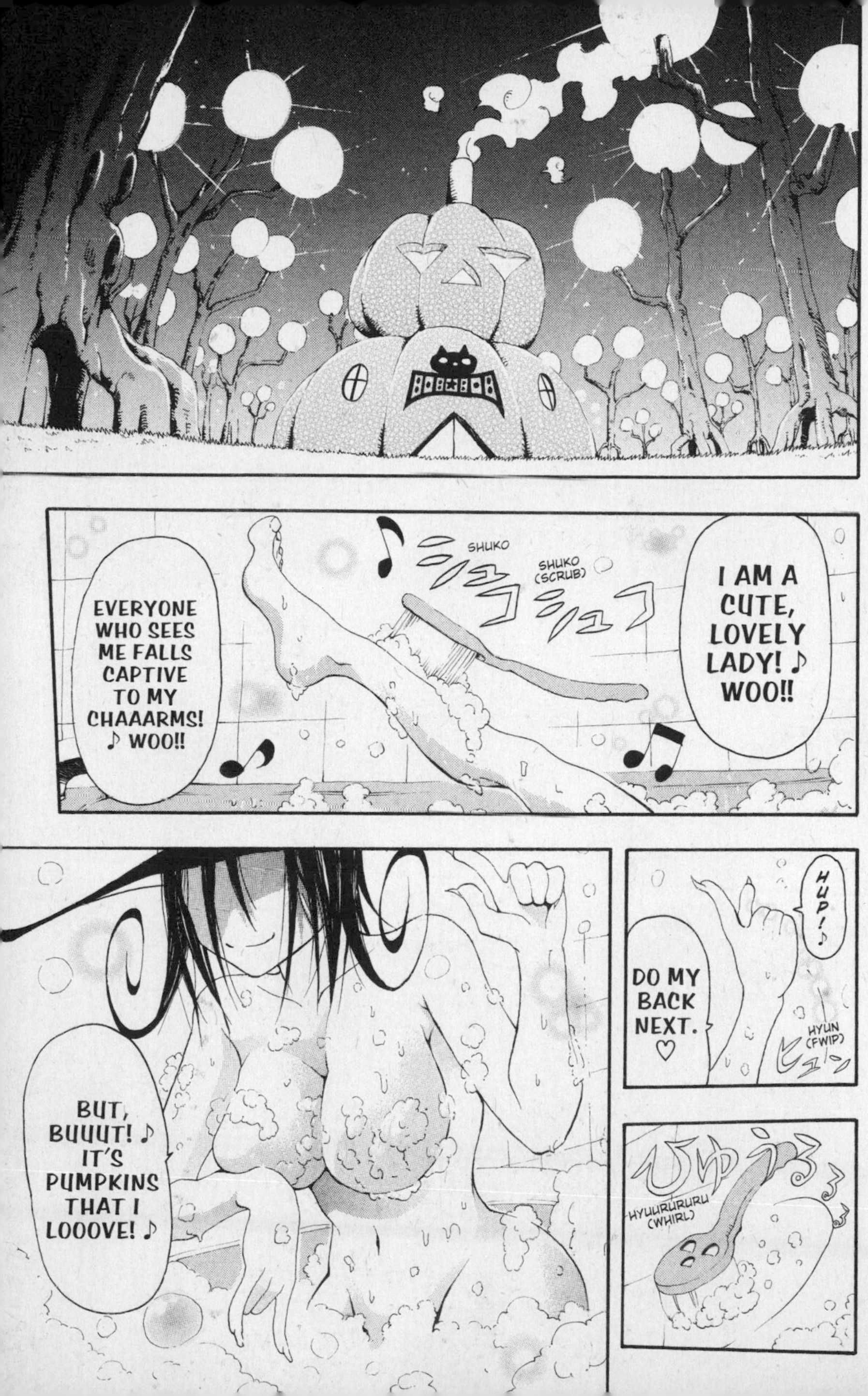
I AM A CUTE, LOVELY LADY! ♪ WOO!!
SHUKO (SCRUB)
SHUKO
EVERYONE WHO SEES ME FALLS CAPTIVE TO MY CHAAARMS! ♪ WOO!!
HUP! ♪
DO MY BACK NEXT. ♡
HYUN (FWIP)
HYUURURURU (WHIRL)
BUT, BUUUT! ♪ IT'S PUMPKINS THAT I LOOOVE! ♪

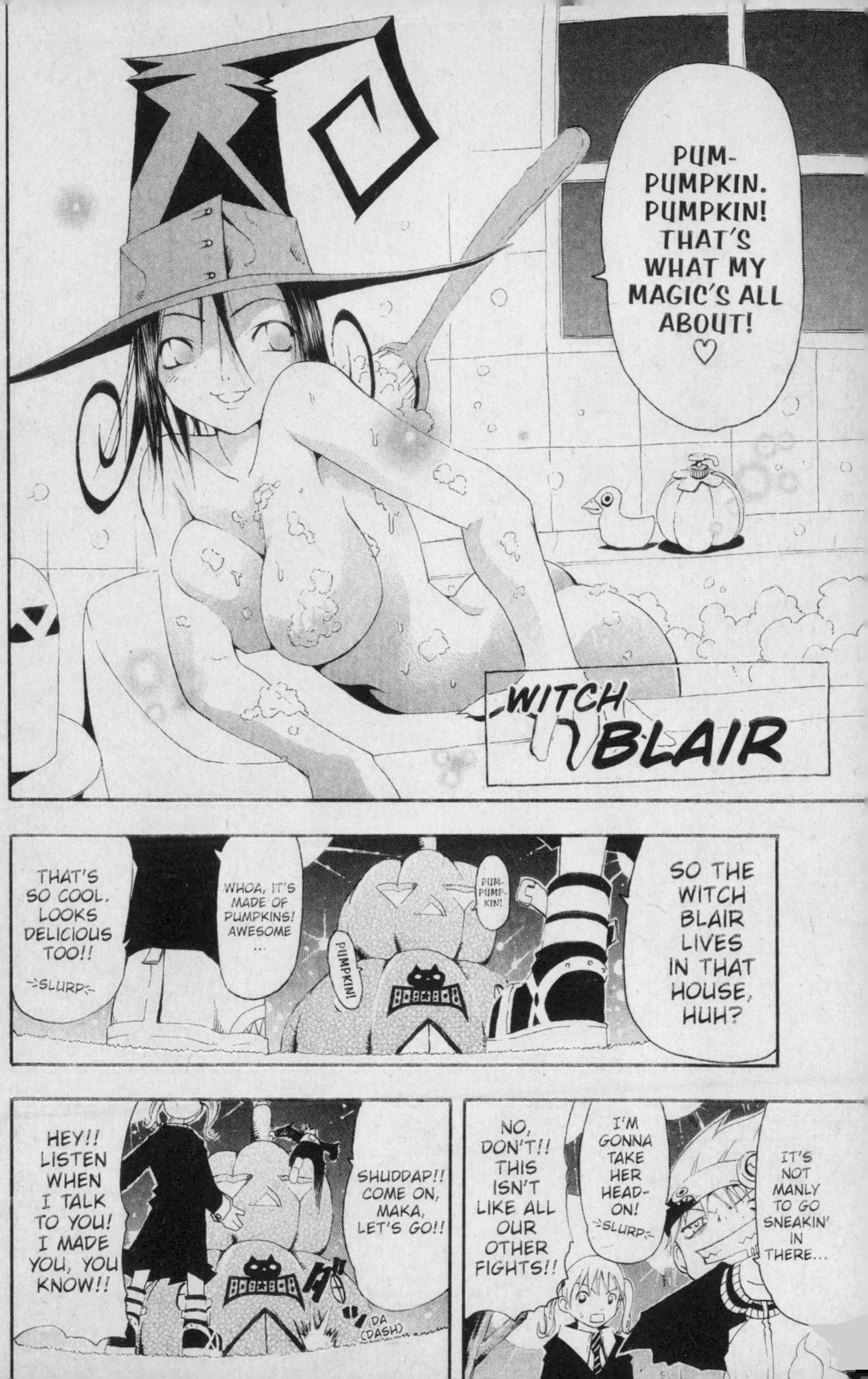

PUM-PUMPKIN. PUMPKIN! THAT'S WHAT MY MAGIC'S ALL ABOUT! ♡
WITCH BLAIR
SO THE WITCH BLAIR LIVES IN THAT HOUSE, HUH?
PUM-PUMPKIN!
PUMPKIN!
WHOA, IT'S MADE OF PUMPKINS! AWESOME ...
THAT'S SO COOL. LOOKS DELICIOUS TOO!!
SLURP
IT'S NOT MANLY TO GO SNEAKIN' IN THERE...
I'M GONNA TAKE HER HEAD-ON!
SLURP
NO, DON'T!! THIS ISN'T LIKE ALL OUR OTHER FIGHTS!!
SHUDDAP!! COME ON, MAKA, LET'S GO!!
HEY!! LISTEN WHEN I TALK TO YOU! I MADE YOU, YOU KNOW!!
DA (DASH)

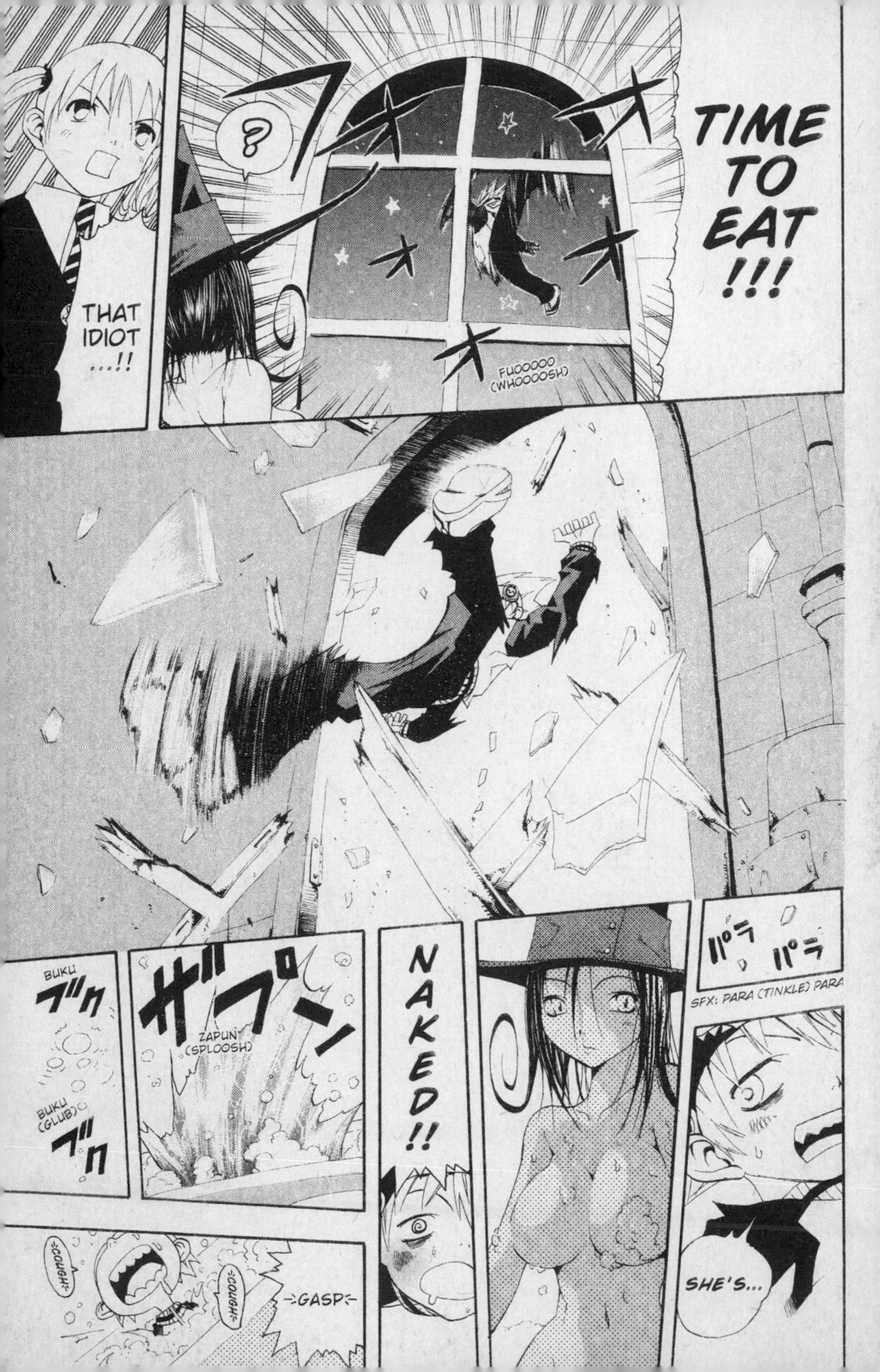
TIME TO EAT!!!
?
FUOOOOO (WHOOOOSH)
THAT IDIOT ...!!
パラ パラ
SFX: PARA (TINKLE) PARA
SHE'S...
NAKED!!
ZAPUN (SPLOOSH)
BUKU
BUKU (GLUB)
-COUGH-
-COUGH-
-GASP-

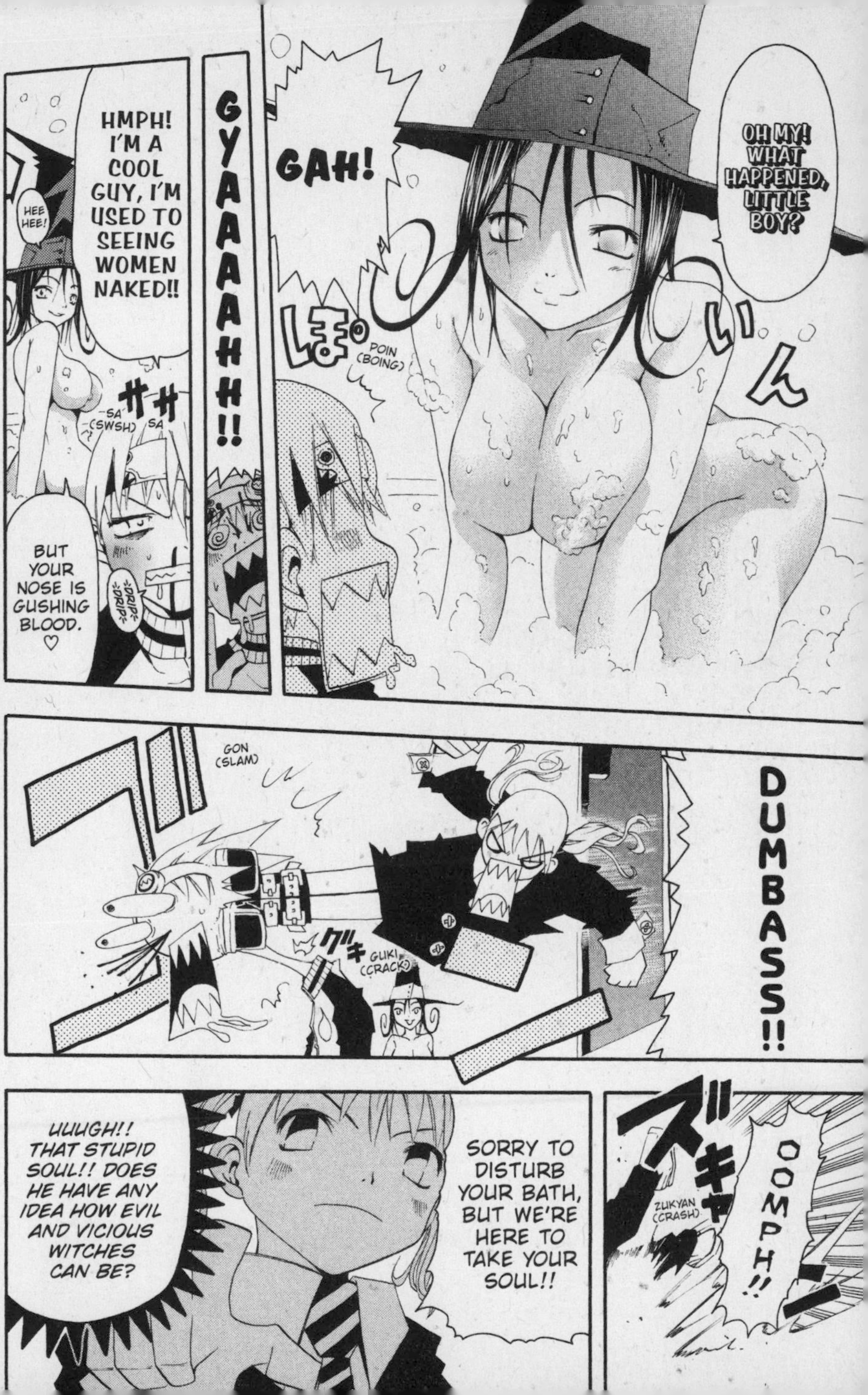

OH MY! WHAT HAPPENED, LITTLE BOY?
GAH!
POIN (BOING)
GYAAAAAHH!!
HMPH! I'M A COOL GUY, I'M USED TO SEEING WOMEN NAKED!!
HEE HEE!
SA SA (SWSH)
BUT YOUR NOSE IS GUSHING BLOOD. ♡
DRIP DRIP
DUMBASS!!
GON (SLAM)
GUKI (CRACK)
OOMPH!!
ZUKYAN (CRASH)
SORRY TO DISTURB YOUR BATH, BUT WE'RE HERE TO TAKE YOUR SOUL!!
UUUGH!! THAT STUPID SOUL!! DOES HE HAVE ANY IDEA HOW EVIL AND VICIOUS WITCHES CAN BE?

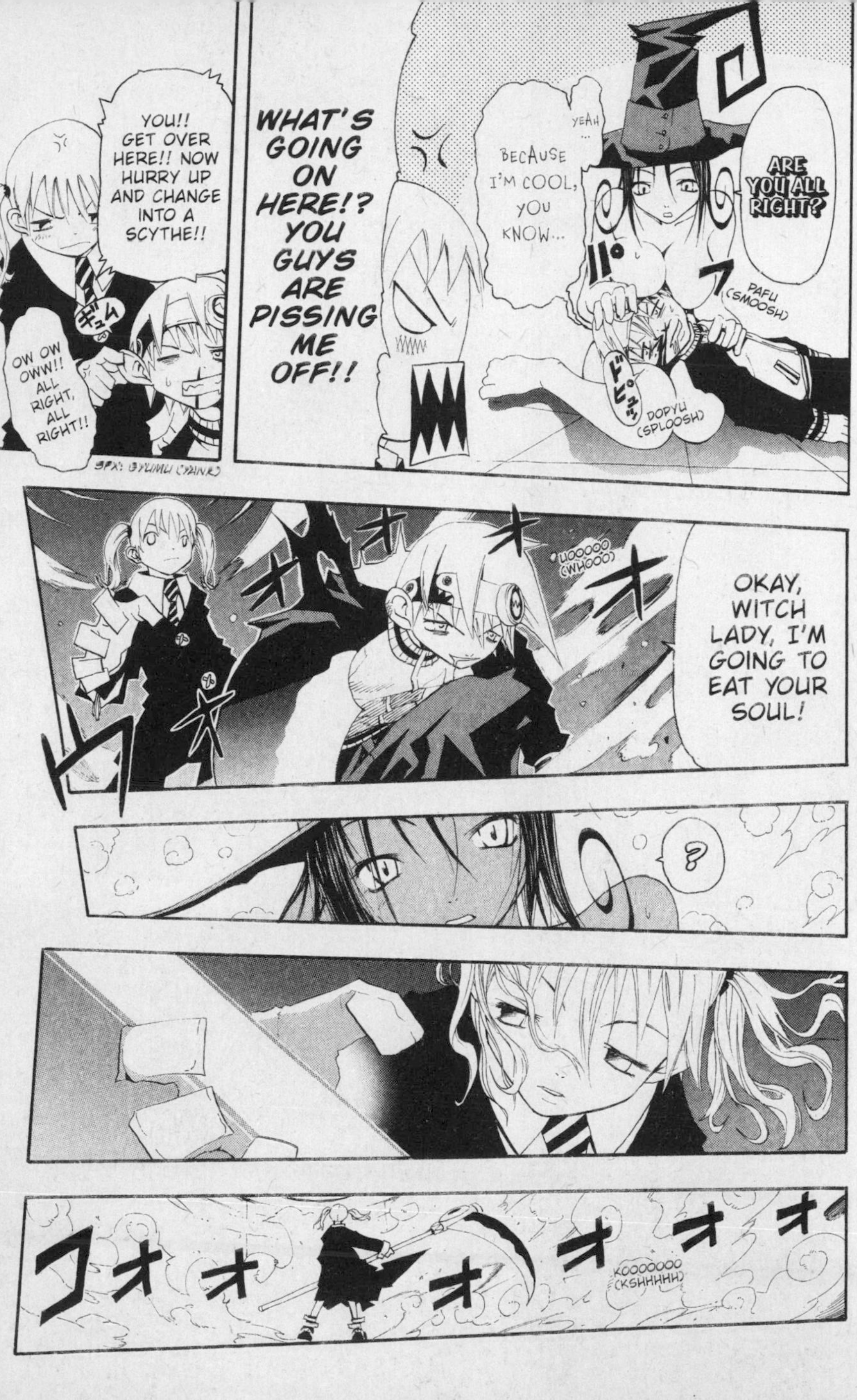
ARE YOU ALL RIGHT?
YEAH ...
BECAUSE I'M COOL, YOU KNOW...
PAFU (SMOOSH)
DOPYU (SPLOOSH)
WHAT'S GOING ON HERE!? YOU GUYS ARE PISSING ME OFF!!
YOU!! GET OVER HERE!! NOW HURRY UP AND CHANGE INTO A SCYTHE!!
OW OW OWW!! ALL RIGHT, ALL RIGHT!!
SFX: GYUMU (YANK)
OKAY, WITCH LADY, I'M GOING TO EAT YOUR SOUL!
UOOOOO (WHOOO)
?
KOOOOOOO (KSHHHHH)

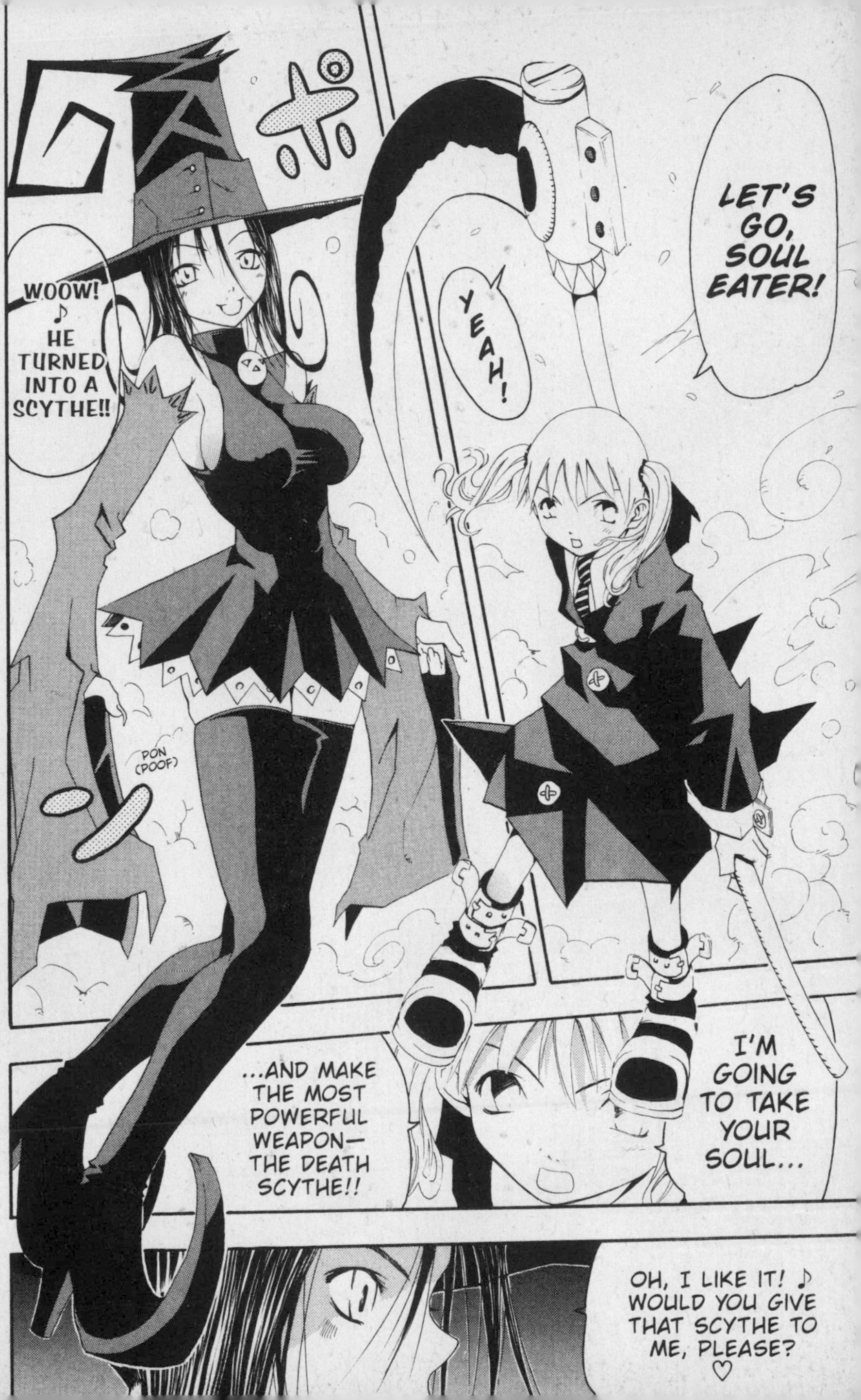
LET'S GO, SOUL EATER!
YEAH!
WOOW! ♪ HE TURNED INTO A SCYTHE!!
PON (POOF)
I'M GOING TO TAKE YOUR SOUL...
...AND MAKE THE MOST POWERFUL WEAPON— THE DEATH SCYTHE!!
OH, I LIKE IT! ♪ WOULD YOU GIVE THAT SCYTHE TO ME, PLEASE? ♡

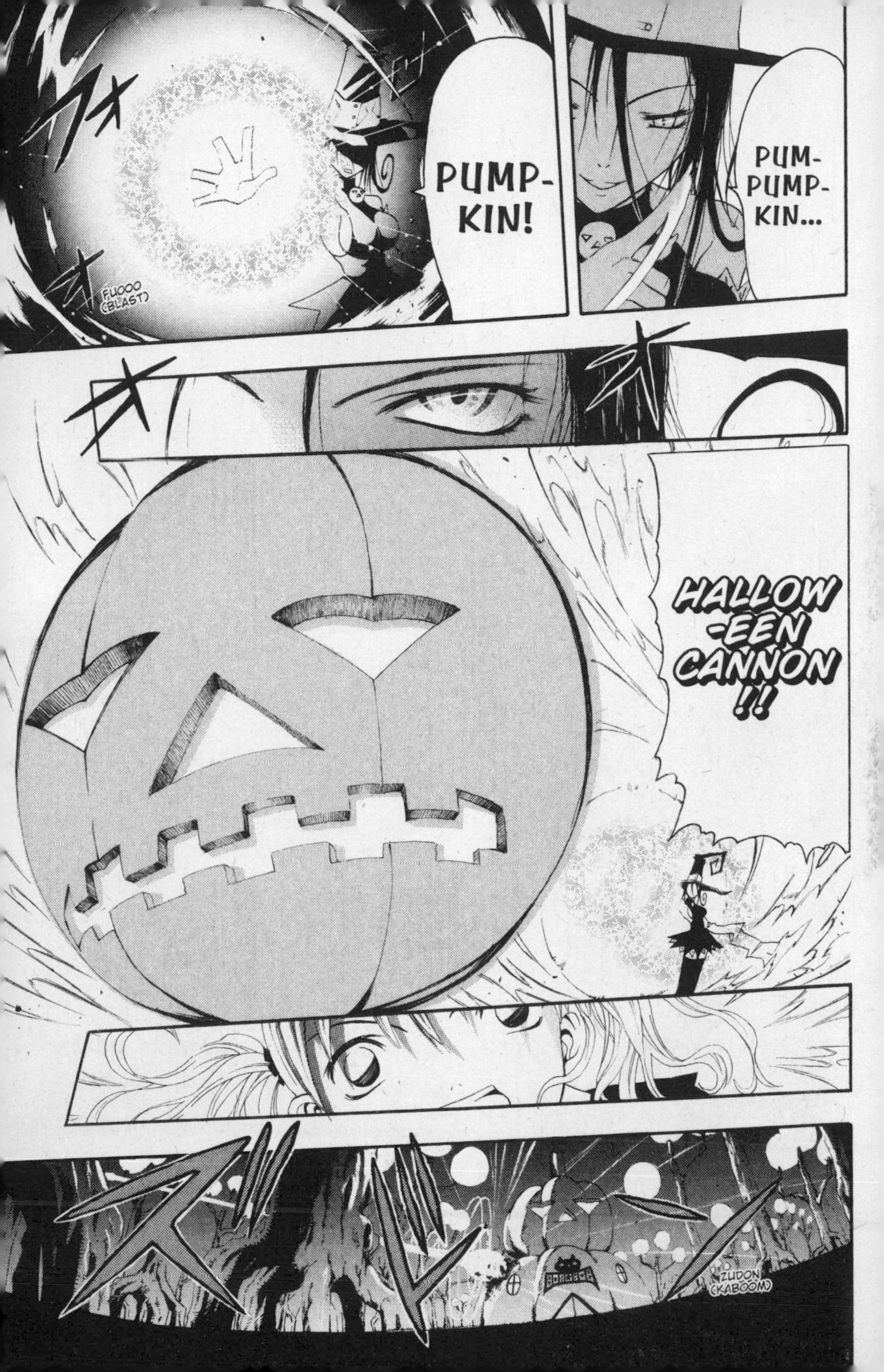
PUM-PUMP-KIN...
PUMP-KIN!
FUOOO (BLAST)
HALLOW-EEN CANNON!!
ZUDON (KABOOM)

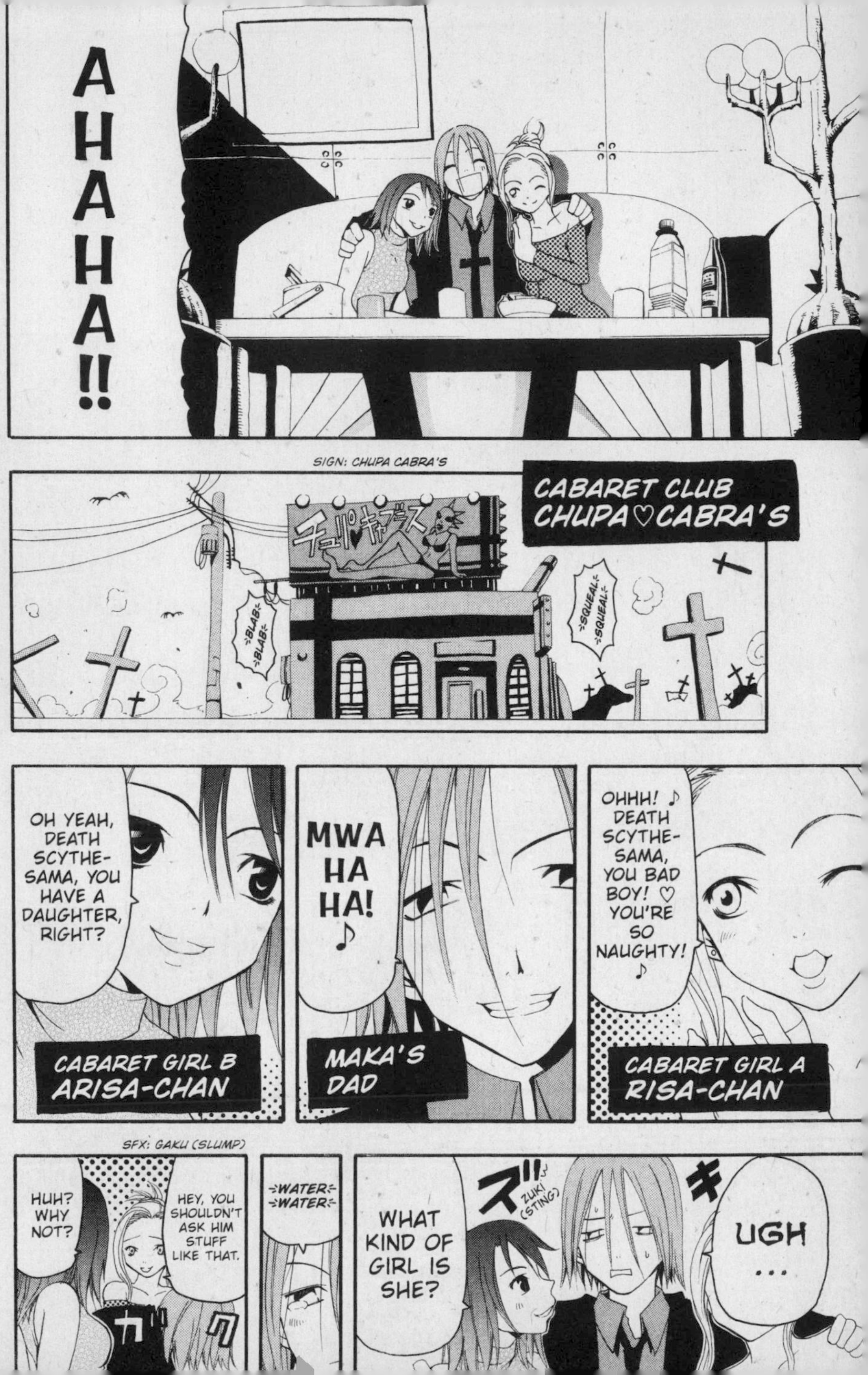
AHAHA!!
SIGN: CHUPA CABRA'S
CABARET CLUB CHUPA♡CABRA'S
SQUEAL SQUEAL
BLAB BLAB
OHHH! ♪ DEATH SCYTHE-SAMA, YOU BAD BOY! ♡ YOU'RE SO NAUGHTY! ♪
CABARET GIRL A RISA-CHAN
MWA HA HA! ♪
MAKA'S DAD
OH YEAH, DEATH SCYTHE-SAMA, YOU HAVE A DAUGHTER, RIGHT?
CABARET GIRL B ARISA-CHAN
SFX: GAKU (SLUMP)
UGH ...
ZUKI (STING)
WHAT KIND OF GIRL IS SHE?
WATER WATER
HEY, YOU SHOULDN'T ASK HIM STUFF LIKE THAT.
HUH? WHY NOT?

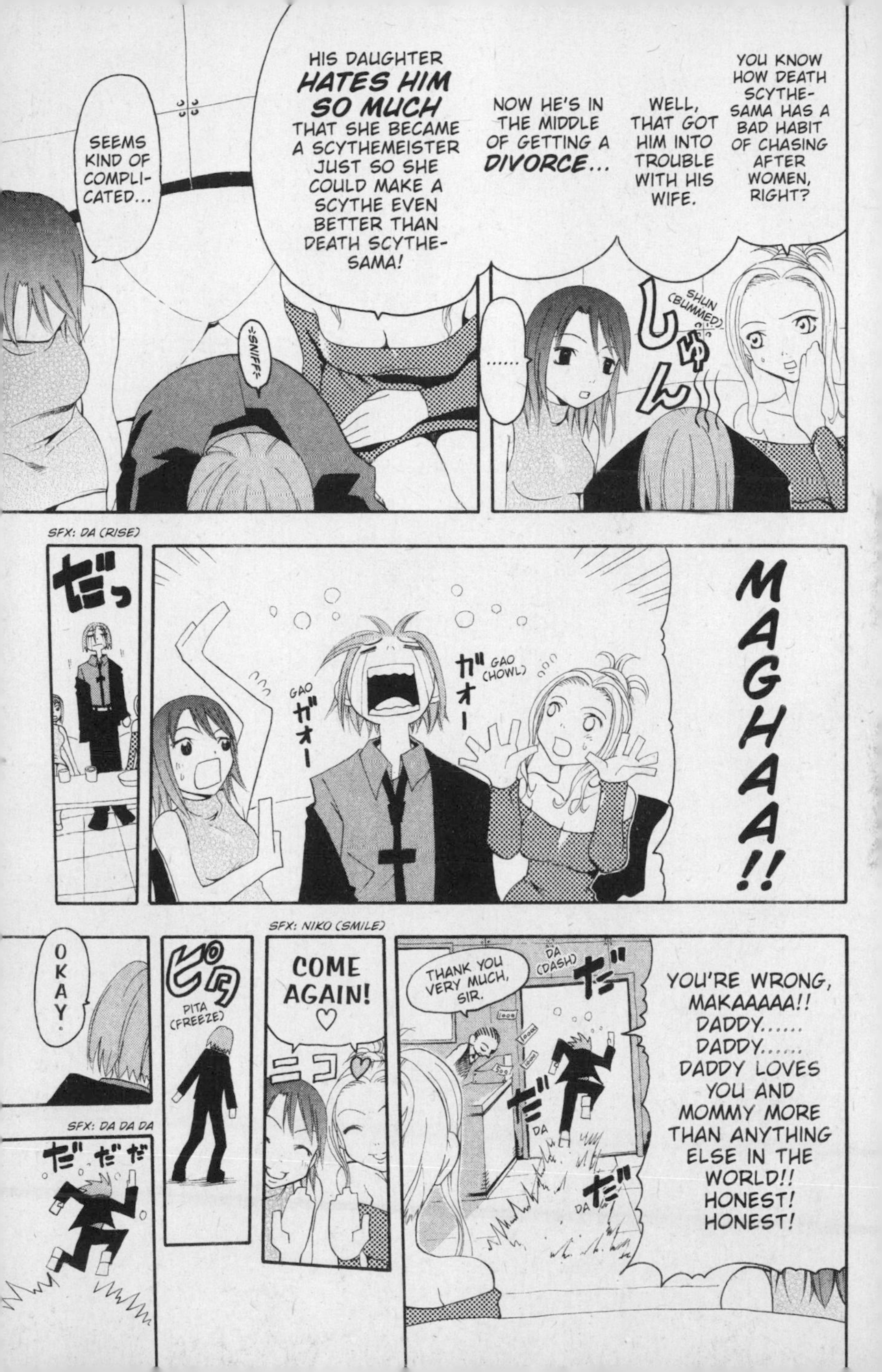
YOU KNOW HOW DEATH SCYTHE-SAMA HAS A BAD HABIT OF CHASING AFTER WOMEN, RIGHT?
WELL, THAT GOT HIM INTO TROUBLE WITH HIS WIFE.
NOW HE'S IN THE MIDDLE OF GETTING A DIVORCE...
HIS DAUGHTER HATES HIM SO MUCH THAT SHE BECAME A SCYTHEMEISTER JUST SO SHE COULD MAKE A SCYTHE EVEN BETTER THAN DEATH SCYTHE-SAMA!
SHUN (BUMMED)
......
SNIFF
SEEMS KIND OF COMPLICATED...
SFX: DA (RISE)
MAGHAAA!!
GAO (HOWL)
GAO
YOU'RE WRONG, MAKAAAAA!! DADDY...... DADDY...... DADDY LOVES YOU AND MOMMY MORE THAN ANYTHING ELSE IN THE WORLD!! HONEST! HONEST!
DA (DASH)
THANK YOU VERY MUCH, SIR.
DA
DA
SFX: NIKO (SMILE)
COME AGAIN! ♡
PITA (FREEZE)
OKAY.
SFX: DA DA DA

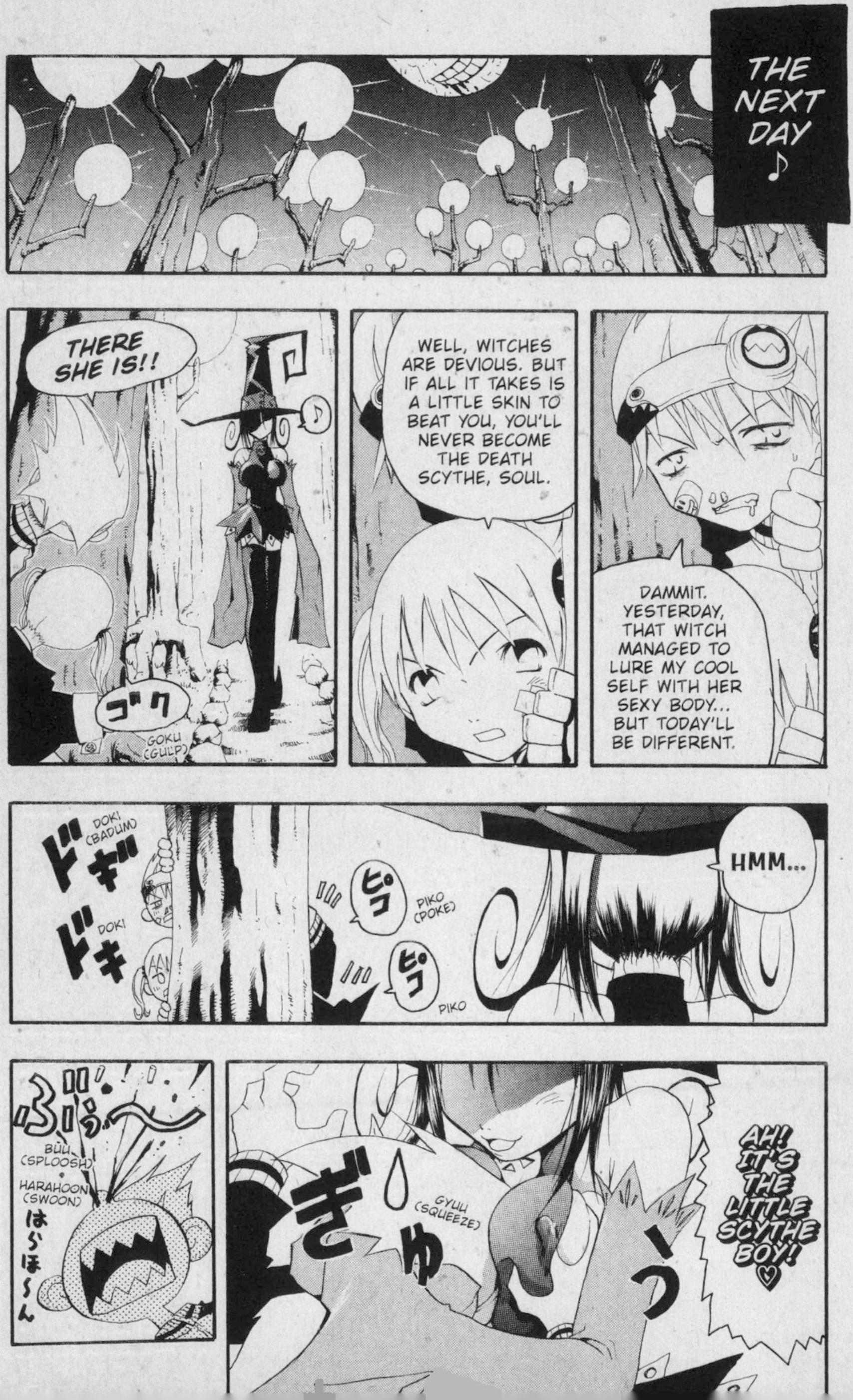
THE NEXT DAY ♪
DAMMIT. YESTERDAY, THAT WITCH MANAGED TO LURE MY COOL SELF WITH HER SEXY BODY... BUT TODAY'LL BE DIFFERENT.
WELL, WITCHES ARE DEVIOUS. BUT IF ALL IT TAKES IS A LITTLE SKIN TO BEAT YOU, YOU'LL NEVER BECOME THE DEATH SCYTHE, SOUL.
THERE SHE IS!!
♪
ゴク
GOKU (GULP)
HMM...
ピコ
PIKO (POKE)
ピコ
PIKO
ドキ
DOKI (BADUM)
ドキ
DOKI
AH! IT'S THE LITTLE SCYTHE BOY! ♡
ぎゅ
GYUU (SQUEEZE)
BUU (SPLOOSH)
HARAHOON (SWOON)
はらほ~ん

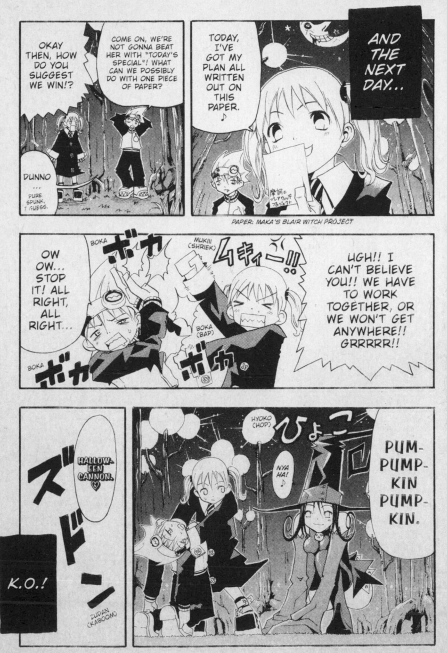

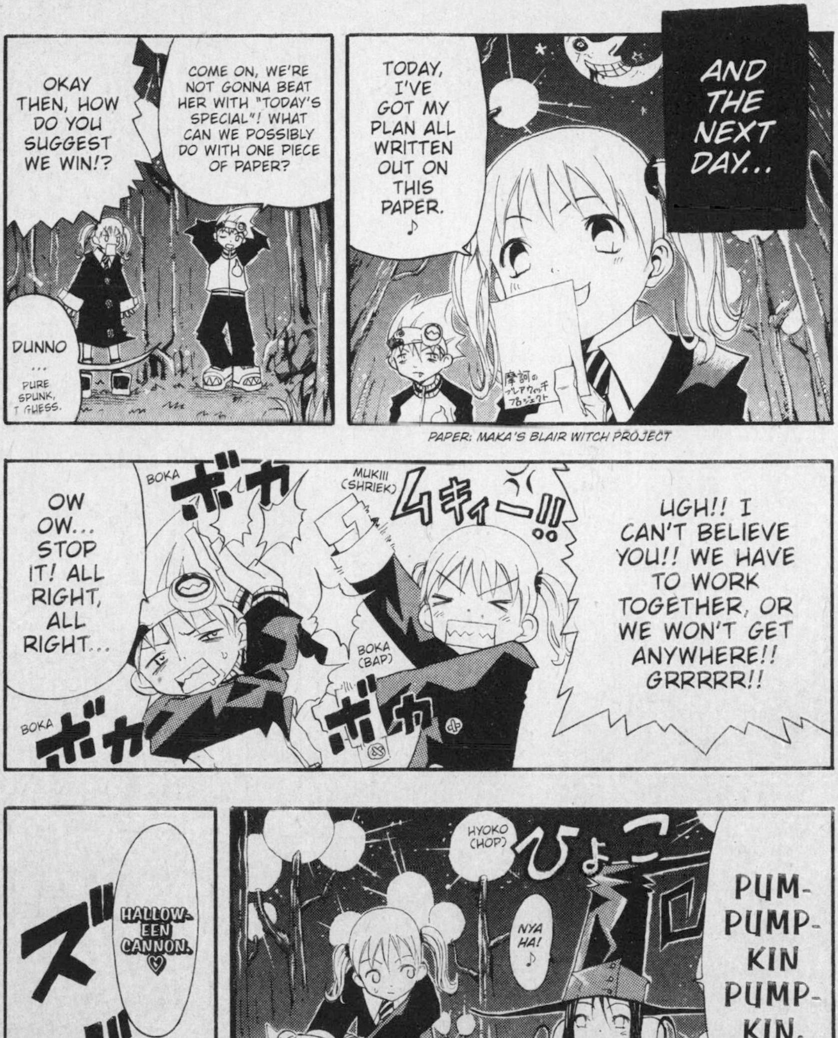
AND THE NEXT DAY...
TODAY, I'VE GOT MY PLAN ALL WRITTEN OUT ON THIS PAPER. ♪
摩訶のブレアウィッチプロジェクト
COME ON, WE'RE NOT GONNA BEAT HER WITH "TODAY'S SPECIAL"! WHAT CAN WE POSSIBLY DO WITH ONE PIECE OF PAPER?
OKAY THEN, HOW DO YOU SUGGEST WE WIN!?
DUNNO ...
PURE SPUNK, I GUESS.
PAPER: MAKA'S BLAIR WITCH PROJECT
UGH!! I CAN'T BELIEVE YOU!! WE HAVE TO WORK TOGETHER, OR WE WON'T GET ANYWHERE!! GRRRRR!!
MUKIII (SHRIEK)
ムキィー!!
BOKA
ボカ
OW OW... STOP IT! ALL RIGHT, ALL RIGHT...
BOKA (BAP)
ボカ
BOKA
ボカ
PUM-PUMP-KIN PUMP-KIN.
HYOKO (HOP)
ひょこ
NYA HA! ♪
HALLOW-EEN CANNON. ♡
ズドーン
ZUDAN (KABOOM)
K.O.!

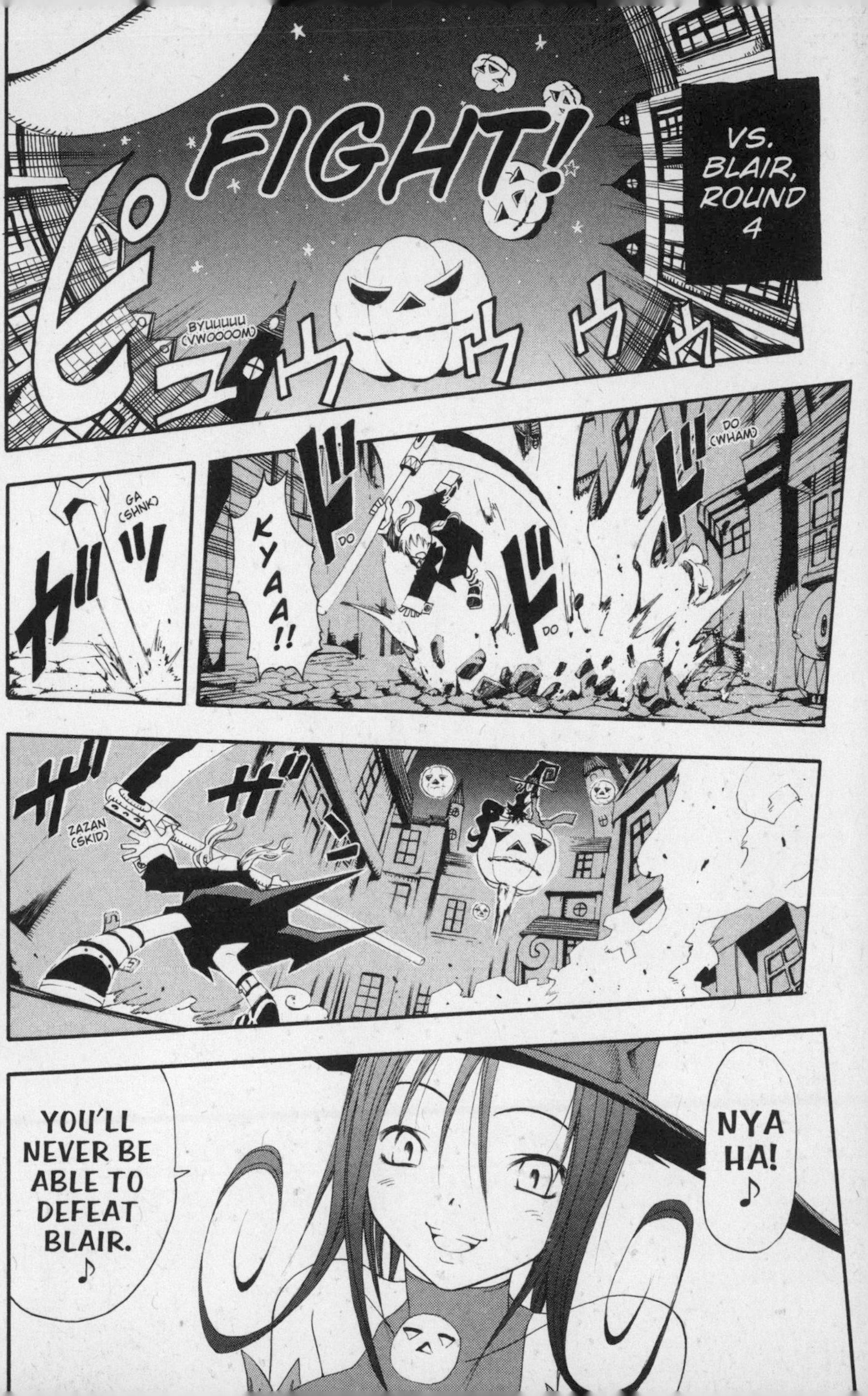
VS. BLAIR, ROUND 4
FIGHT!
BYUUUUU (VWOOOOM)
DO (WHAM)
KYAA!!
DO
DO
GA (SHNK)
ZAZAN (SKID)
NYA HA! ♪
YOU'LL NEVER BE ABLE TO DEFEAT BLAIR. ♪

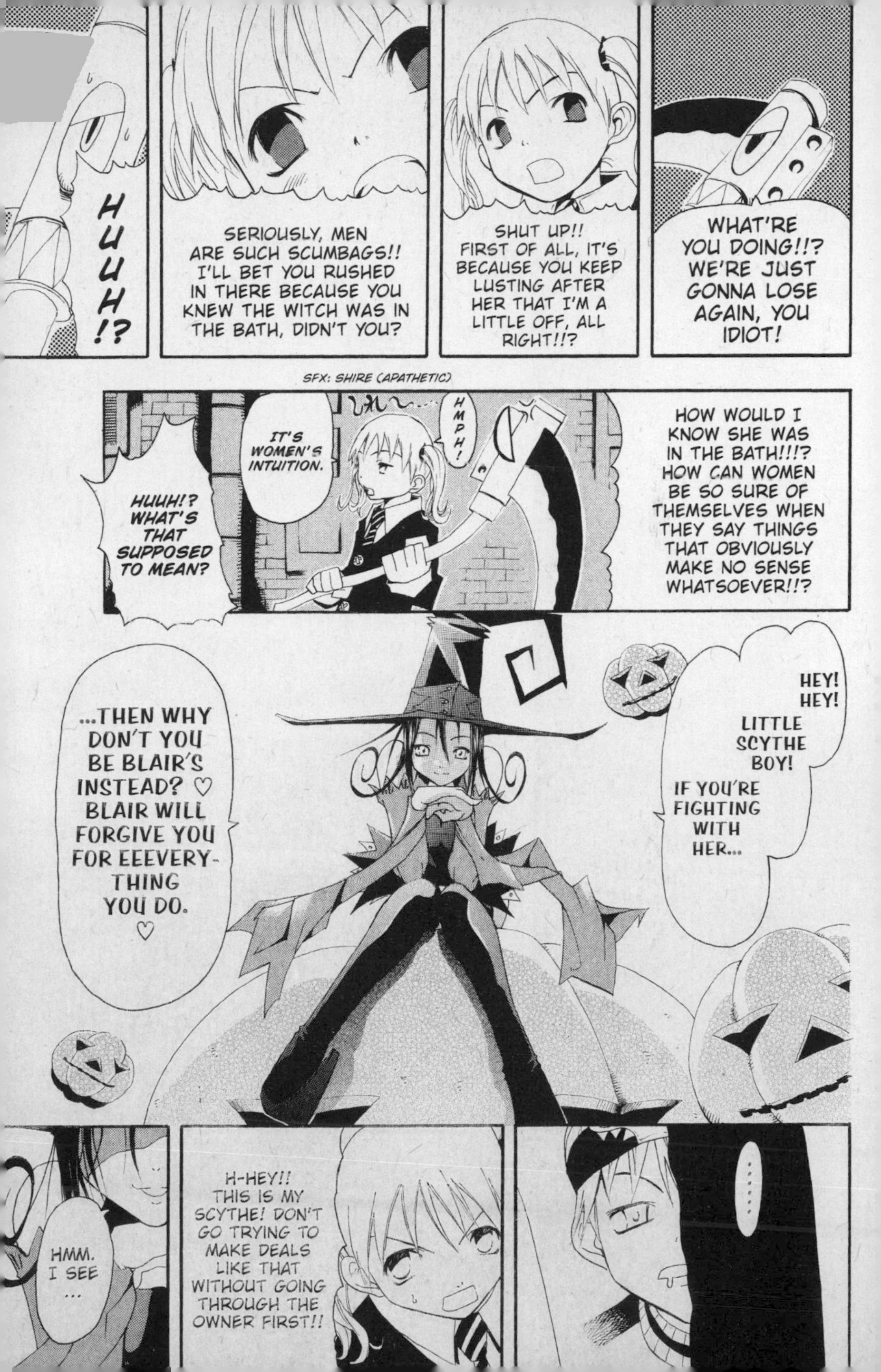
WHAT'RE YOU DOING!!? WE'RE JUST GONNA LOSE AGAIN, YOU IDIOT!
SHUT UP!! FIRST OF ALL, IT'S BECAUSE YOU KEEP LUSTING AFTER HER THAT I'M A LITTLE OFF, ALL RIGHT!!?
SERIOUSLY, MEN ARE SUCH SCUMBAGS!! I'LL BET YOU RUSHED IN THERE BECAUSE YOU KNEW THE WITCH WAS IN THE BATH, DIDN'T YOU?
HUUH!?
SFX: SHIRE (APATHETIC)
HOW WOULD I KNOW SHE WAS IN THE BATH!!!? HOW CAN WOMEN BE SO SURE OF THEMSELVES WHEN THEY SAY THINGS THAT OBVIOUSLY MAKE NO SENSE WHATSOEVER!!?
HMPH!
IT'S WOMEN'S INTUITION.
HUUH!? WHAT'S THAT SUPPOSED TO MEAN?
HEY! HEY! LITTLE SCYTHE BOY!
IF YOU'RE FIGHTING WITH HER...
...THEN WHY DON'T YOU BE BLAIR'S INSTEAD? ♡ BLAIR WILL FORGIVE YOU FOR EEEVERY-THING YOU DO. ♡
......
H-HEY!! THIS IS MY SCYTHE! DON'T GO TRYING TO MAKE DEALS LIKE THAT WITHOUT GOING THROUGH THE OWNER FIRST!!
HMM. I SEE ...

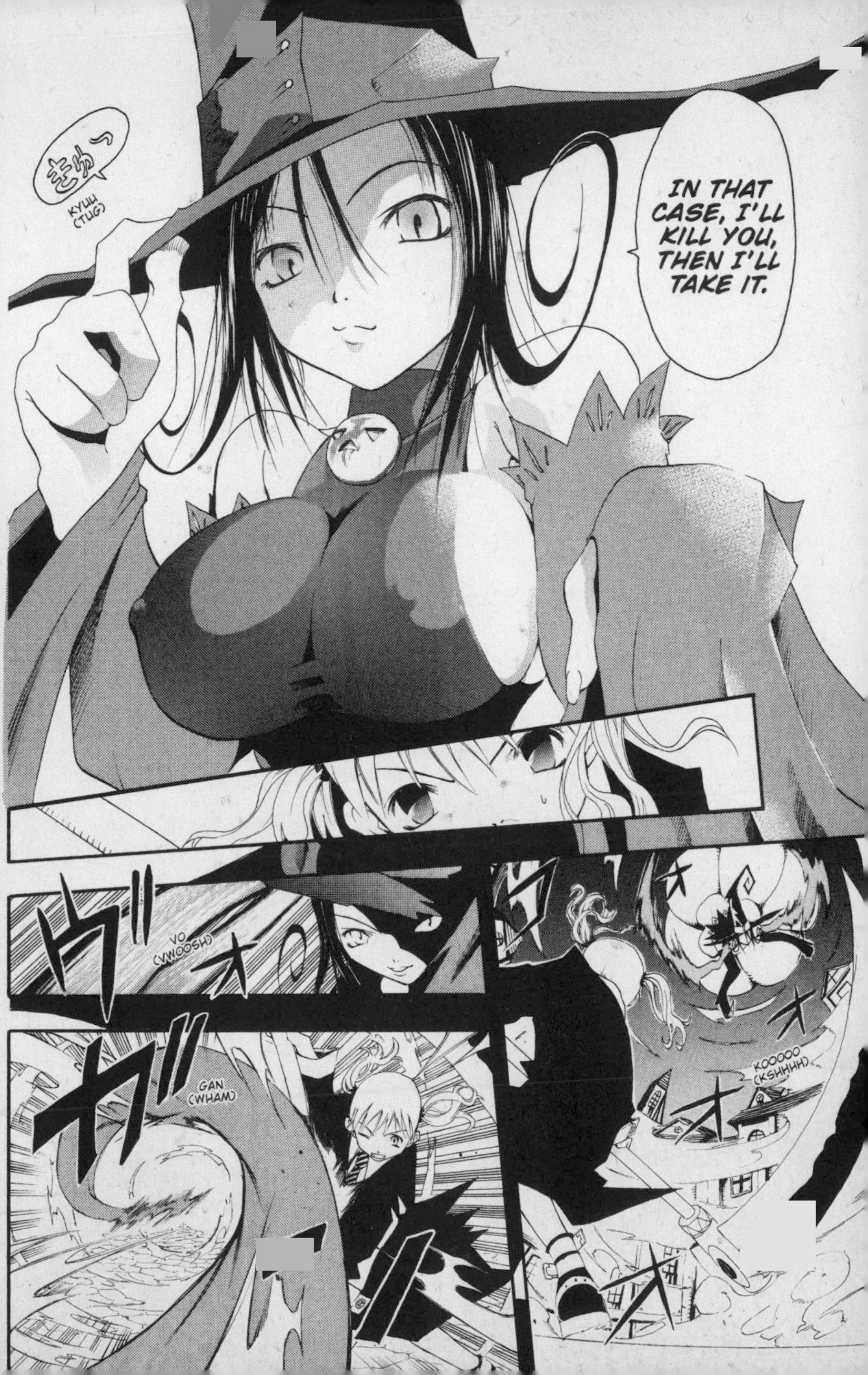

IN THAT CASE, I'LL KILL YOU, THEN I'LL TAKE IT.
きゅっ
KYUU (TUG)
KOOOOO (KSHHHH)
VO (VWOOSH)
GAN (WHAM)

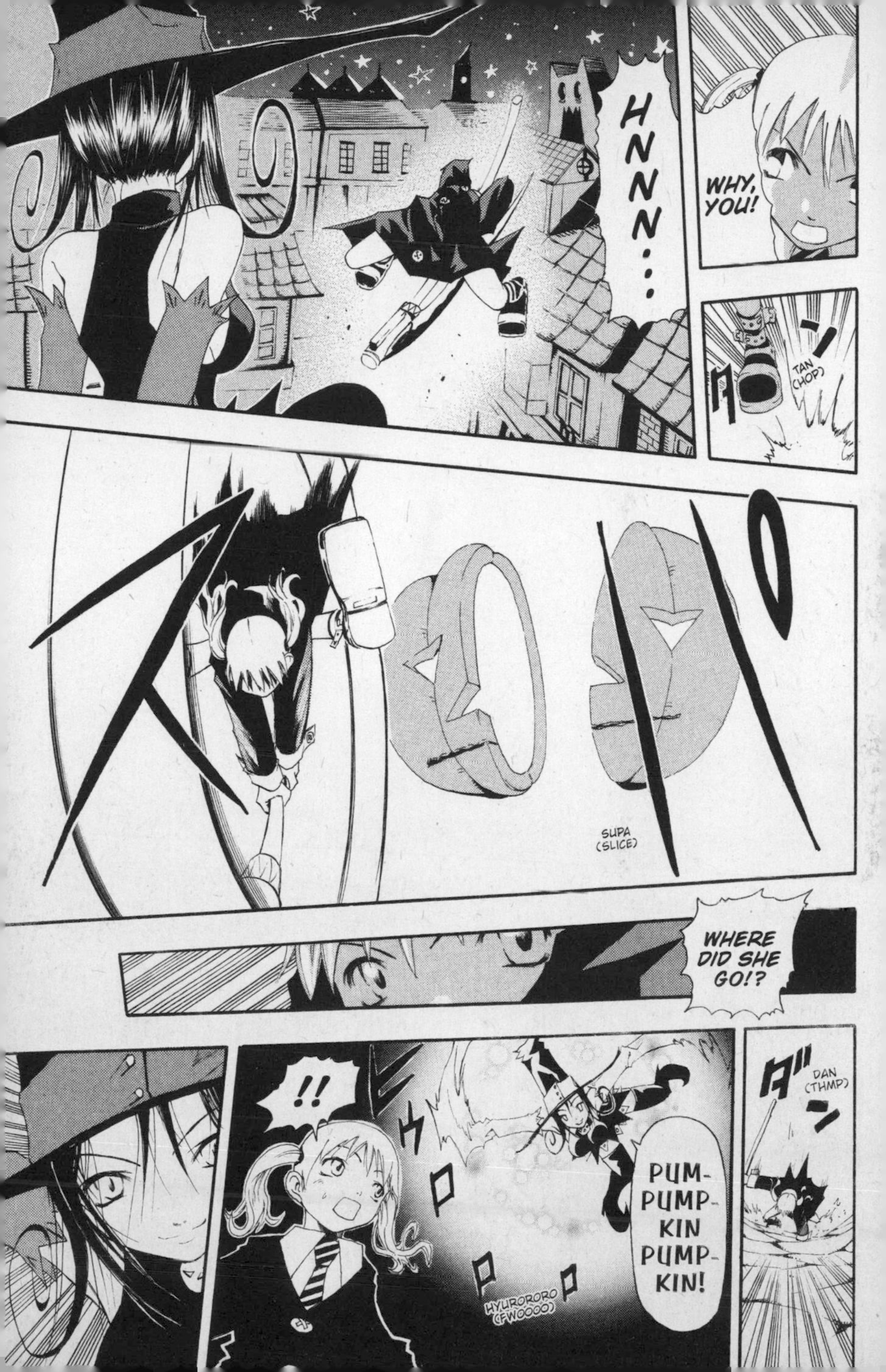
WHY, YOU!
TAN (CHOP)
HNNN...
SUPA (SLICE)
WHERE DID SHE GO!?
DAN (THMP)
!!
PUM-PUMP-KIN PUMP-KIN!
HYURORORO (FWOOOO)

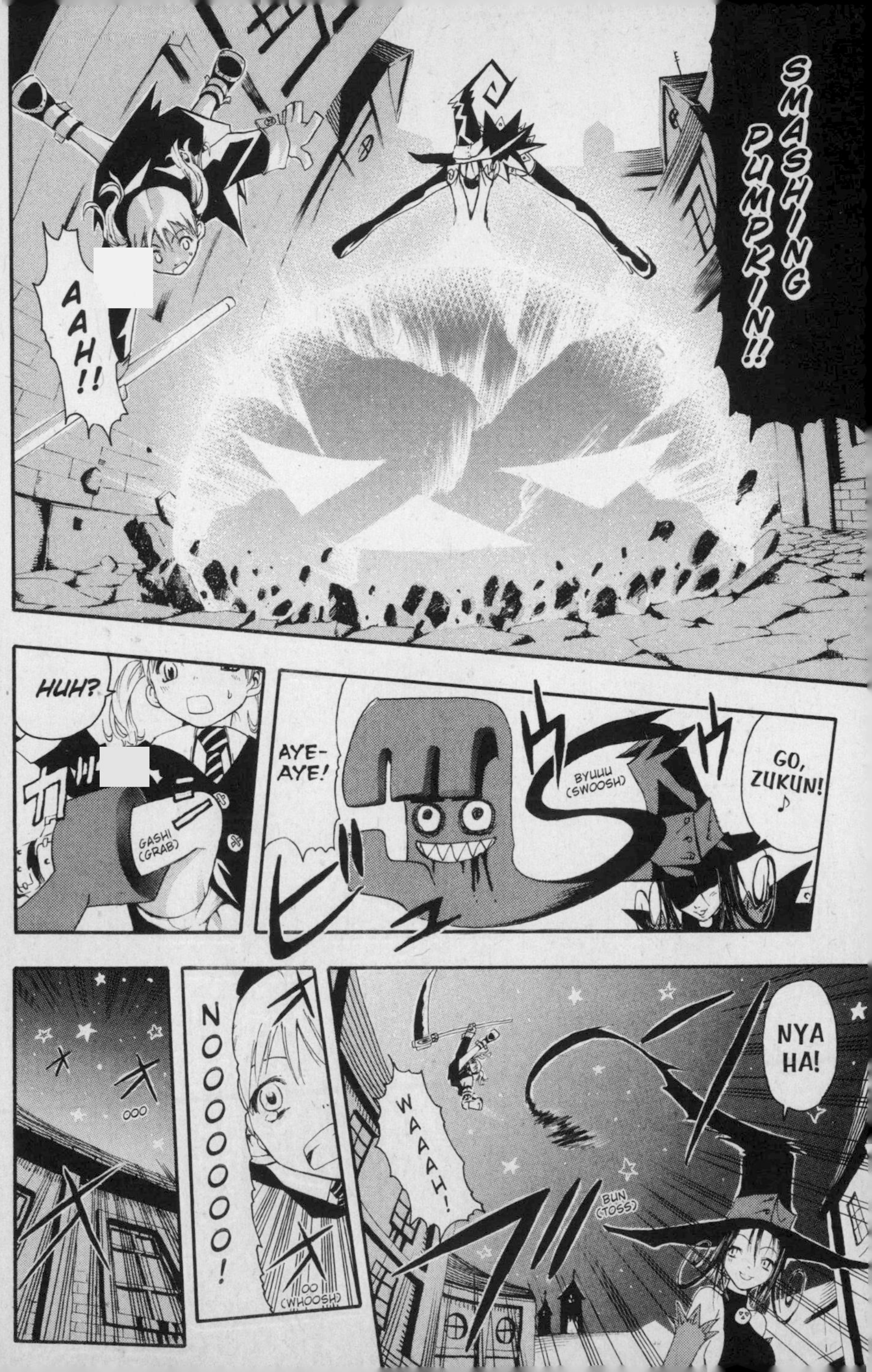
SMASHING PUMPKIN!!
AAH!!
GO, ZUKUN! ♪
BYUUU (SWOOSH)
AYE-AYE!
HUH?
GASHI (GRAB)
NYA HA!
BUN (TOSS)
WAAAAH!
NOOOOOOOO!
OO (WHOOSH)
OOO

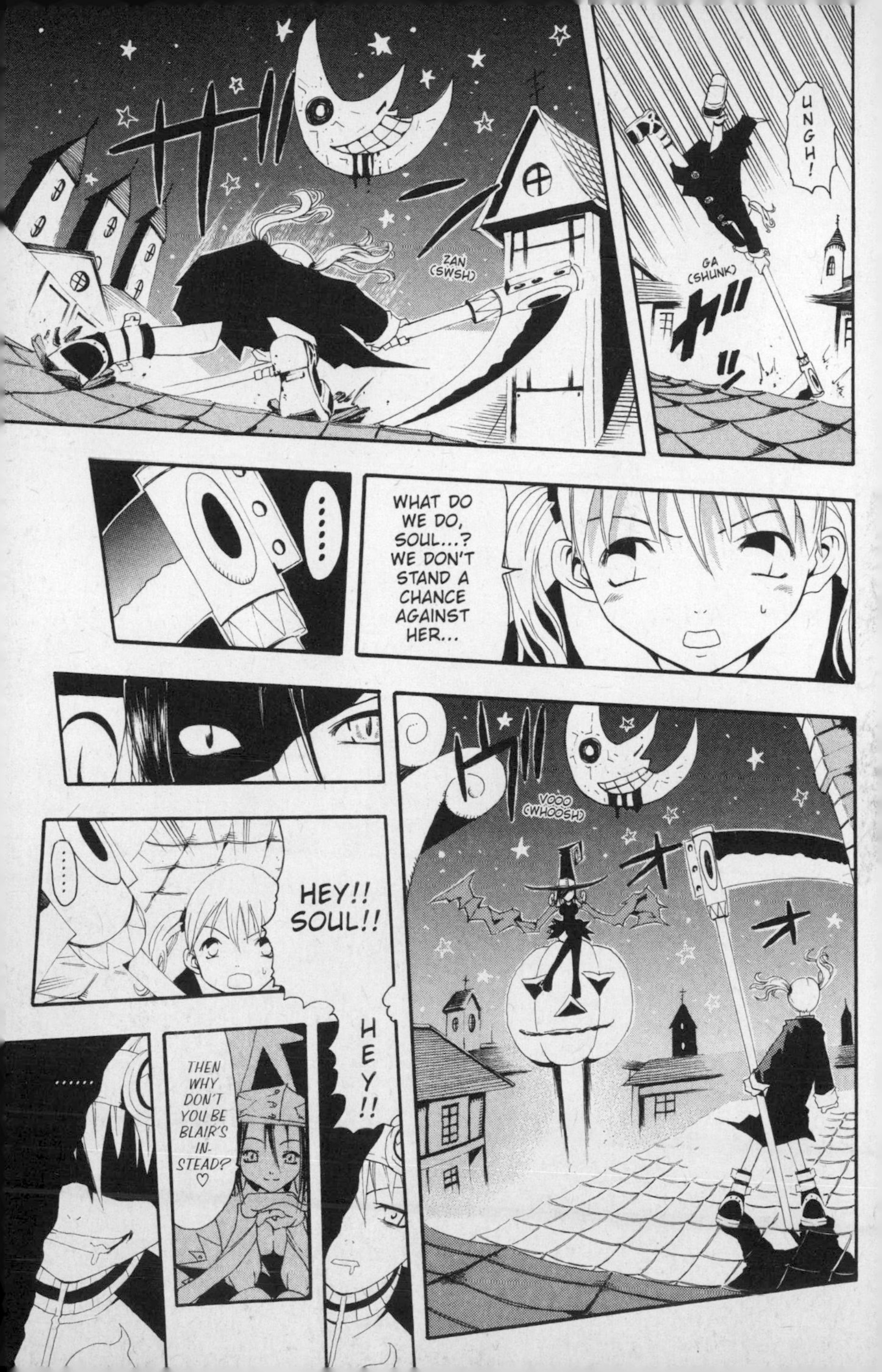
UNGH!
GA (SHUNK)
ZAN (SWSH)
WHAT DO WE DO, SOUL...? WE DON'T STAND A CHANCE AGAINST HER...
......
VOOO (WHOOSH)
HEY!! SOUL!!
......
HEY!!
THEN WHY DON'T YOU BE BLAIR'S IN-STEAD? ♡
......

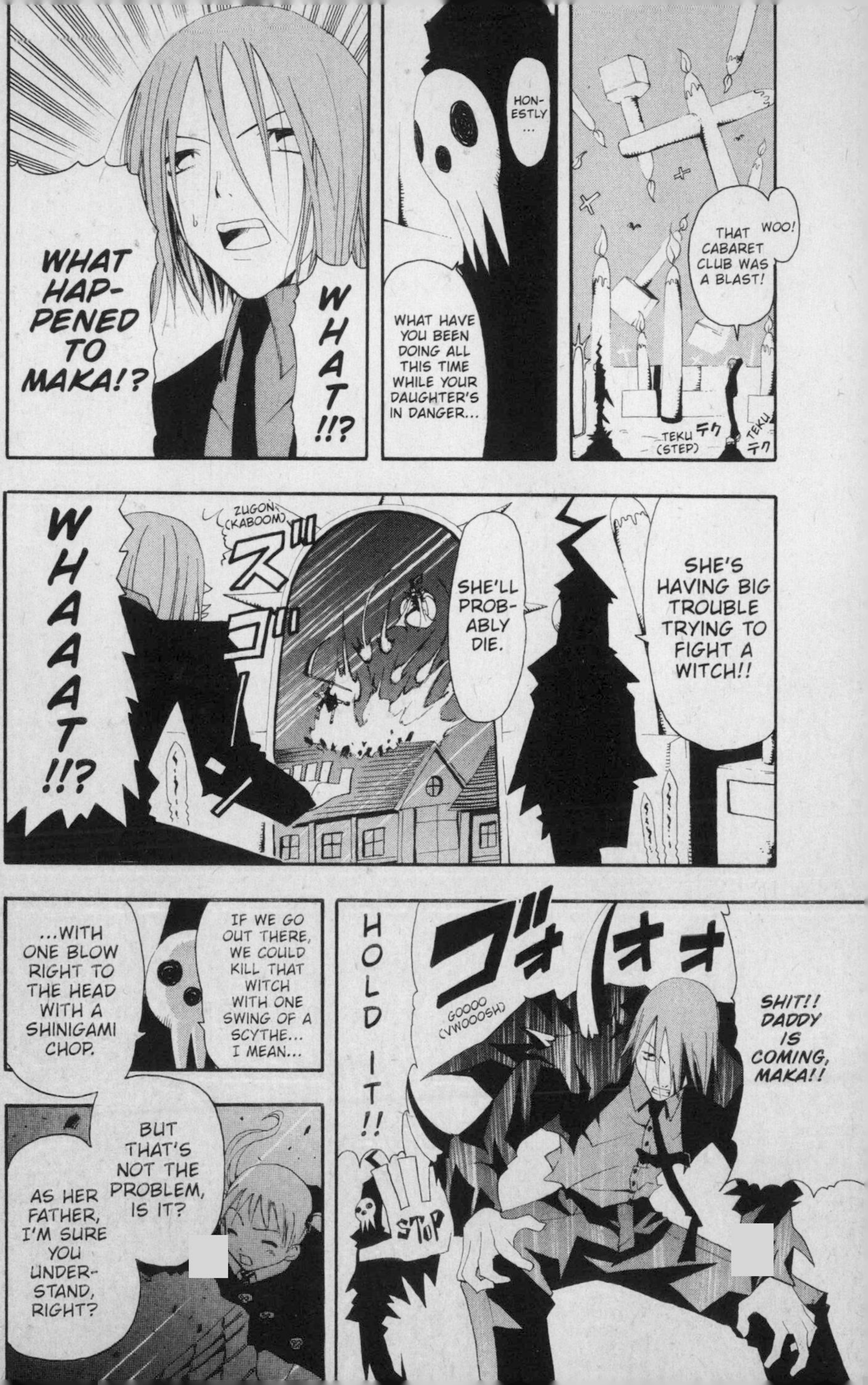
THAT CABARET CLUB WAS A BLAST! WOO!
TEKU テク (STEP) TEKU テク
HON-ESTLY...
WHAT HAVE YOU BEEN DOING ALL THIS TIME WHILE YOUR DAUGHTER'S IN DANGER...
WHAT!!?
WHAT HAP-PENED TO MAKA!?
SHE'S HAVING BIG TROUBLE TRYING TO FIGHT A WITCH!!
SHE'LL PROBABLY DIE.
ZUGON (KABOOM) ズゴ
WHAAAAT!!?
SHIT!! DADDY IS COMING, MAKA!!
ゴォオオ
GOOOO (VWOOOSH)
HOLD IT!!
STOP
IF WE GO OUT THERE, WE COULD KILL THAT WITCH WITH ONE SWING OF A SCYTHE... I MEAN...
...WITH ONE BLOW RIGHT TO THE HEAD WITH A SHINIGAMI CHOP.
BUT THAT'S NOT THE PROBLEM, IS IT?
AS HER FATHER, I'M SURE YOU UNDERSTAND, RIGHT?

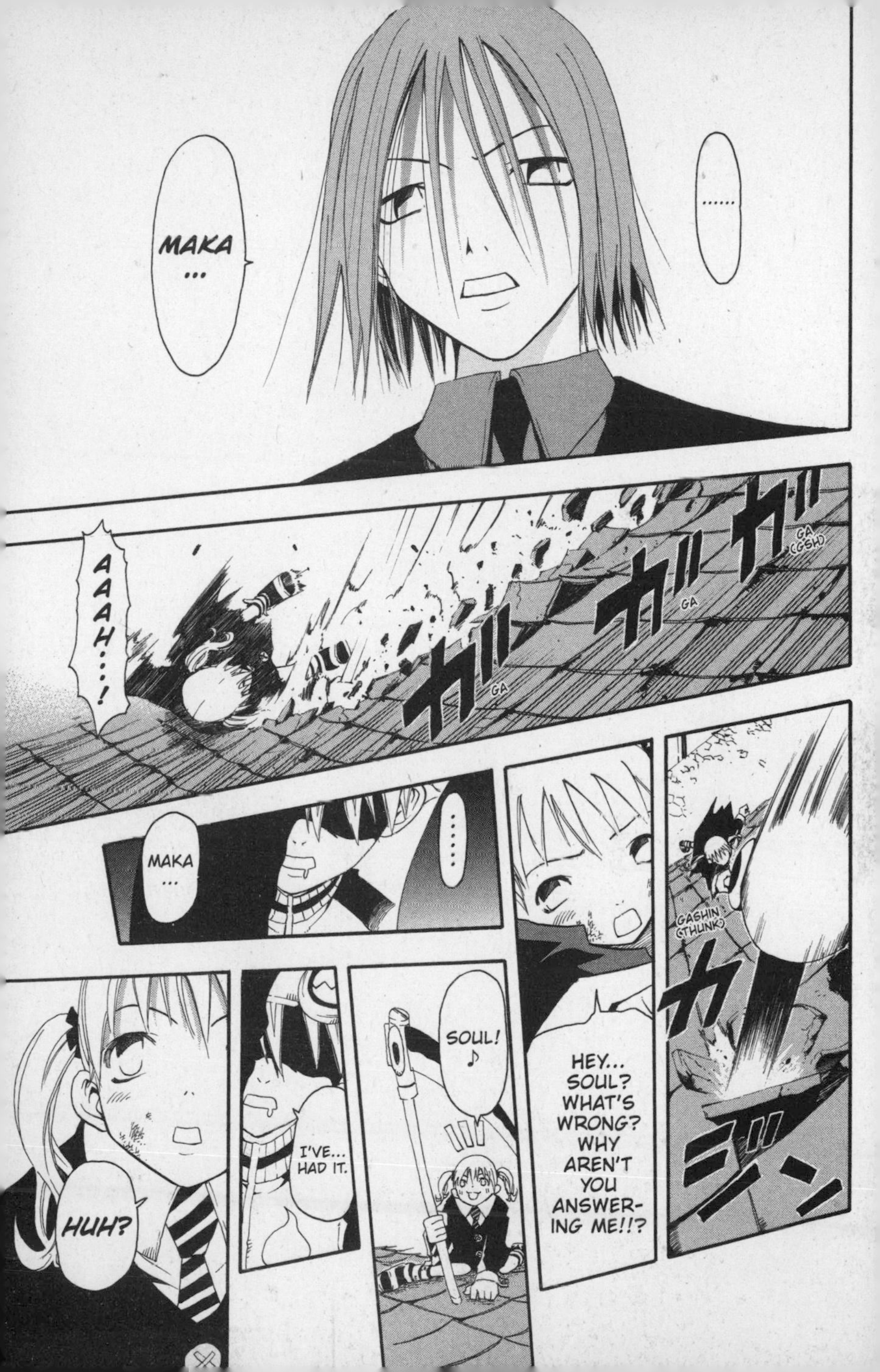
......
MAKA ...
GA (GSH)
GA
GA
AAAH...!
GASHIN (THUNK)
HEY... SOUL? WHAT'S WRONG? WHY AREN'T YOU ANSWERING ME!!?
......
MAKA ...
SOUL! ♪
I'VE... HAD IT.
HUH?

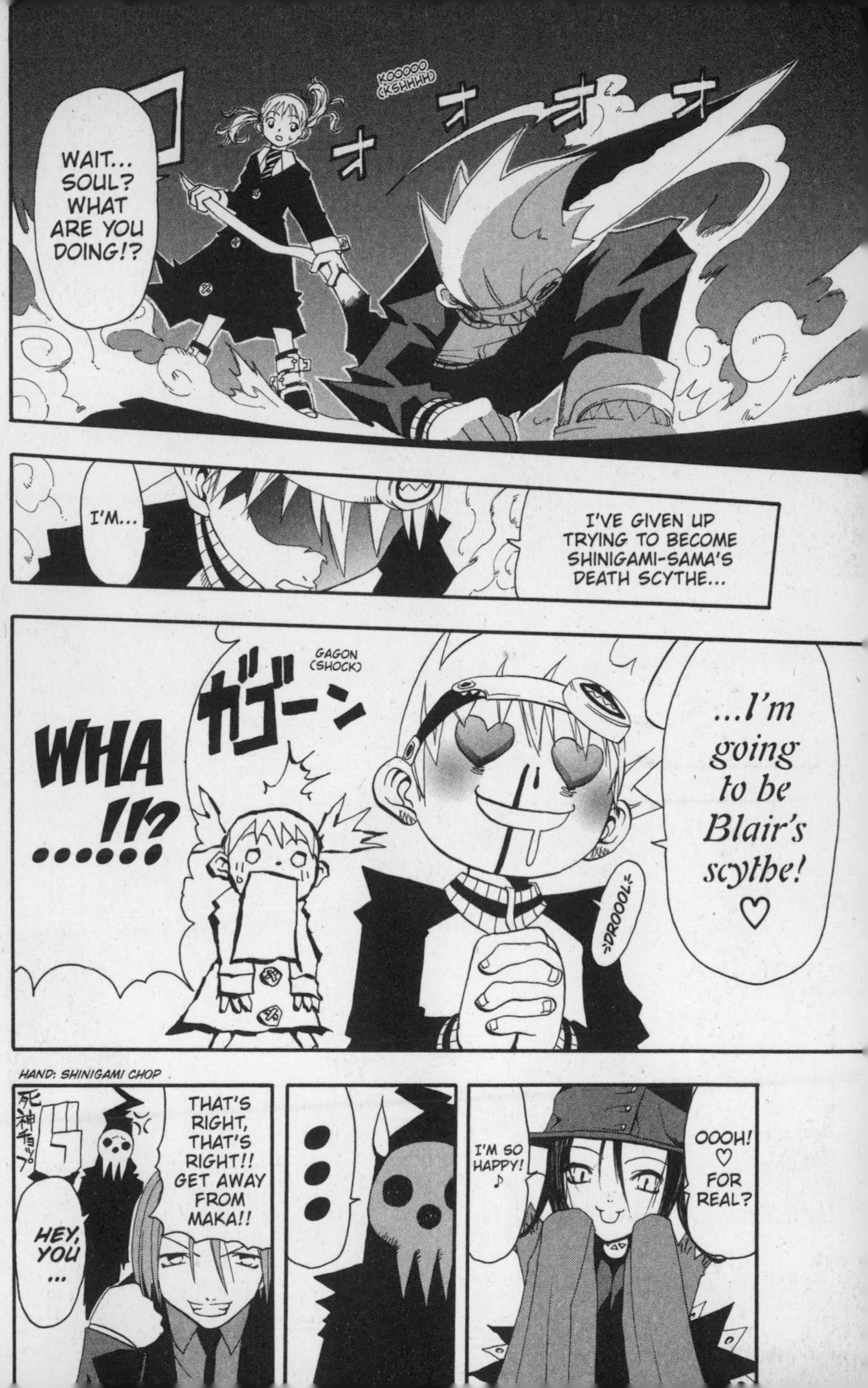
KOOOOO (KSHHHH)
WAIT... SOUL? WHAT ARE YOU DOING!?
I'VE GIVEN UP TRYING TO BECOME SHINIGAMI-SAMA'S DEATH SCYTHE...
I'M...
...I'm going to be Blair's scythe! ♡
DROOOL
GAGON (SHOCK)
ガゴーン
WHA ......!!?
HAND: SHINIGAMI CHOP
OOOH! ♡ FOR REAL?
I'M SO HAPPY! ♪
•••
THAT'S RIGHT, THAT'S RIGHT!! GET AWAY FROM MAKA!!
死神チョップ
HEY, YOU ...

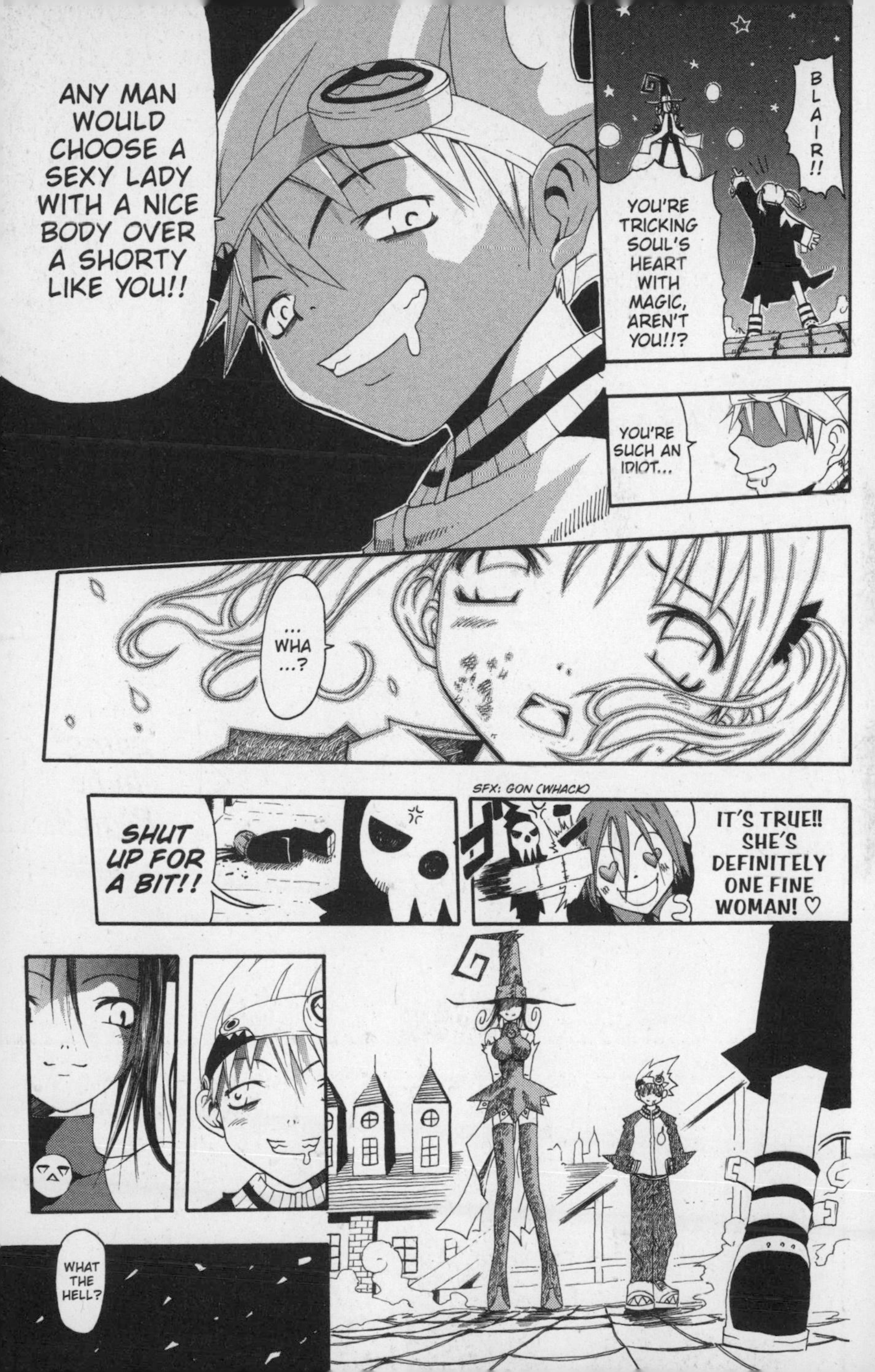
BLAIR!!
YOU'RE TRICKING SOUL'S HEART WITH MAGIC, AREN'T YOU!!?
YOU'RE SUCH AN IDIOT...
ANY MAN WOULD CHOOSE A SEXY LADY WITH A NICE BODY OVER A SHORTY LIKE YOU!!
... WHA ...?
IT'S TRUE!! SHE'S DEFINITELY ONE FINE WOMAN! ♡
SFX: GON (WHACK)
SHUT UP FOR A BIT!!
WHAT THE HELL?

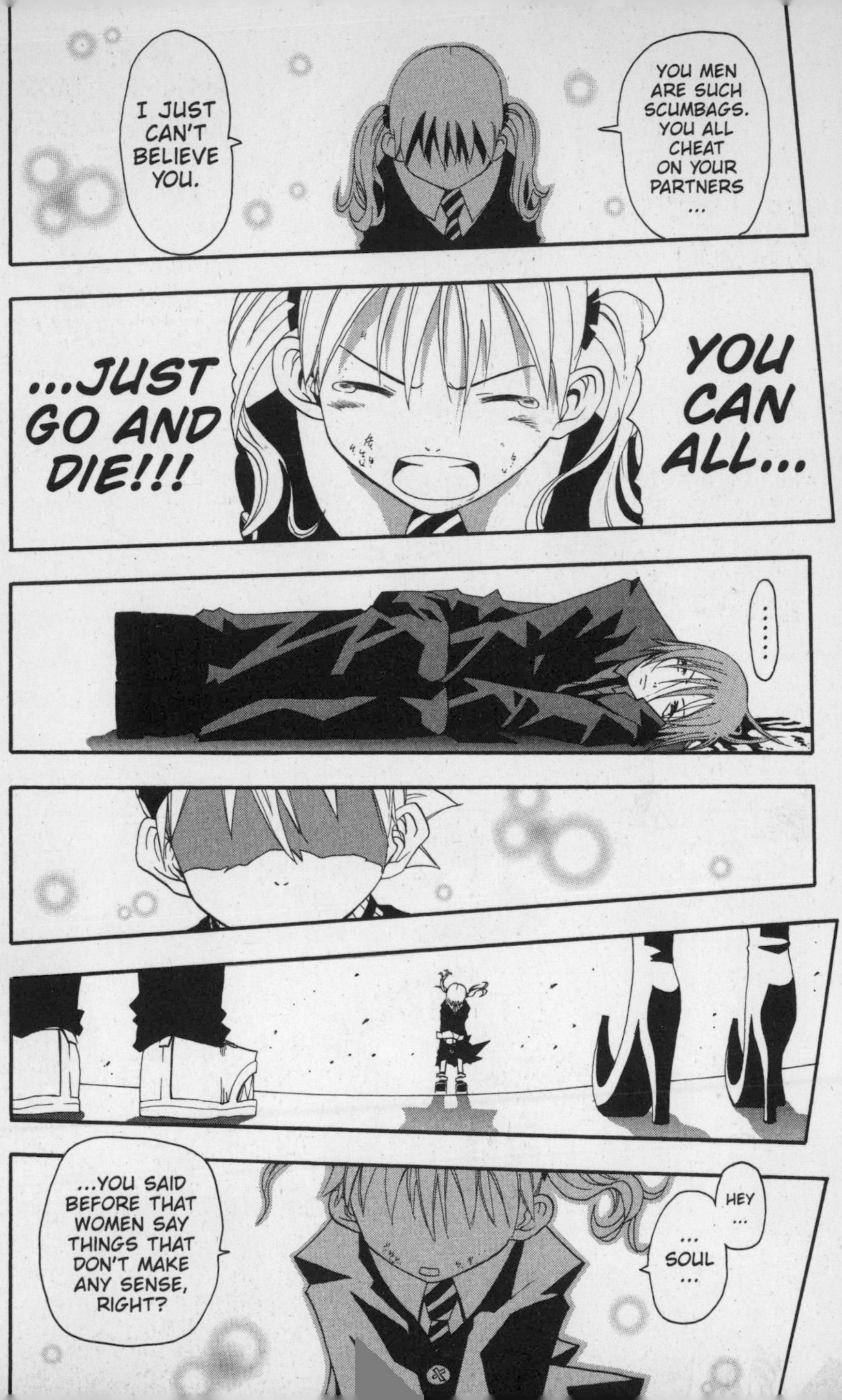
YOU MEN ARE SUCH SCUMBAGS. YOU ALL CHEAT ON YOUR PARTNERS ...
I JUST CAN'T BELIEVE YOU.
YOU CAN ALL...
...JUST GO AND DIE!!!
......
HEY ... ... SOUL ...
...YOU SAID BEFORE THAT WOMEN SAY THINGS THAT DON'T MAKE ANY SENSE, RIGHT?

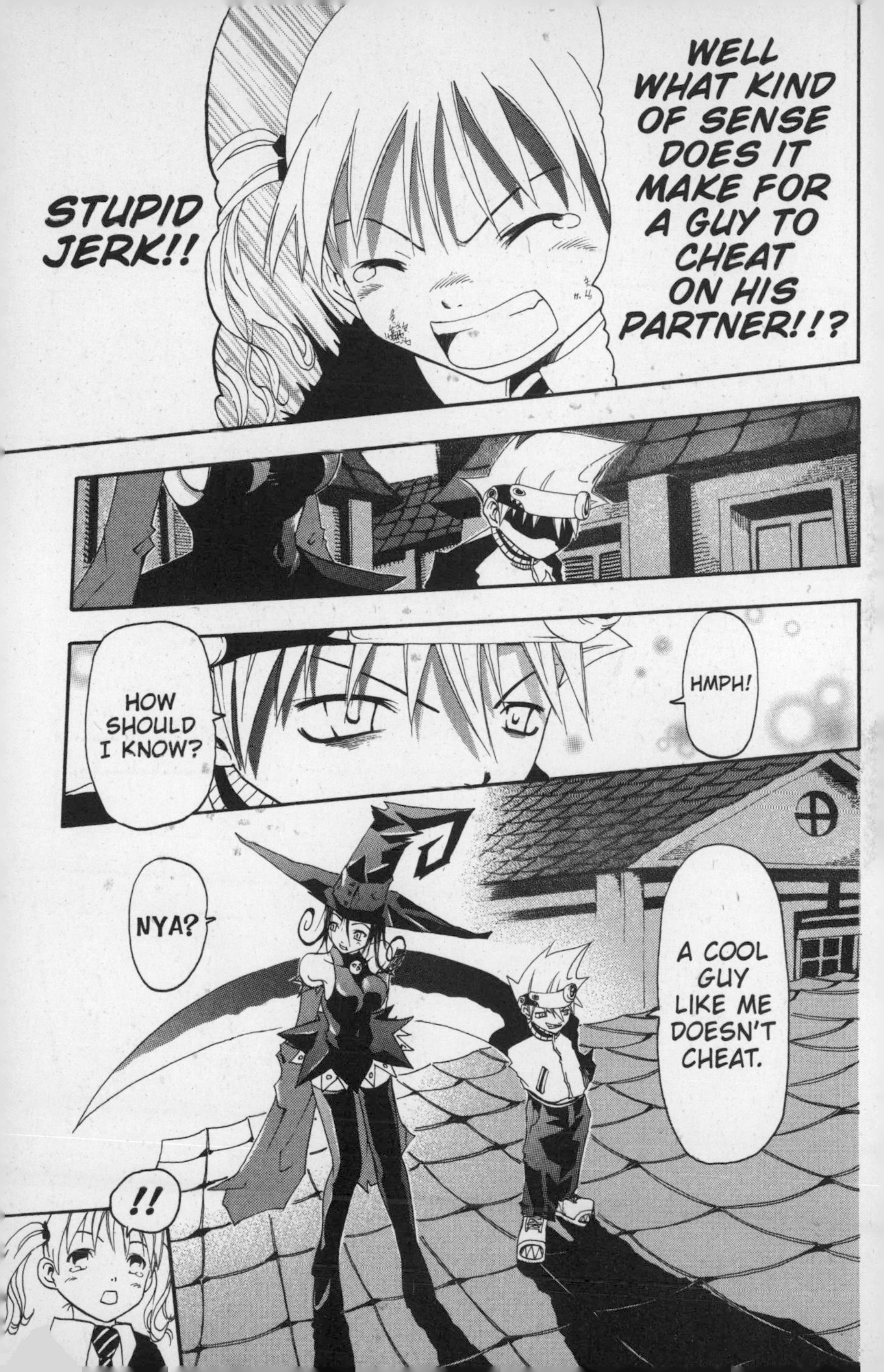
WELL WHAT KIND OF SENSE DOES IT MAKE FOR A GUY TO CHEAT ON HIS PARTNER!!?
STUPID JERK!!
HMPH!
HOW SHOULD I KNOW?
A COOL GUY LIKE ME DOESN'T CHEAT.
NYA?
!!

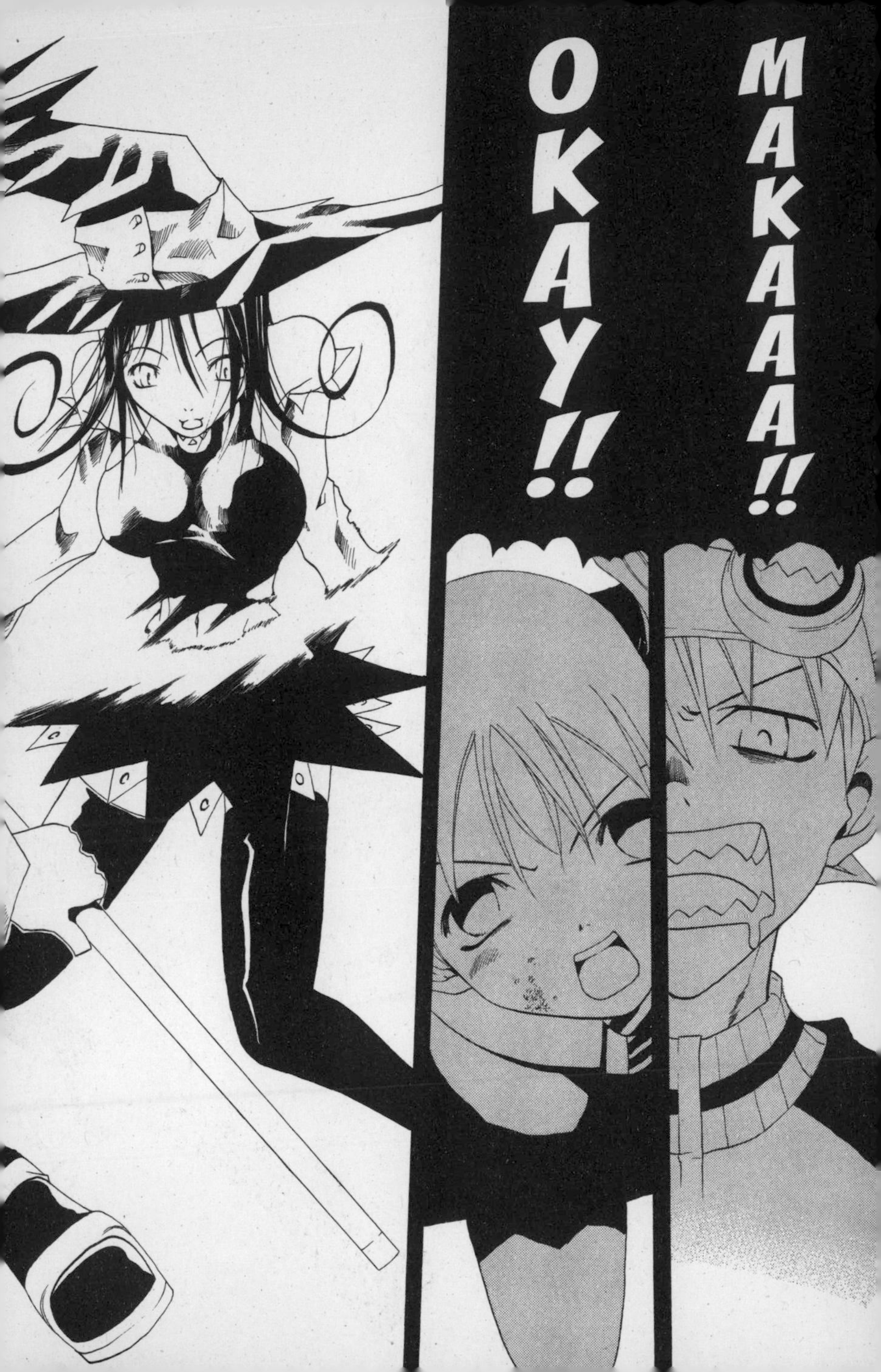
MAKAAAA!!
OKAY!!

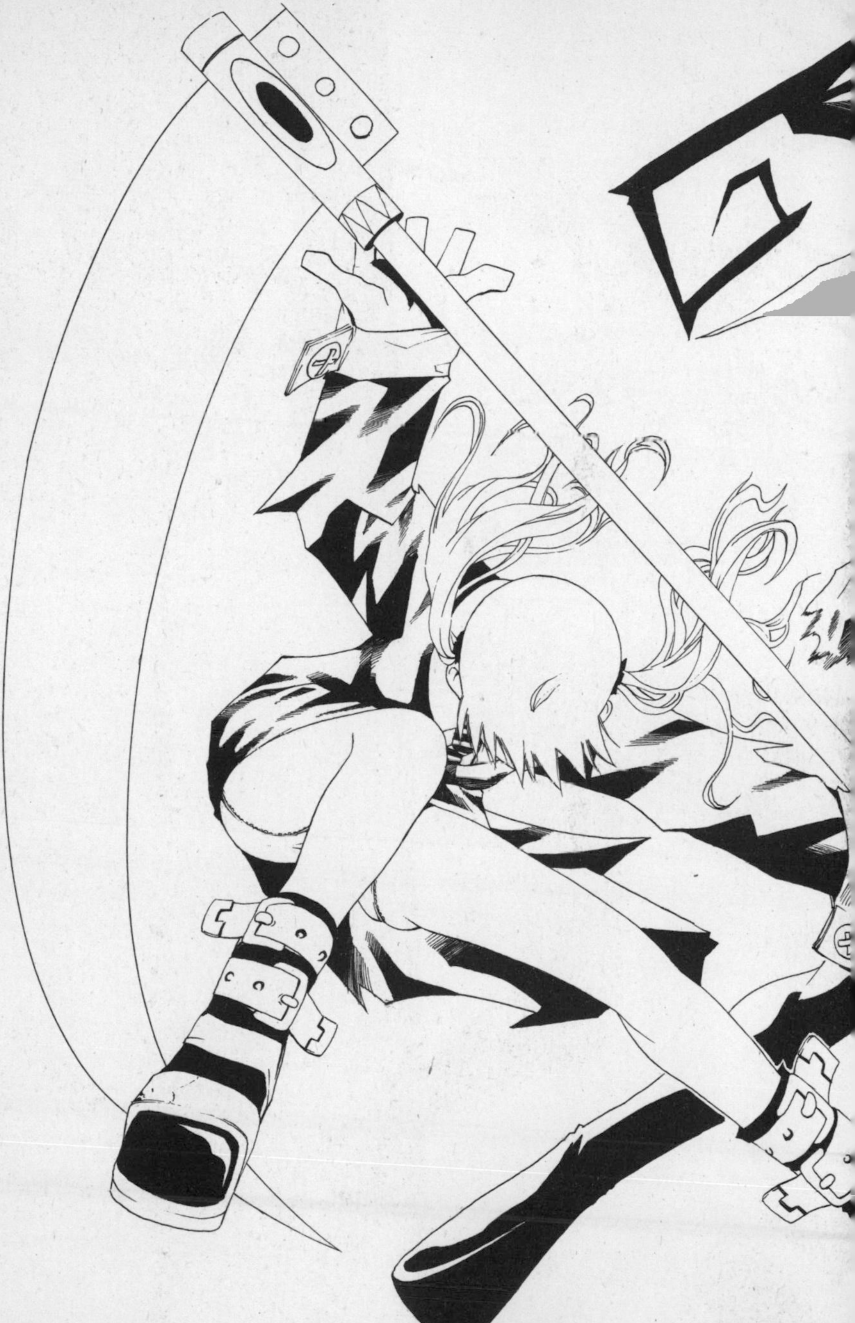

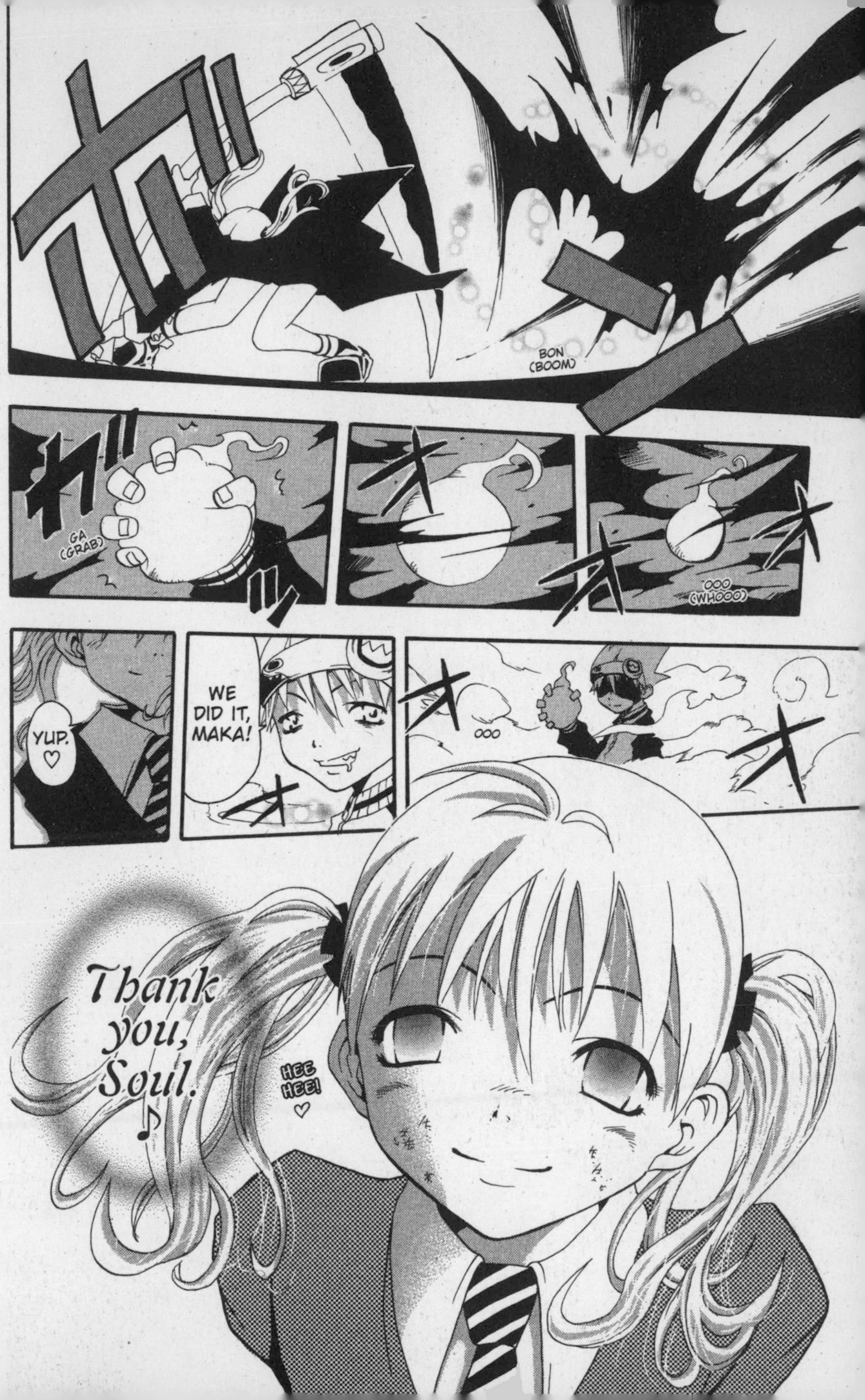
BON (BOOM)
OOO (WHOOO)
GA (GRAB)
OOO
WE DID IT, MAKA!
YUP. ♡
Thank you, Soul. ♪
HEE HEE! ♡

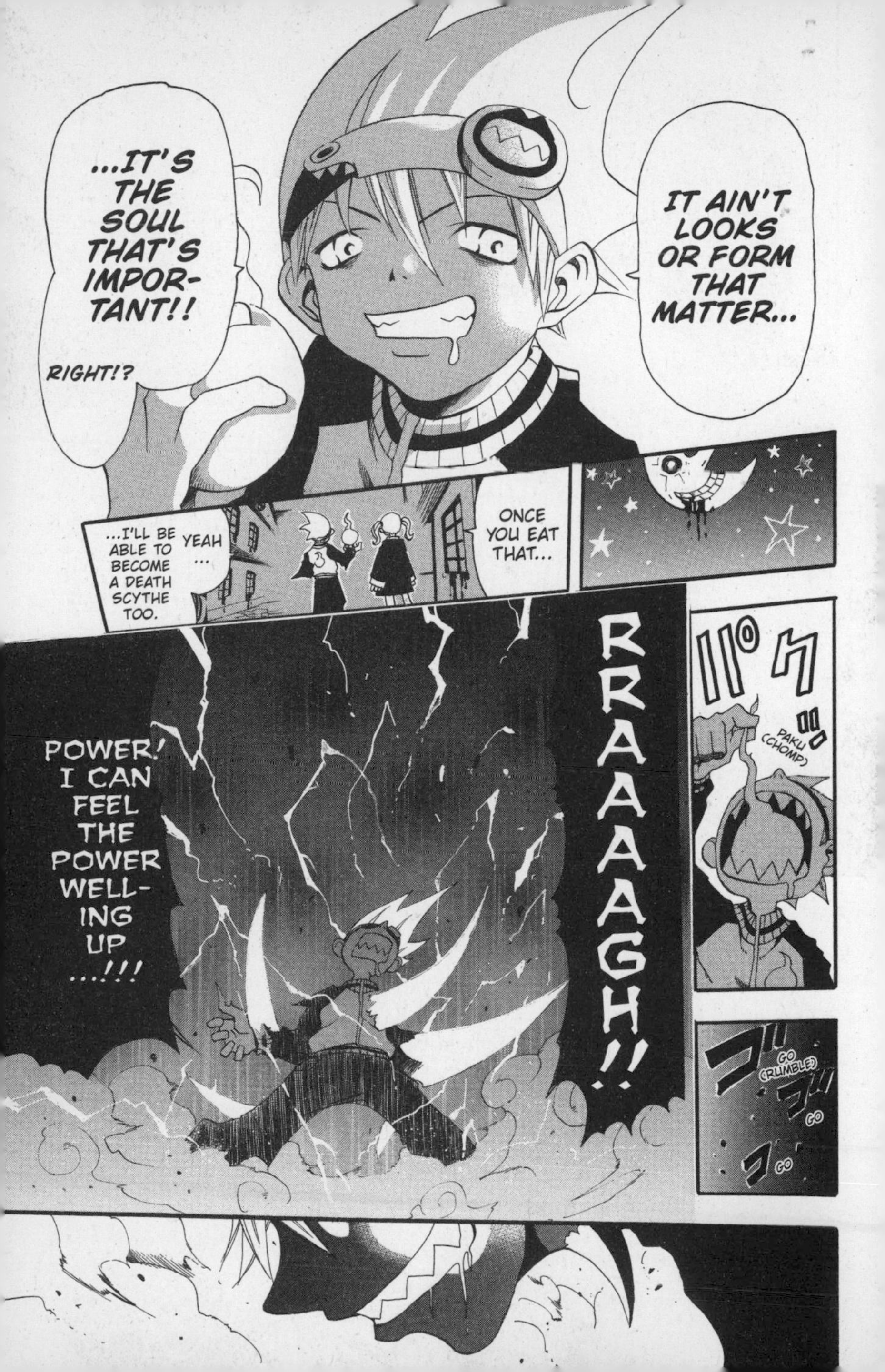
IT AIN'T LOOKS OR FORM THAT MATTER...
...IT'S THE SOUL THAT'S IMPOR-TANT!!
RIGHT!?
ONCE YOU EAT THAT...
YEAH ...
...I'LL BE ABLE TO BECOME A DEATH SCYTHE TOO.
パク
PAKU (CHOMP)
ゴゴゴ
GO (RUMBLE) GO GO
RRAAAAGH!!
POWER! I CAN FEEL THE POWER WELL-ING UP ...!!!

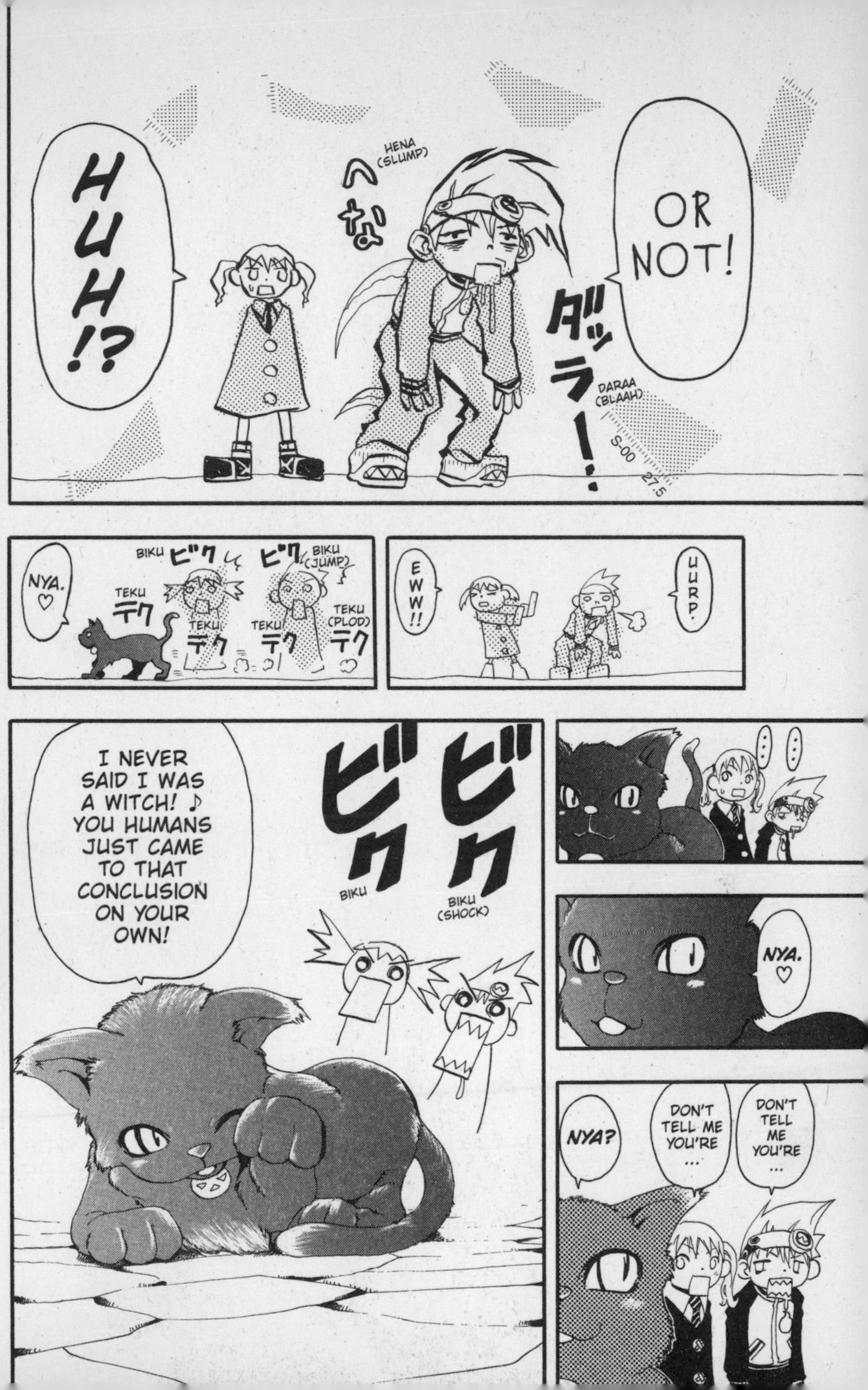
OR NOT!
ダッラー!!
DARAA (BLAAH)
へな
HENA (SLUMP)
HUH!?
UURP.
EWW!!
テク
TEKU (PLOD)
ビク
BIKU (JUMP)
テク
TEKU
ビク
BIKU
テク
TEKU
テク
TEKU
NYA. ♡
...
...
NYA. ♡
DON'T TELL ME YOU'RE ...
DON'T TELL ME YOU'RE ...
NYA?
ビク
BIKU (SHOCK)
ビク
BIKU
I NEVER SAID I WAS A WITCH! ♪ YOU HUMANS JUST CAME TO THAT CONCLUSION ON YOUR OWN!

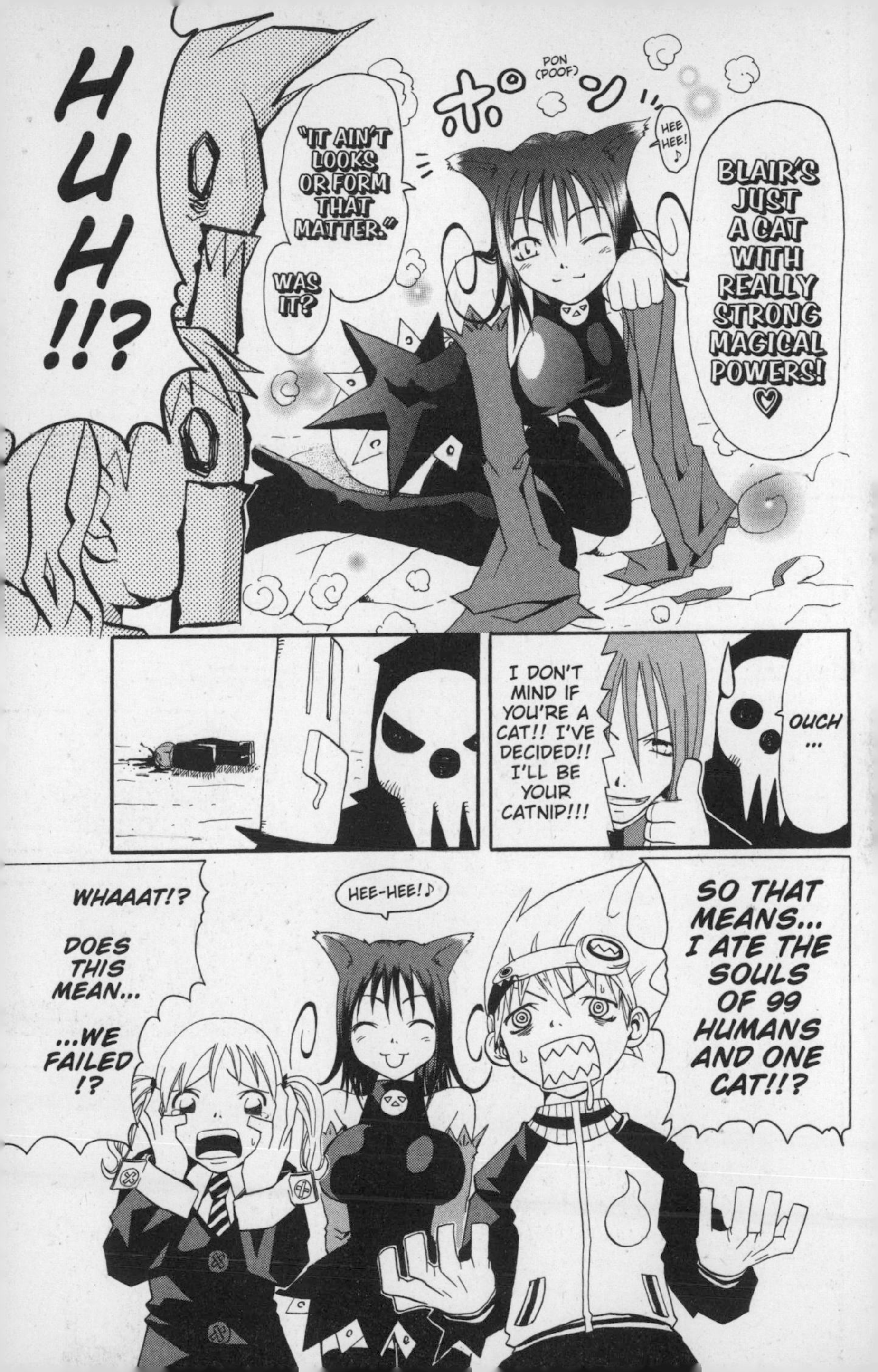
BLAIR'S JUST A CAT WITH REALLY STRONG MAGICAL POWERS! ♡
HEE HEE! ♪
PON (POOF)
ポン
"IT AIN'T LOOKS OR FORM THAT MATTER."
WAS IT?
HUH!!?
OUCH ...
I DON'T MIND IF YOU'RE A CAT!! I'VE DECIDED!! I'LL BE YOUR CATNIP!!!
SO THAT MEANS... I ATE THE SOULS OF 99 HUMANS AND ONE CAT!!?
HEE-HEE!♪
WHAAAT!?
DOES THIS MEAN...
...WE FAILED !?

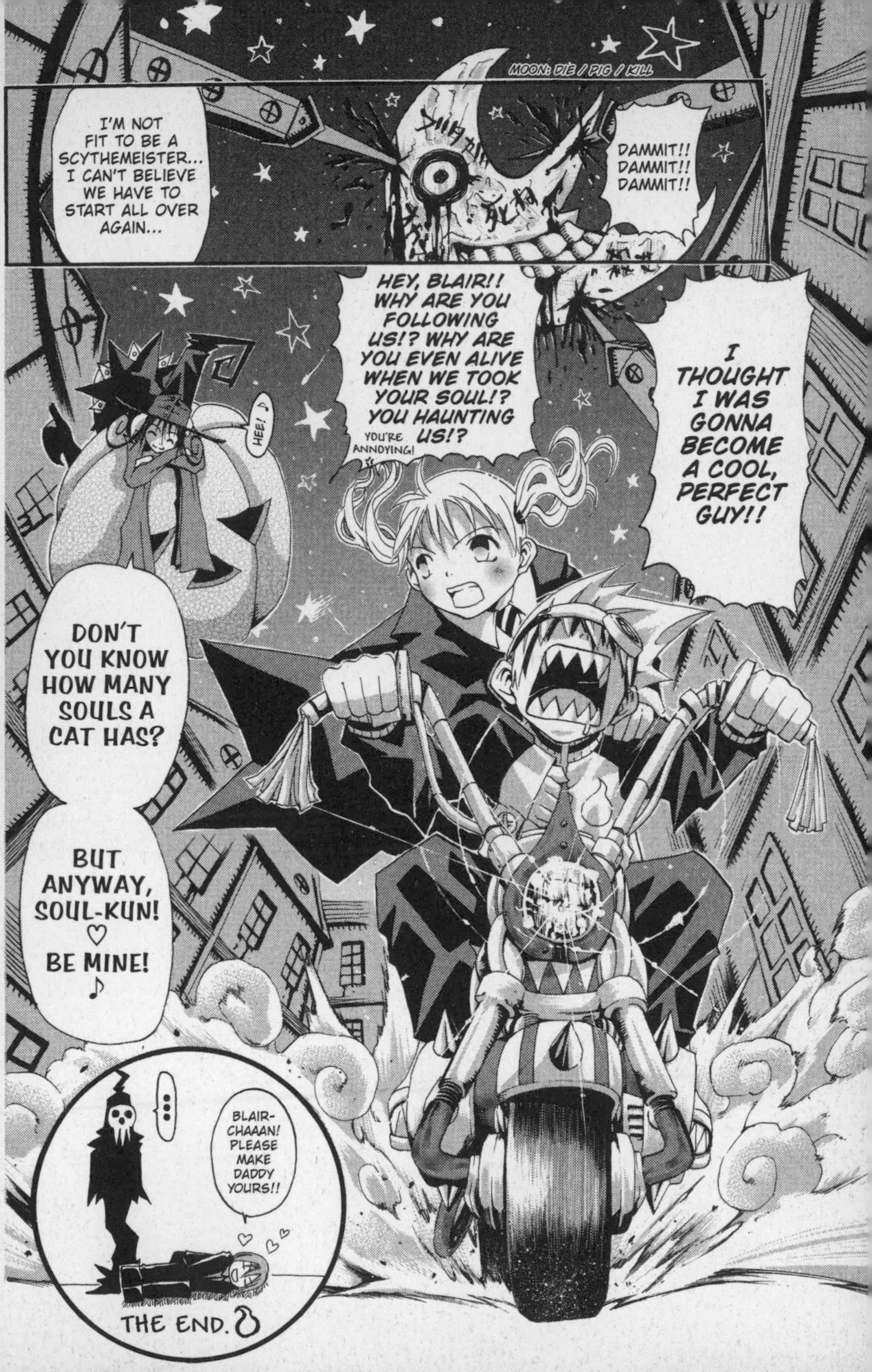
MOON: DIE / PIG / KILL
DAMMIT!! DAMMIT!! DAMMIT!!
I'M NOT FIT TO BE A SCYTHEMEISTER... I CAN'T BELIEVE WE HAVE TO START ALL OVER AGAIN...
I THOUGHT I WAS GONNA BECOME A COOL, PERFECT GUY!!
HEY, BLAIR!! WHY ARE YOU FOLLOWING US!? WHY ARE YOU EVEN ALIVE WHEN WE TOOK YOUR SOUL!? YOU HAUNTING US!?
YOU'RE ANNOYING!
HEE! ♪
DON'T YOU KNOW HOW MANY SOULS A CAT HAS?
BUT ANYWAY, SOUL-KUN! ♡ BE MINE! ♪
BLAIR-CHAAAN! PLEASE MAKE DADDY YOURS!!
...
THE END.

SOUL EATER

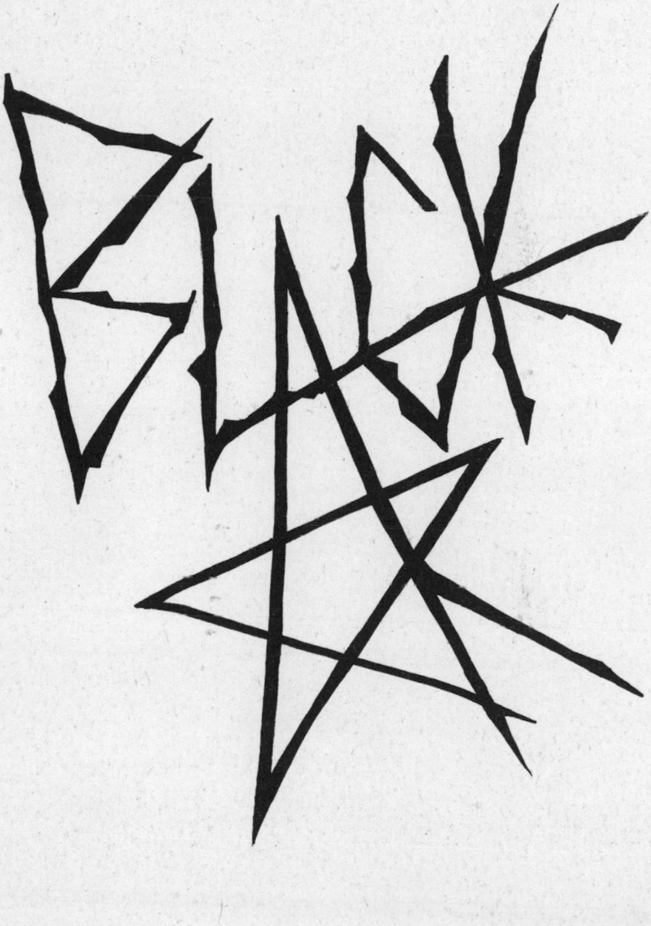
BLACK

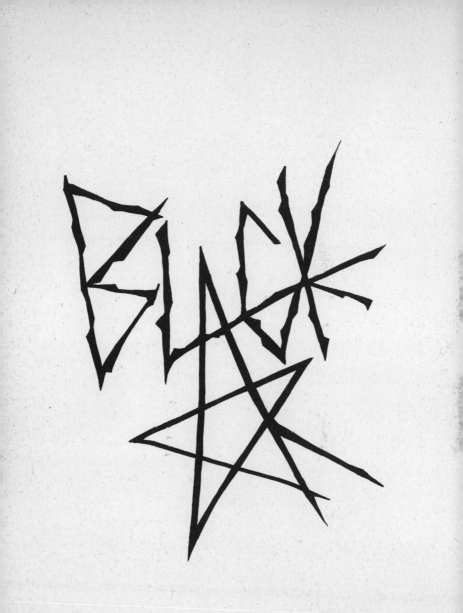

PROLOGUE 2: BLACK☆STAR

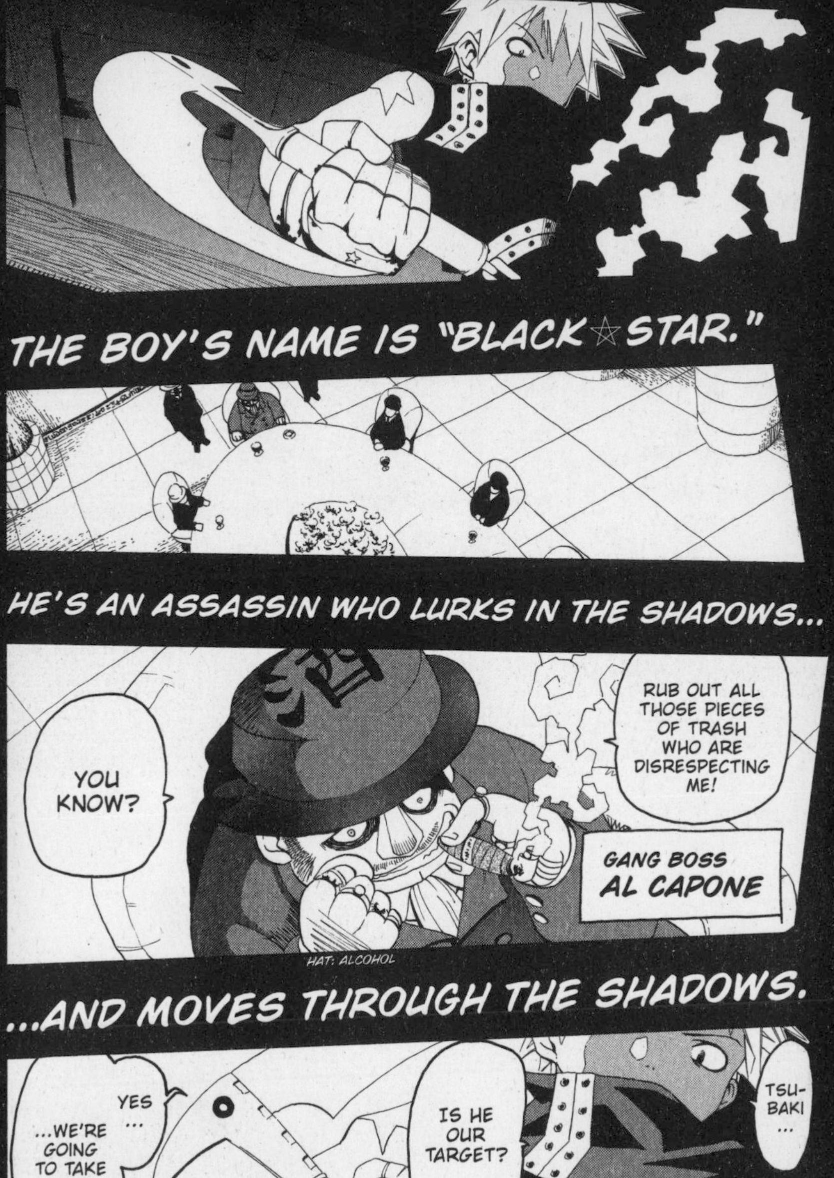
THE BOY'S NAME IS "BLACK☆STAR."
HE'S AN ASSASSIN WHO LURKS IN THE SHADOWS...
RUB OUT ALL THOSE PIECES OF TRASH WHO ARE DISRESPECTING ME!
GANG BOSS AL CAPONE
YOU KNOW?
HAT: ALCOHOL
...AND MOVES THROUGH THE SHADOWS.
TSU-BAKI ...
IS HE OUR TARGET?
YES ...
...WE'RE GOING TO TAKE HIS SOUL!!

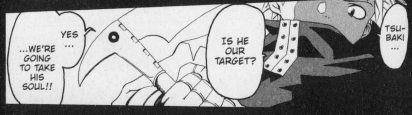

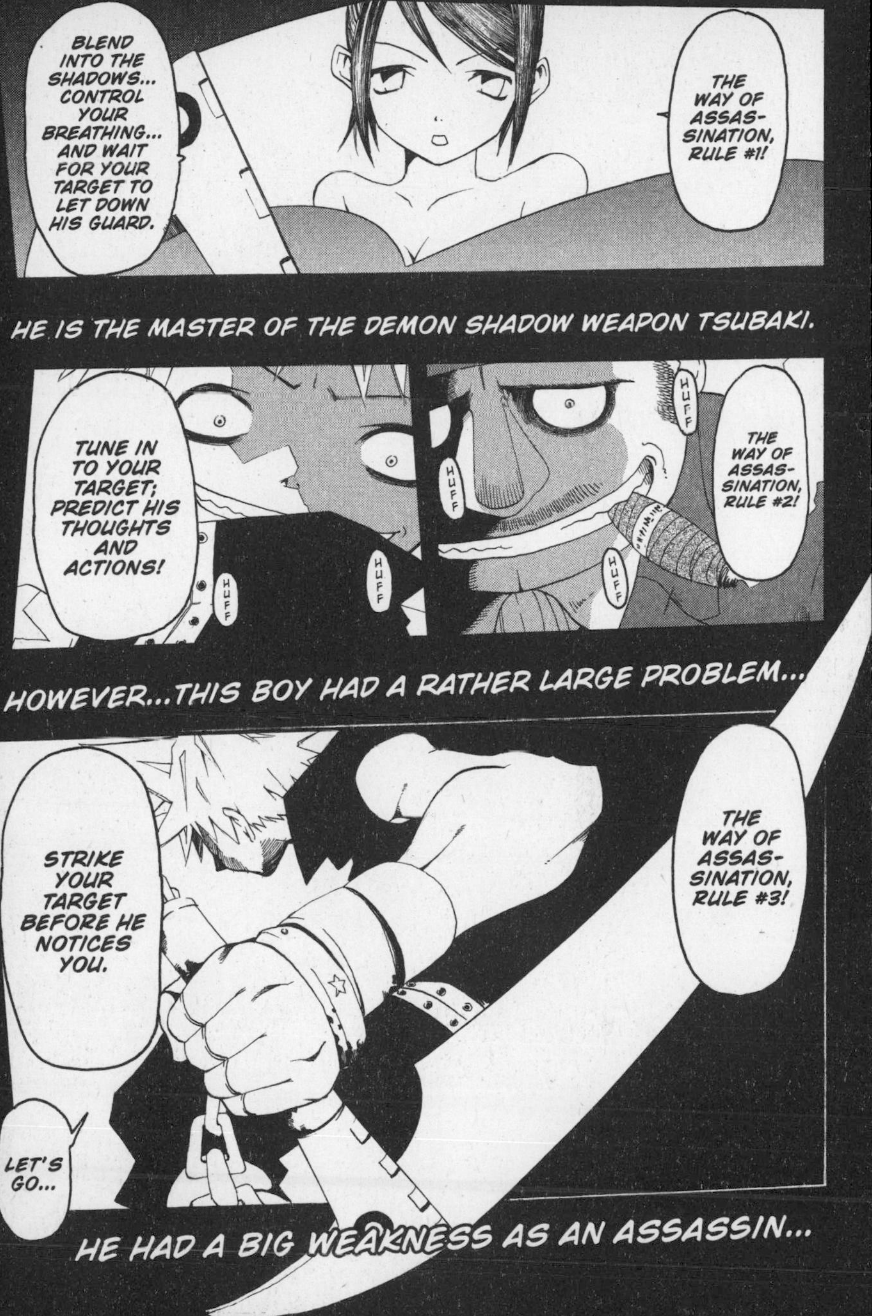
THE WAY OF ASSAS-SINATION, RULE #1!
BLEND INTO THE SHADOWS... CONTROL YOUR BREATHING... AND WAIT FOR YOUR TARGET TO LET DOWN HIS GUARD.
HE IS THE MASTER OF THE DEMON SHADOW WEAPON TSUBAKI.
HUFF
THE WAY OF ASSAS-SINATION, RULE #2!
HUFF
HUFF
TUNE IN TO YOUR TARGET; PREDICT HIS THOUGHTS AND ACTIONS!
HUFF
HUFF
HOWEVER...THIS BOY HAD A RATHER LARGE PROBLEM...
THE WAY OF ASSAS-SINATION, RULE #3!
STRIKE YOUR TARGET BEFORE HE NOTICES YOU.
LET'S GO...
HE HAD A BIG WEAKNESS AS AN ASSASSIN...

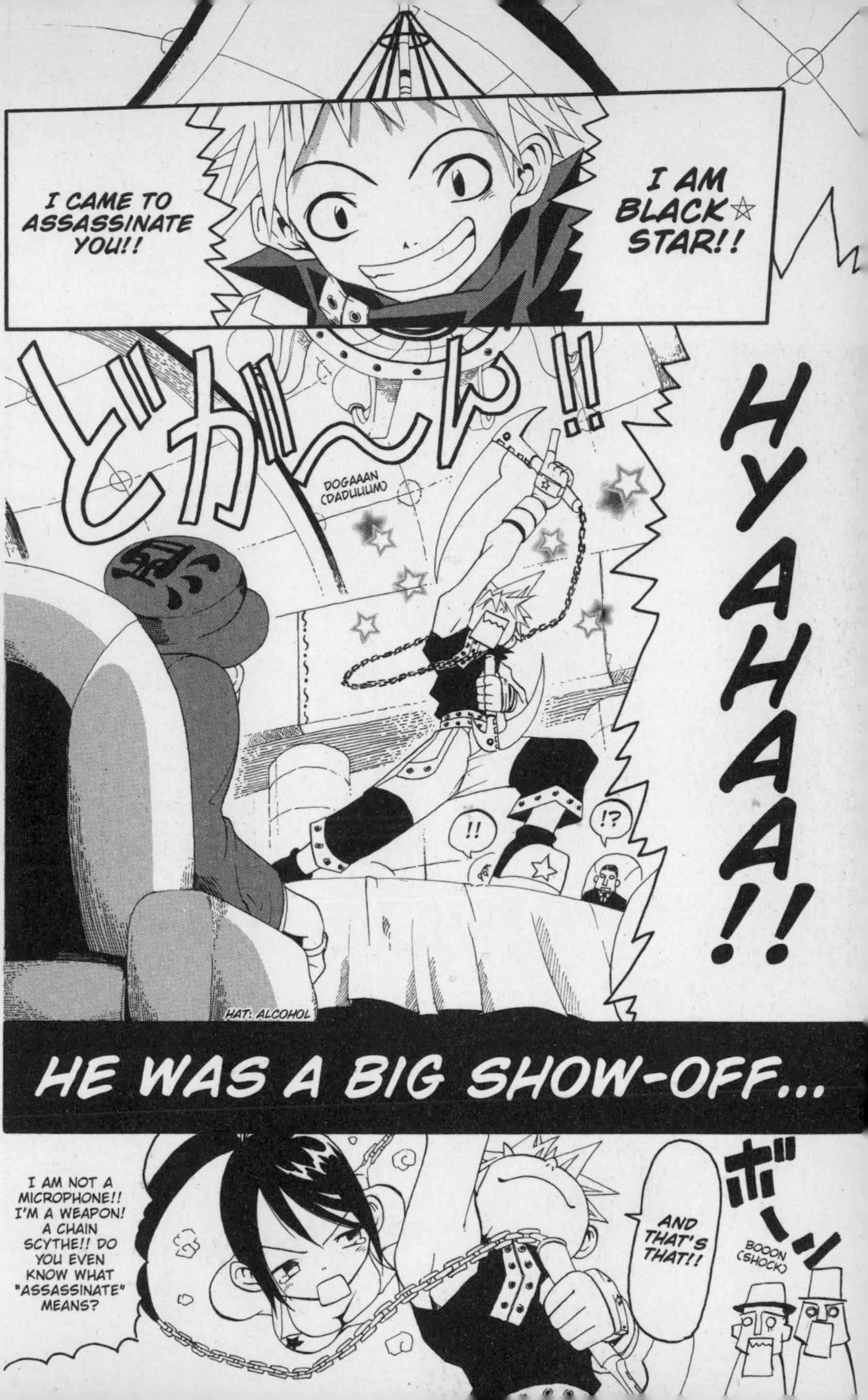

I AM BLACK☆STAR!!
I CAME TO ASSASSINATE YOU!!
HYAHAHA!!
どが〜ん!!
DOGAAAN (DADUUUM)
!?
!!
HAT: ALCOHOL
HE WAS A BIG SHOW-OFF...
ボーンッ
BOOON (SHOCK)
AND THAT'S THAT!!
I AM NOT A MICROPHONE!! I'M A WEAPON! A CHAIN SCYTHE!! DO YOU EVEN KNOW WHAT "ASSASSINATE" MEANS?

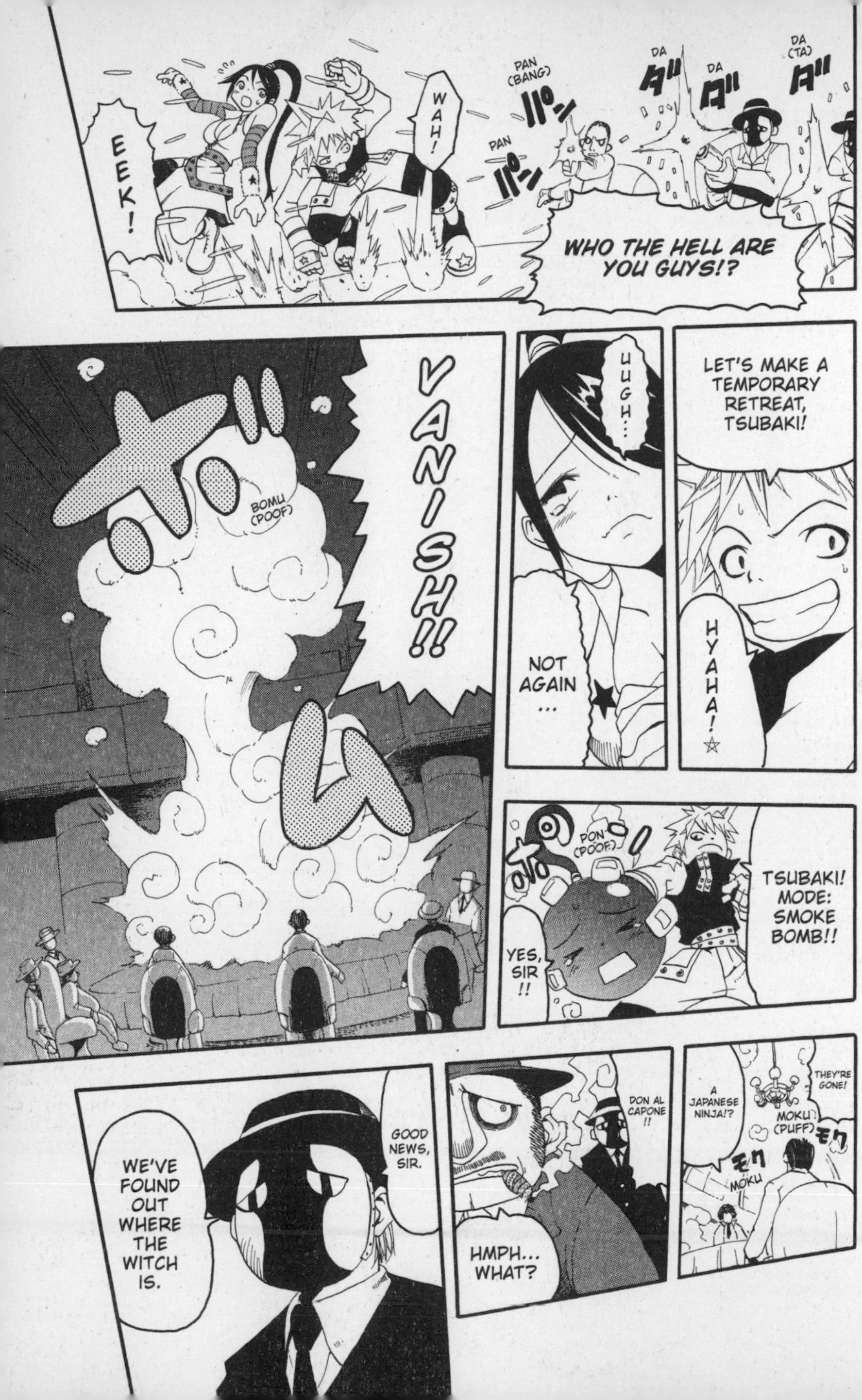
DA (TA)
DA
DA
PAN (BANG)
WHO THE HELL ARE YOU GUYS!?
PAN
WAH!
EEK!
LET'S MAKE A TEMPORARY RETREAT, TSUBAKI!
HYAHA!☆
UUGH...
NOT AGAIN ...
TSUBAKI! MODE: SMOKE BOMB!!
PON (POOF)
YES, SIR!!
VANISH!!
BOMU (POOF)
THEY'RE GONE!
A JAPANESE NINJA!?
MOKU (PUFF)
MOKU
DON AL CAPONE!!
HMPH... WHAT?
GOOD NEWS, SIR.
WE'VE FOUND OUT WHERE THE WITCH IS.

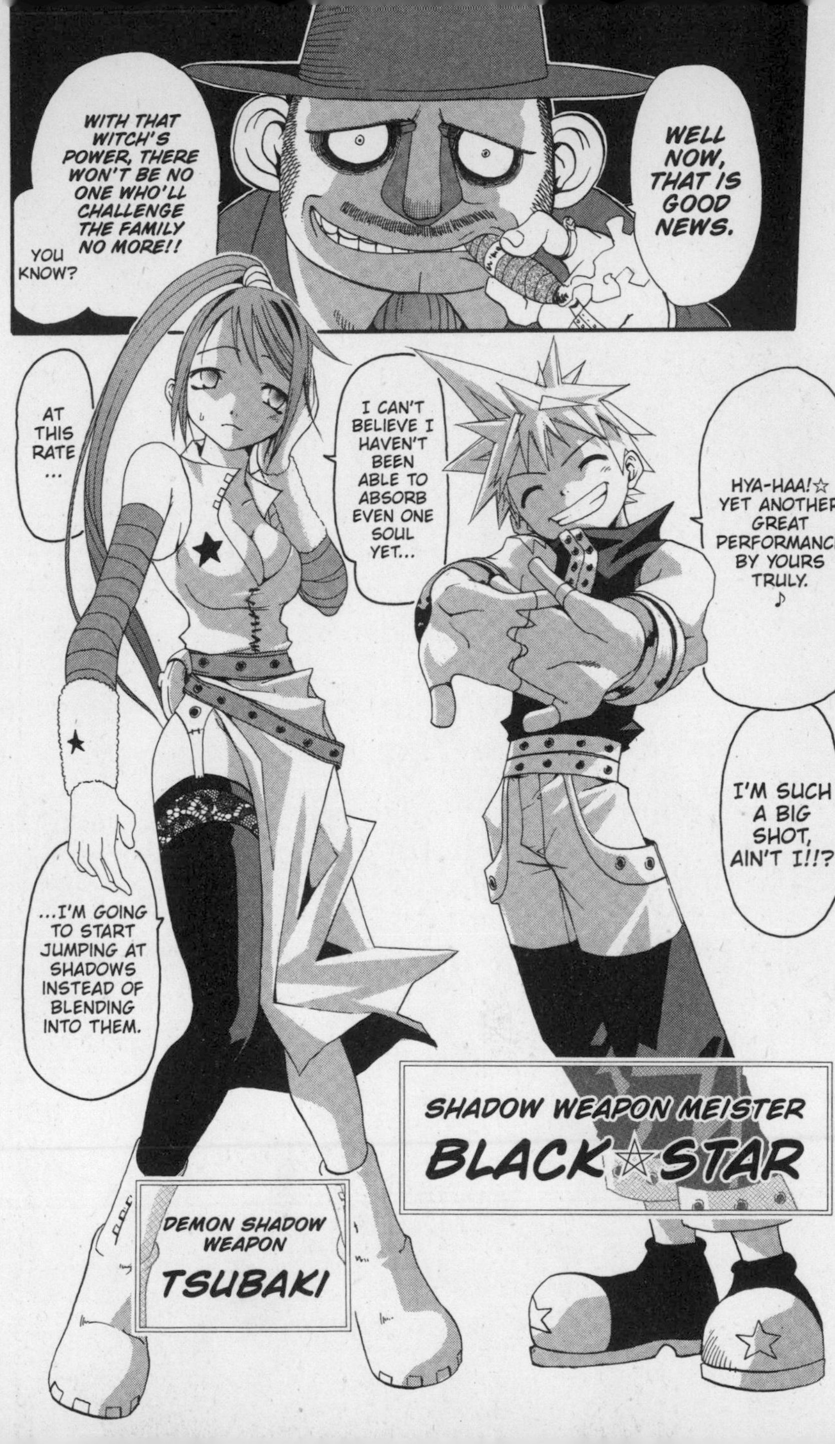
WELL NOW, THAT IS GOOD NEWS.
WITH THAT WITCH'S POWER, THERE WON'T BE NO ONE WHO'LL CHALLENGE THE FAMILY NO MORE!!
YOU KNOW?
HYA-HAA!☆ YET ANOTHER GREAT PERFORMANCE BY YOURS TRULY. ♪
I'M SUCH A BIG SHOT, AIN'T I!!?
I CAN'T BELIEVE I HAVEN'T BEEN ABLE TO ABSORB EVEN ONE SOUL YET...
AT THIS RATE ...
...I'M GOING TO START JUMPING AT SHADOWS INSTEAD OF BLENDING INTO THEM.
SHADOW WEAPON MEISTER
BLACK☆STAR
DEMON SHADOW WEAPON
TSUBAKI

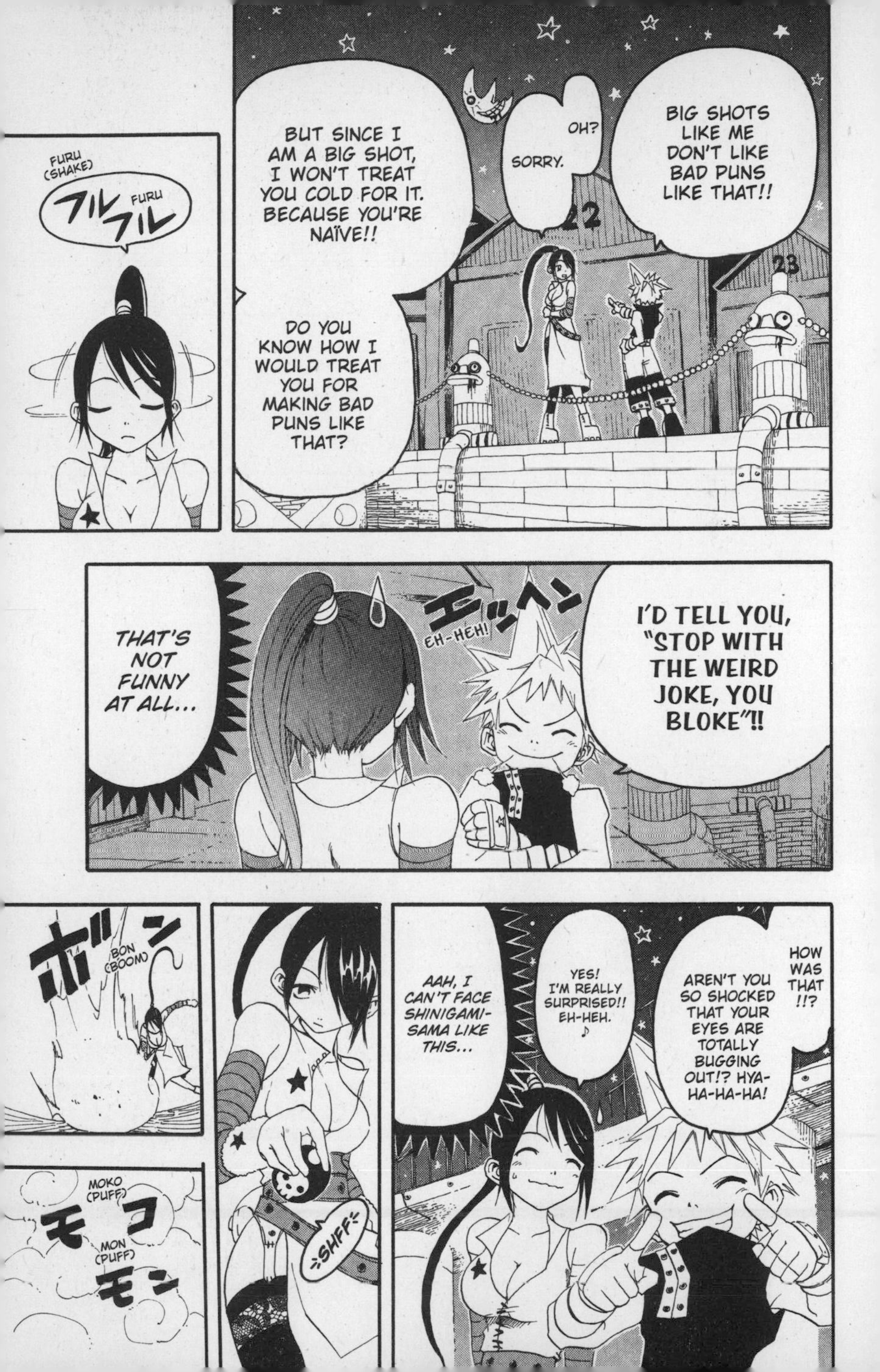
BIG SHOTS LIKE ME DON'T LIKE BAD PUNS LIKE THAT!!
OH?
SORRY.
BUT SINCE I AM A BIG SHOT, I WON'T TREAT YOU COLD FOR IT. BECAUSE YOU'RE NAÏVE!!
DO YOU KNOW HOW I WOULD TREAT YOU FOR MAKING BAD PUNS LIKE THAT?
22
23
フルフル
FURU (SHAKE)
FURU
I'D TELL YOU, "STOP WITH THE WEIRD JOKE, YOU BLOKE"!!
エッヘン
EH-HEH!
THAT'S NOT FUNNY AT ALL...
HOW WAS THAT!!?
AREN'T YOU SO SHOCKED THAT YOUR EYES ARE TOTALLY BUGGING OUT!? HYA-HA-HA-HA!
YES! I'M REALLY SURPRISED!! EH-HEH. ♪
AAH, I CAN'T FACE SHINIGAMI-SAMA LIKE THIS...
SHFF
ボン
BON (BOOM)
モコ
MOKO (PUFF)
モン
MON (PUFF)

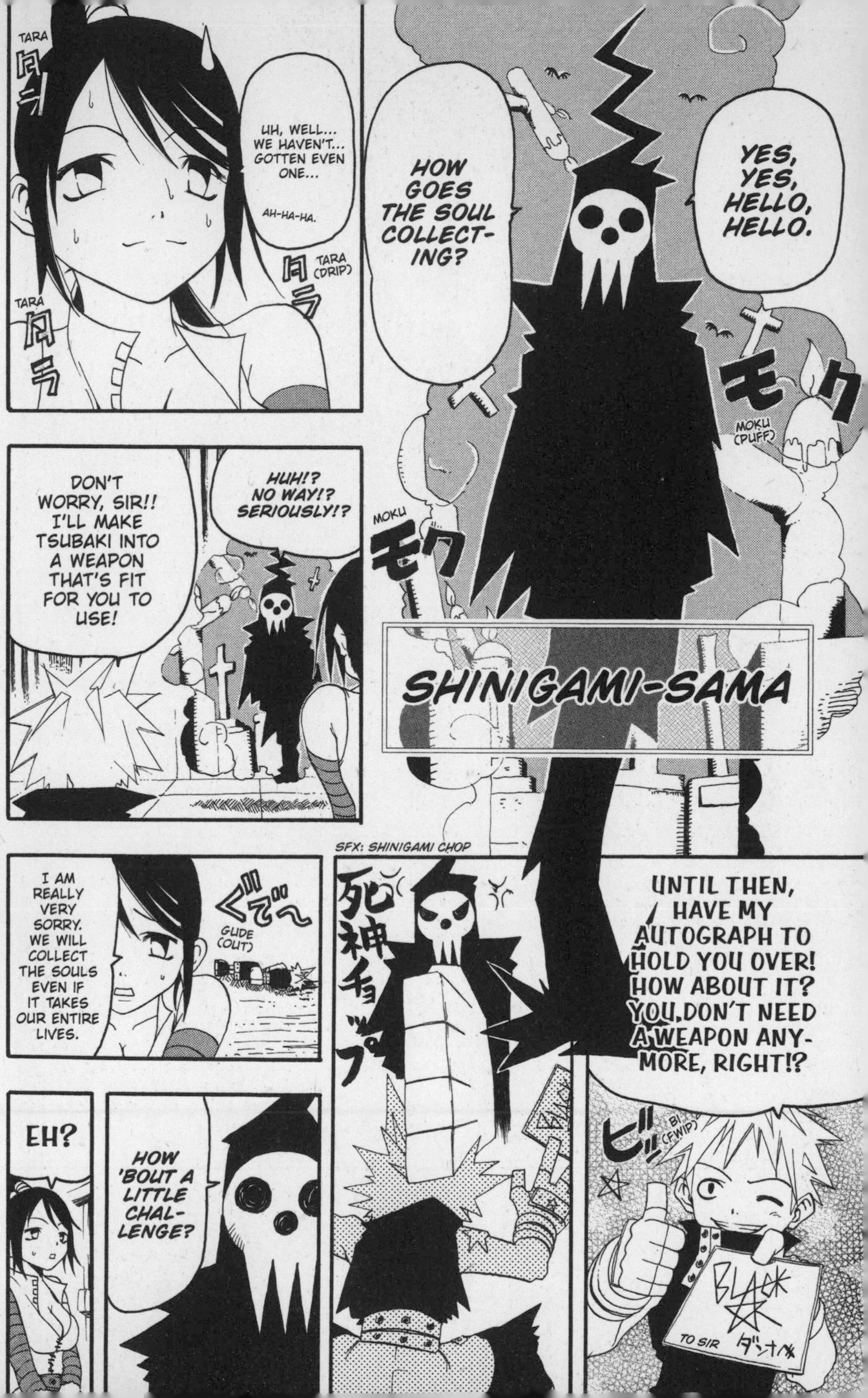
YES, YES, HELLO, HELLO.
HOW GOES THE SOUL COLLECTING?
MOKU (PUFF)
MOKU
SHINIGAMI-SAMA
TARA
TARA
UH, WELL... WE HAVEN'T... GOTTEN EVEN ONE...
AH-HA-HA.
TARA (DRIP)
HUH!? NO WAY!? SERIOUSLY!?
DON'T WORRY, SIR!! I'LL MAKE TSUBAKI INTO A WEAPON THAT'S FIT FOR YOU TO USE!
UNTIL THEN, HAVE MY AUTOGRAPH TO HOLD YOU OVER! HOW ABOUT IT? YOU DON'T NEED A WEAPON ANYMORE, RIGHT!?
BI (FWIP)
TO SIR
SFX: SHINIGAMI CHOP
GUDE (OUT)
I AM REALLY VERY SORRY. WE WILL COLLECT THE SOULS EVEN IF IT TAKES OUR ENTIRE LIVES.
HOW 'BOUT A LITTLE CHALLENGE?
EH?

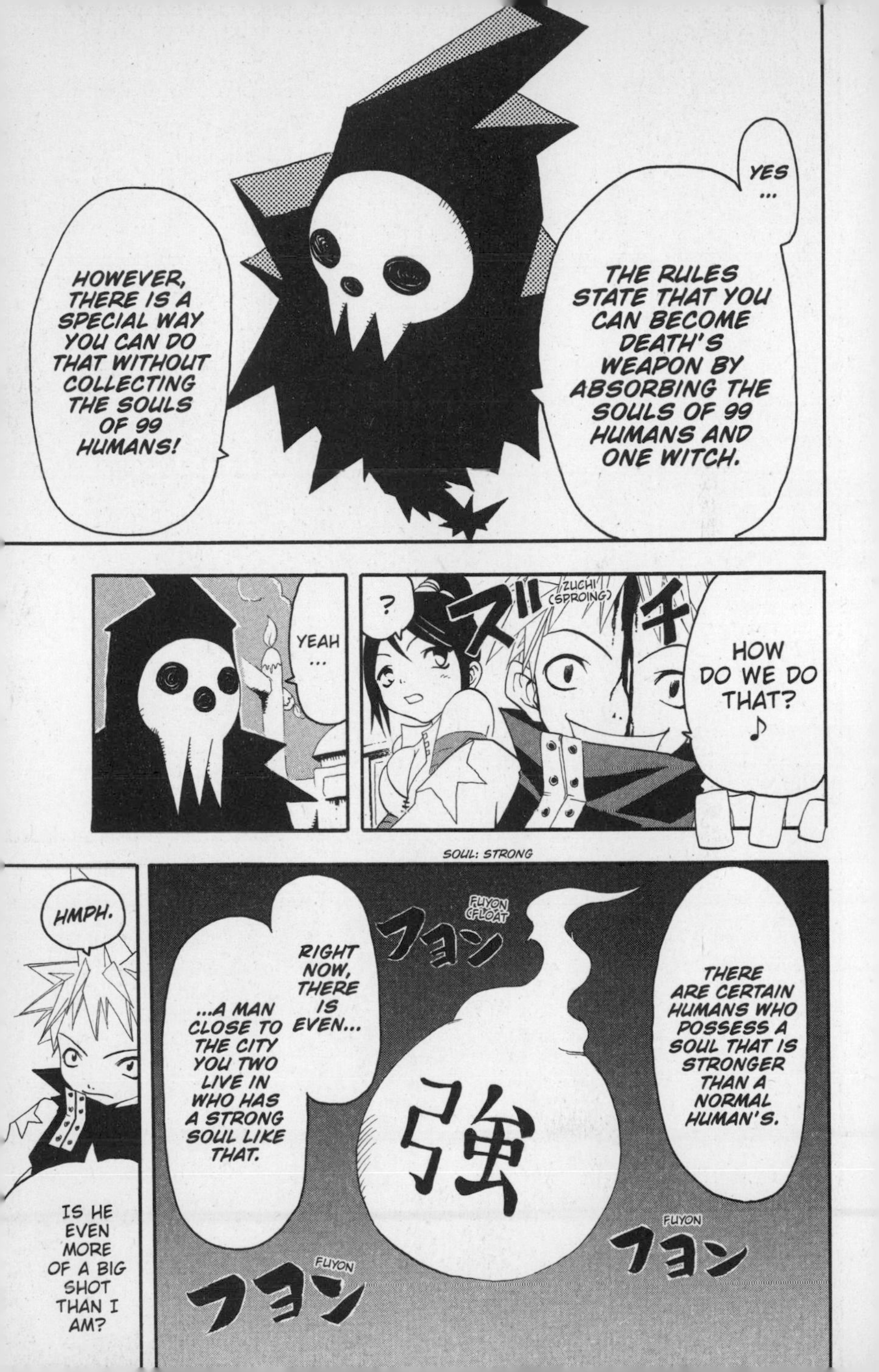
YES ...
THE RULES STATE THAT YOU CAN BECOME DEATH'S WEAPON BY ABSORBING THE SOULS OF 99 HUMANS AND ONE WITCH.
HOWEVER, THERE IS A SPECIAL WAY YOU CAN DO THAT WITHOUT COLLECTING THE SOULS OF 99 HUMANS!
HOW DO WE DO THAT? ♪
ZUCHI (SPROING)
?
YEAH ...
SOUL: STRONG
THERE ARE CERTAIN HUMANS WHO POSSESS A SOUL THAT IS STRONGER THAN A NORMAL HUMAN'S.
FUYON (FLOAT)
RIGHT NOW, THERE IS EVEN...
...A MAN CLOSE TO THE CITY YOU TWO LIVE IN WHO HAS A STRONG SOUL LIKE THAT.
強
FUYON
FUYON
HMPH.
IS HE EVEN MORE OF A BIG SHOT THAN I AM?

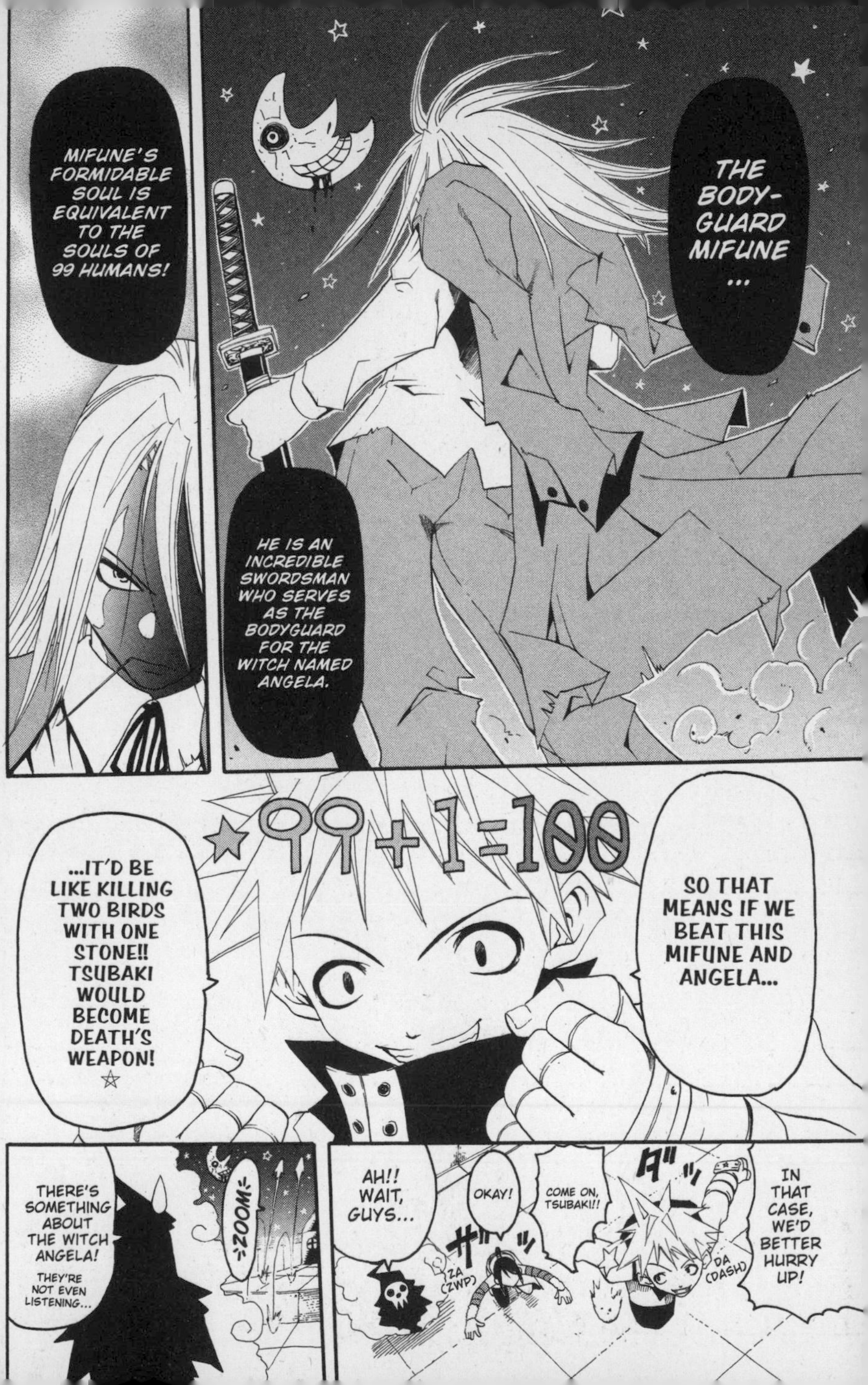
THE BODY-GUARD MIFUNE ...
HE IS AN INCREDIBLE SWORDSMAN WHO SERVES AS THE BODYGUARD FOR THE WITCH NAMED ANGELA.
MIFUNE'S FORMIDABLE SOUL IS EQUIVALENT TO THE SOULS OF 99 HUMANS!
★99 + 1 = 100
SO THAT MEANS IF WE BEAT THIS MIFUNE AND ANGELA...
...IT'D BE LIKE KILLING TWO BIRDS WITH ONE STONE!! TSUBAKI WOULD BECOME DEATH'S WEAPON! ☆
IN THAT CASE, WE'D BETTER HURRY UP!
ダッ
DA (DASH)
COME ON, TSUBAKI!!
OKAY!
ザッ
ZA (ZWP)
AH!! WAIT, GUYS...
ZOOM
THERE'S SOMETHING ABOUT THE WITCH ANGELA!
THEY'RE NOT EVEN LISTENING...

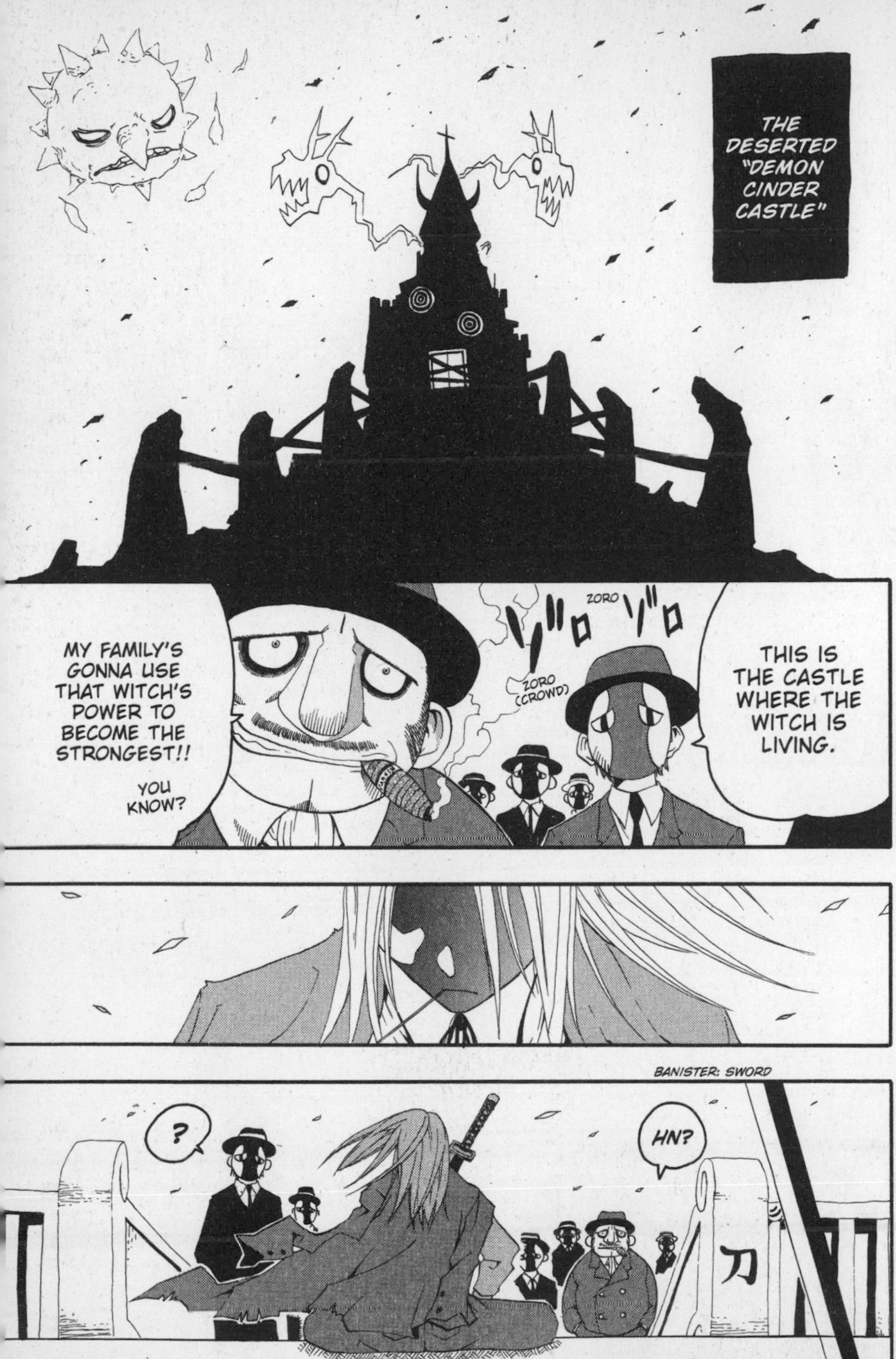
THE DESERTED "DEMON CINDER CASTLE"
THIS IS THE CASTLE WHERE THE WITCH IS LIVING.
ZORO
ゾロ ゾロ
ZORO (CROWD)
MY FAMILY'S GONNA USE THAT WITCH'S POWER TO BECOME THE STRONGEST!!
YOU KNOW?
BANISTER: SWORD
HN?
刀
?

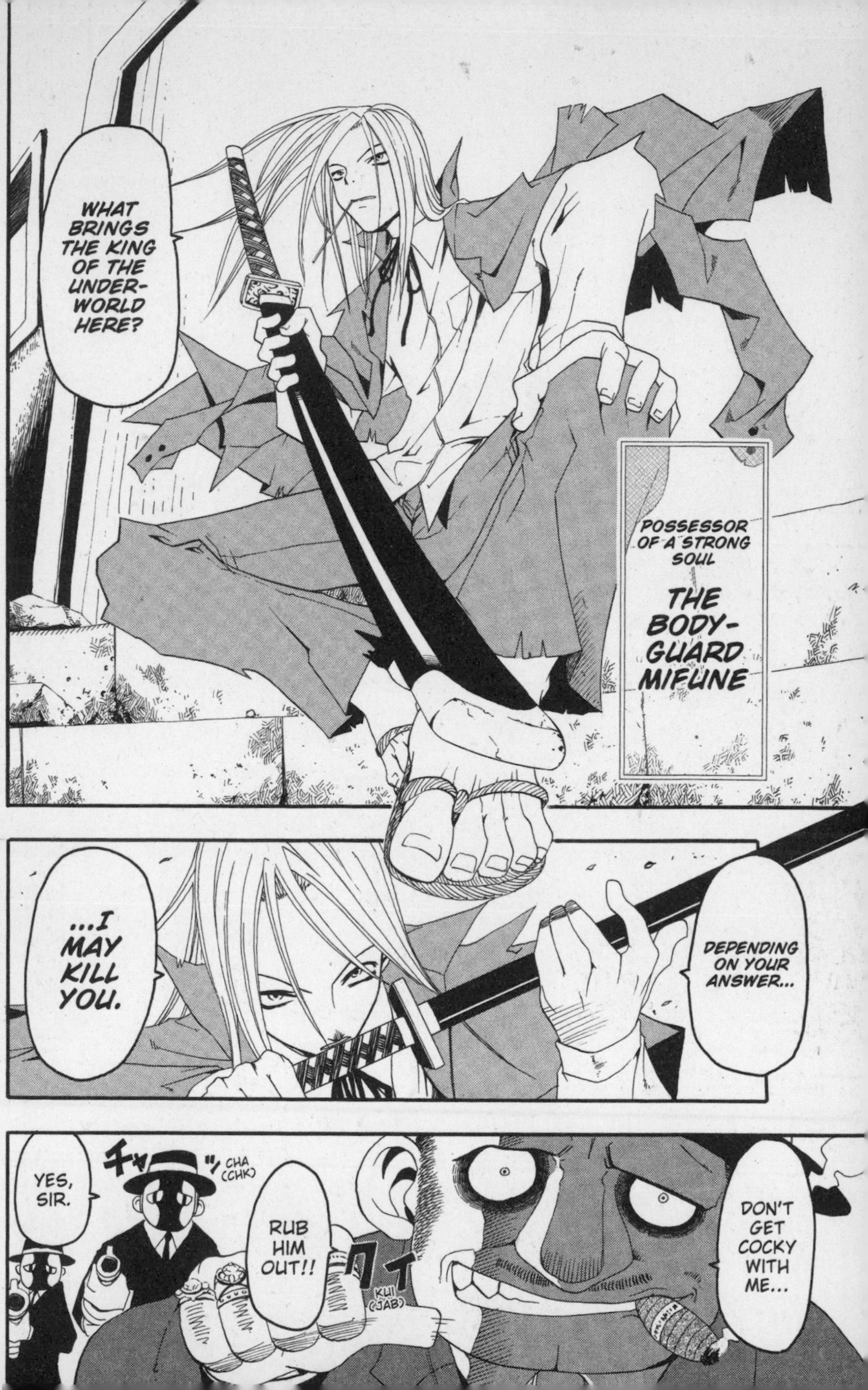
WHAT BRINGS THE KING OF THE UNDER-WORLD HERE?
POSSESSOR OF A STRONG SOUL
THE BODY-GUARD MIFUNE
DEPENDING ON YOUR ANSWER...
...I MAY KILL YOU.
DON'T GET COCKY WITH ME...
クイ
KUI (JAB)
RUB HIM OUT!!
チャッ
CHA (CHK)
YES, SIR.

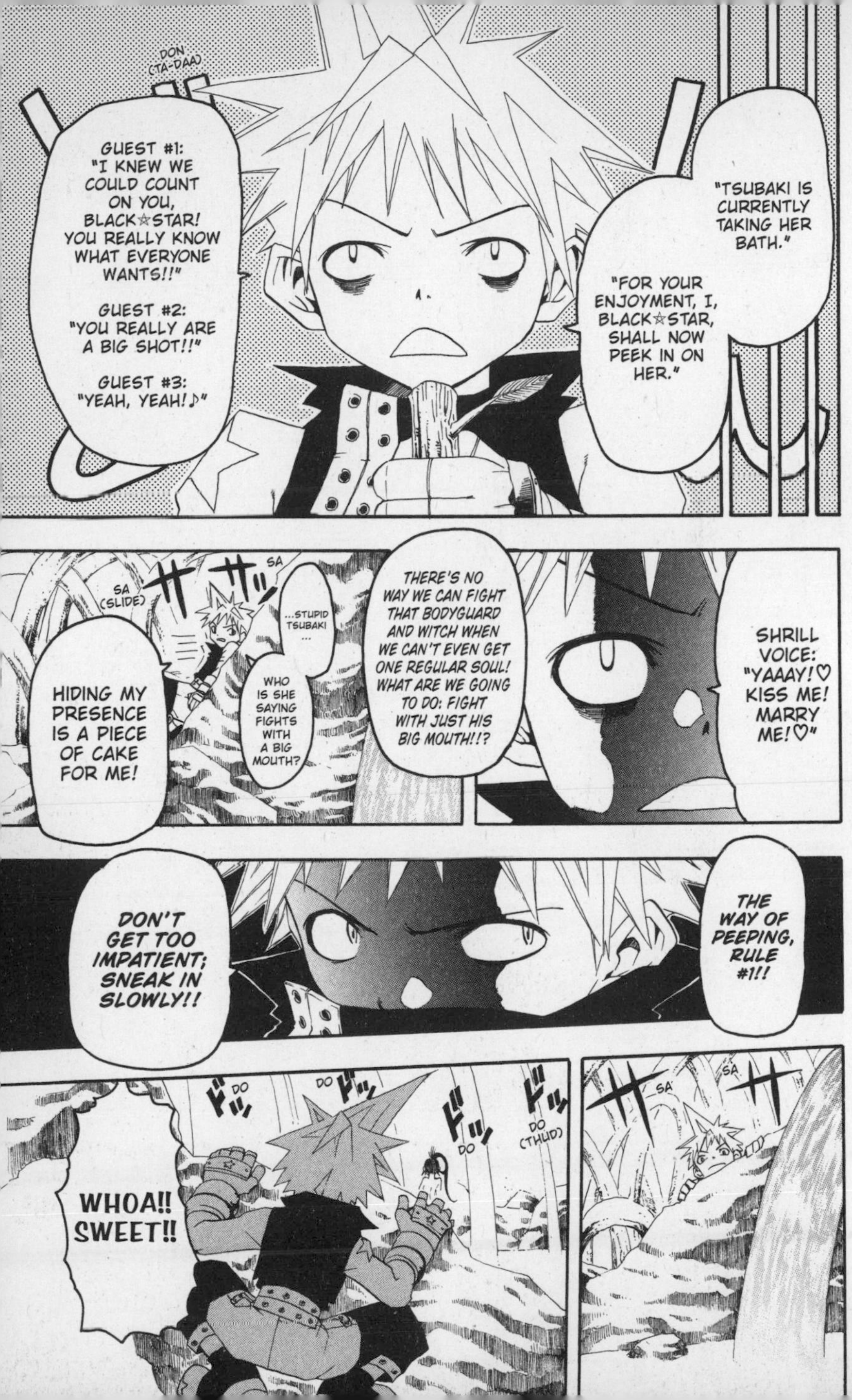
"TSUBAKI IS CURRENTLY TAKING HER BATH."
"FOR YOUR ENJOYMENT, I, BLACK☆STAR, SHALL NOW PEEK IN ON HER."
DON (TA-DAA)
GUEST #1: "I KNEW WE COULD COUNT ON YOU, BLACK☆STAR! YOU REALLY KNOW WHAT EVERYONE WANTS!!"
GUEST #2: "YOU REALLY ARE A BIG SHOT!!"
GUEST #3: "YEAH, YEAH!♪"
SHRILL VOICE: "YAAAY!♡ KISS ME! MARRY ME!♡"
THERE'S NO WAY WE CAN FIGHT THAT BODYGUARD AND WITCH WHEN WE CAN'T EVEN GET ONE REGULAR SOUL! WHAT ARE WE GOING TO DO: FIGHT WITH JUST HIS BIG MOUTH!!?
SA
SA (SLIDE)
...STUPID TSUBAKI ...
WHO IS SHE SAYING FIGHTS WITH A BIG MOUTH?
HIDING MY PRESENCE IS A PIECE OF CAKE FOR ME!
THE WAY OF PEEPING, RULE #1!!
DON'T GET TOO IMPATIENT; SNEAK IN SLOWLY!!
SA
SA
DO
DO
DO
DO (THUD)
WHOA!! SWEET!!

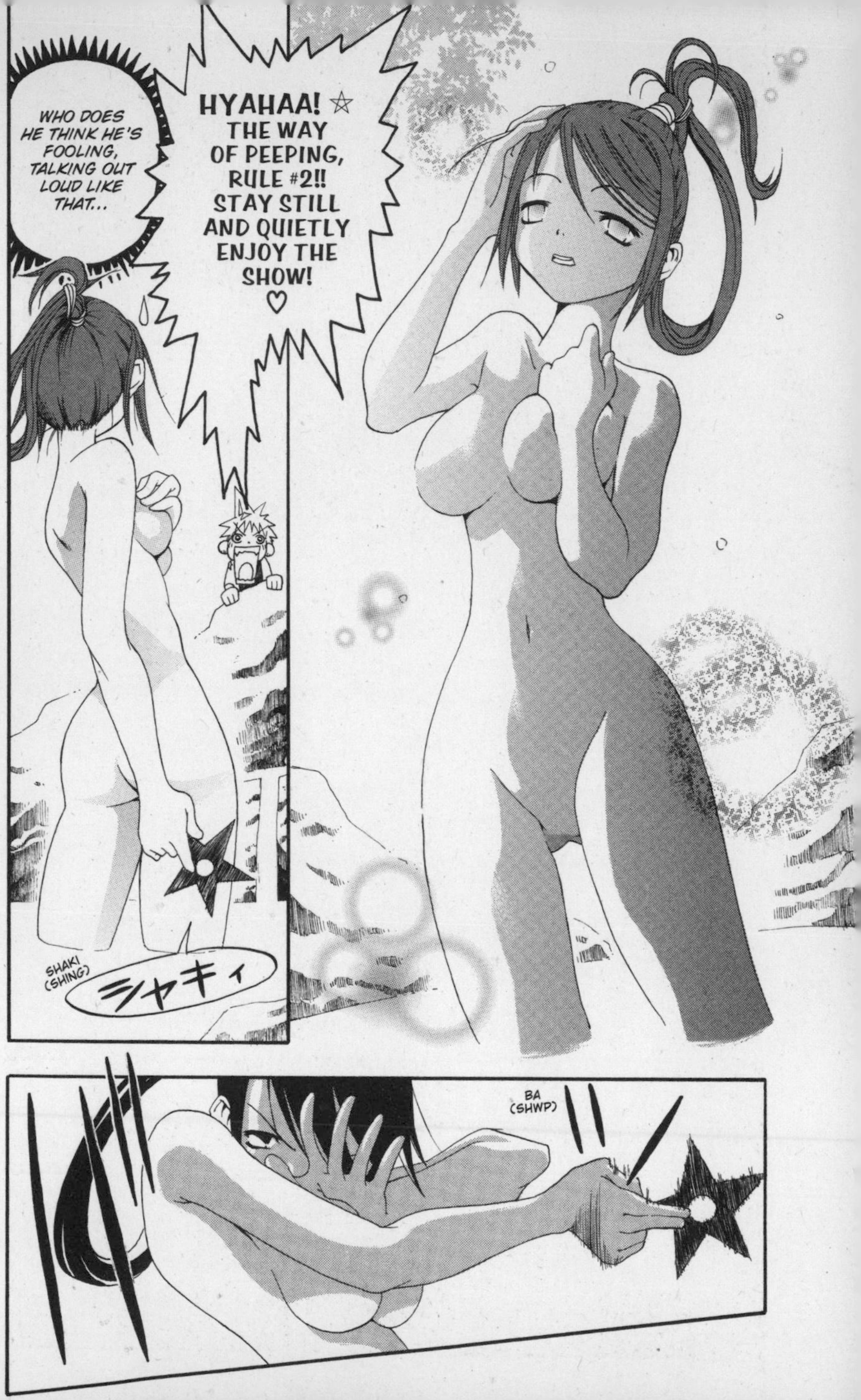
HYAHAA! ☆ THE WAY OF PEEPING, RULE #2!! STAY STILL AND QUIETLY ENJOY THE SHOW! ♡
WHO DOES HE THINK HE'S FOOLING, TALKING OUT LOUD LIKE THAT...
シャキィ
SHAKI (SHING)
BA (SHWP)

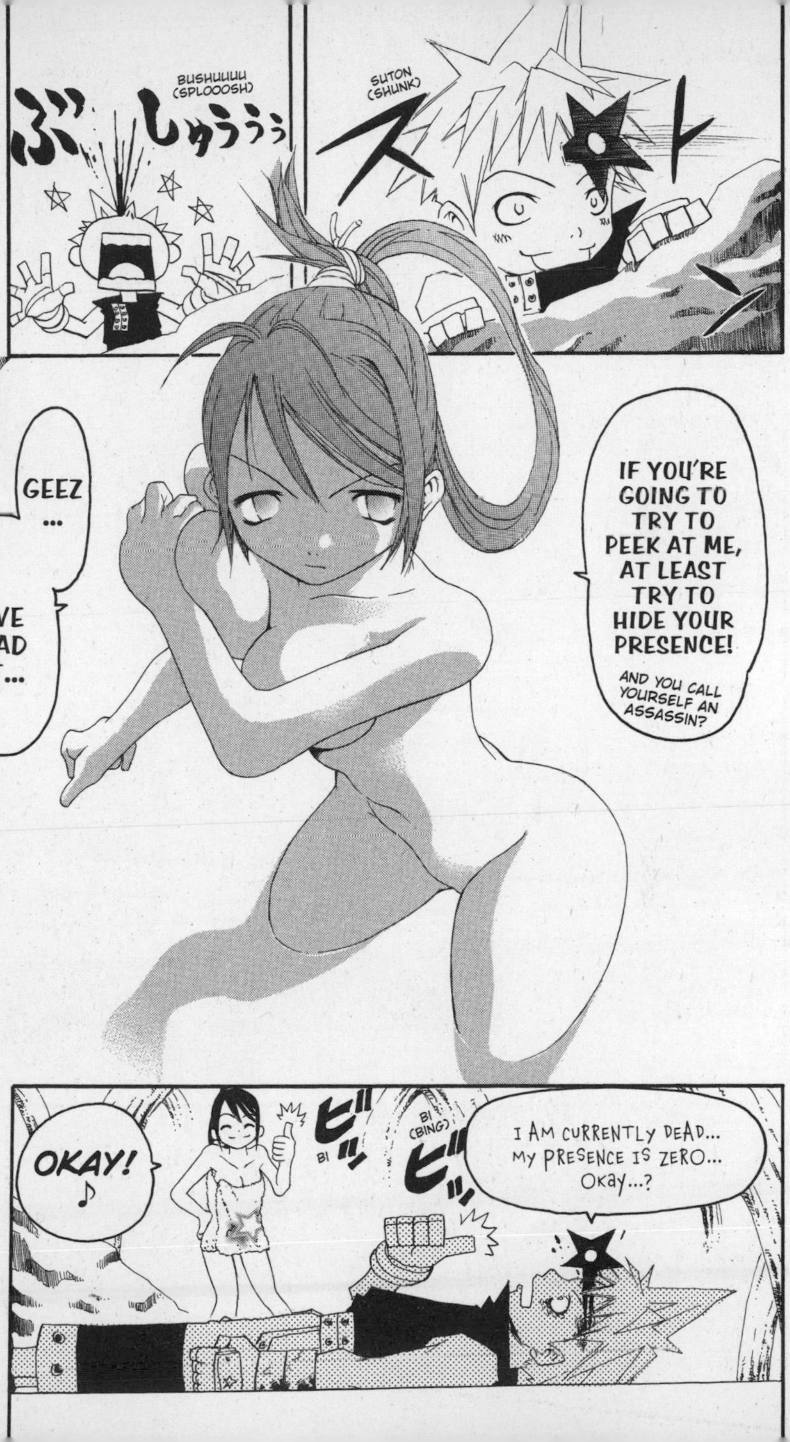

SUTON (SHUNK)
BUSHUUUU (SPLOOOSH)
IF YOU'RE GOING TO TRY TO PEEK AT ME, AT LEAST TRY TO HIDE YOUR PRESENCE!
AND YOU CALL YOURSELF AN ASSASSIN?
GEEZ ... I'VE HAD IT...
I AM CURRENTLY DEAD... MY PRESENCE IS ZERO... Okay...?
BI (BING)
BI
OKAY! ♪

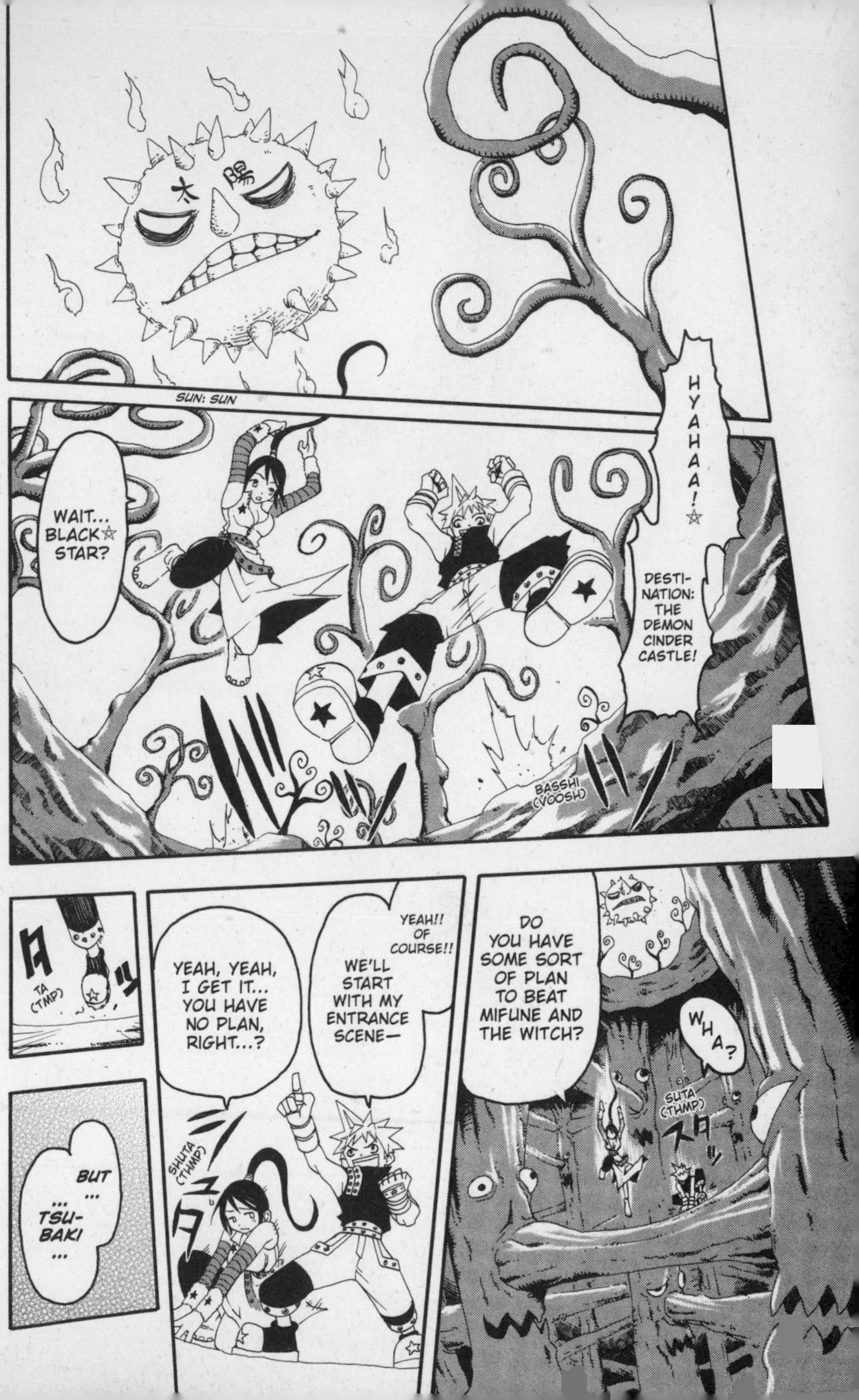
SUN: SUN
HYAHAAA!☆
DESTINATION: THE DEMON CINDER CASTLE!
WAIT... BLACK☆ STAR?
BASSHI (VOOSH)
DO YOU HAVE SOME SORT OF PLAN TO BEAT MIFUNE AND THE WITCH?
WHA?
SUTA (THMP)
YEAH!! OF COURSE!!
WE'LL START WITH MY ENTRANCE SCENE—
YEAH, YEAH, I GET IT... YOU HAVE NO PLAN, RIGHT...?
SHUTA (THMP)
TA (TMP)
BUT... ...TSUBAKI...

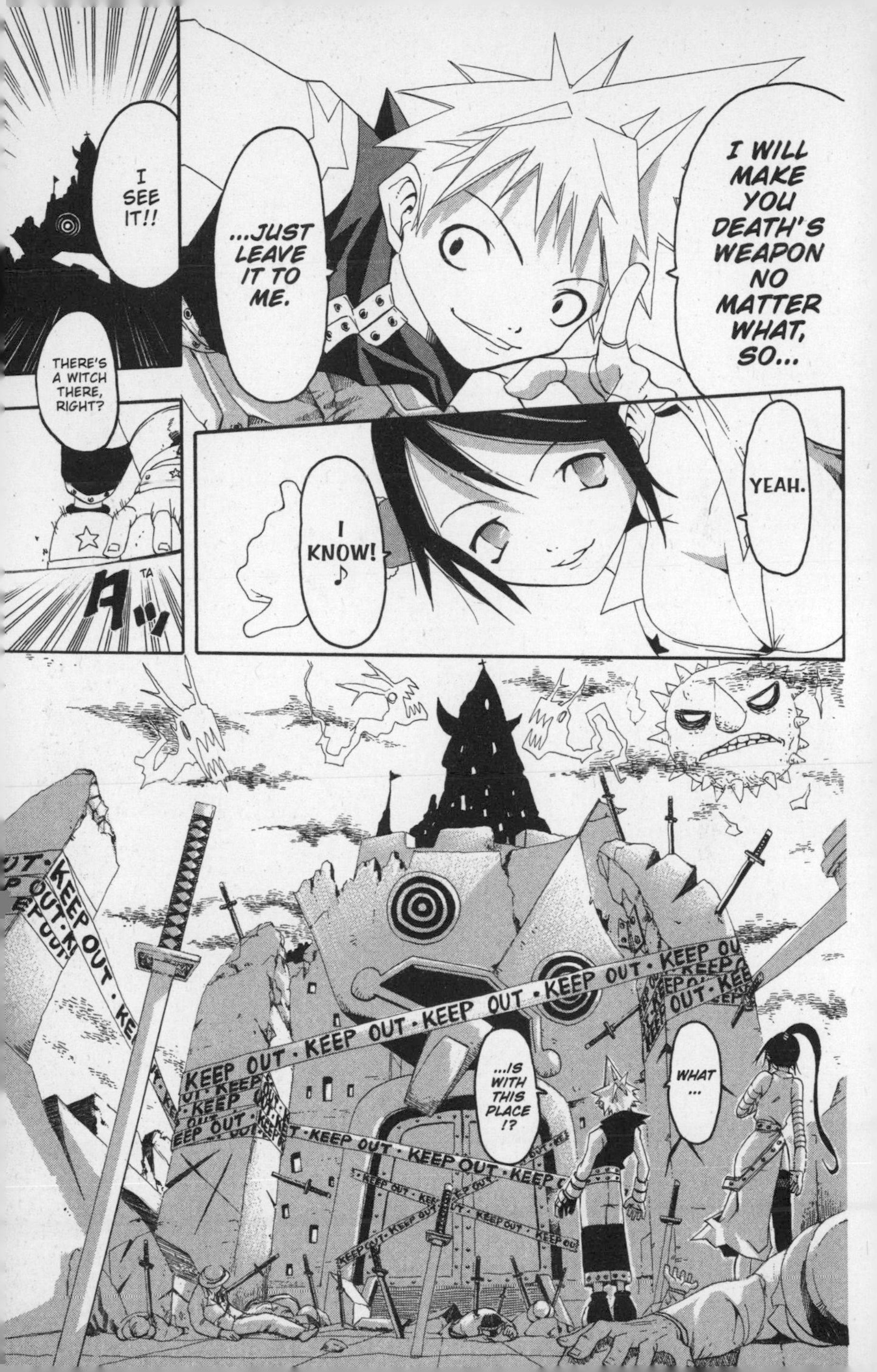
I WILL MAKE YOU DEATH'S WEAPON NO MATTER WHAT, SO...
...JUST LEAVE IT TO ME.
YEAH.
I KNOW! ♪
I SEE IT!!
THERE'S A WITCH THERE, RIGHT?
TA
WHAT ...
...IS WITH THIS PLACE !?
KEEP OUT · KEEP OUT · KEEP OUT · KEEP OUT

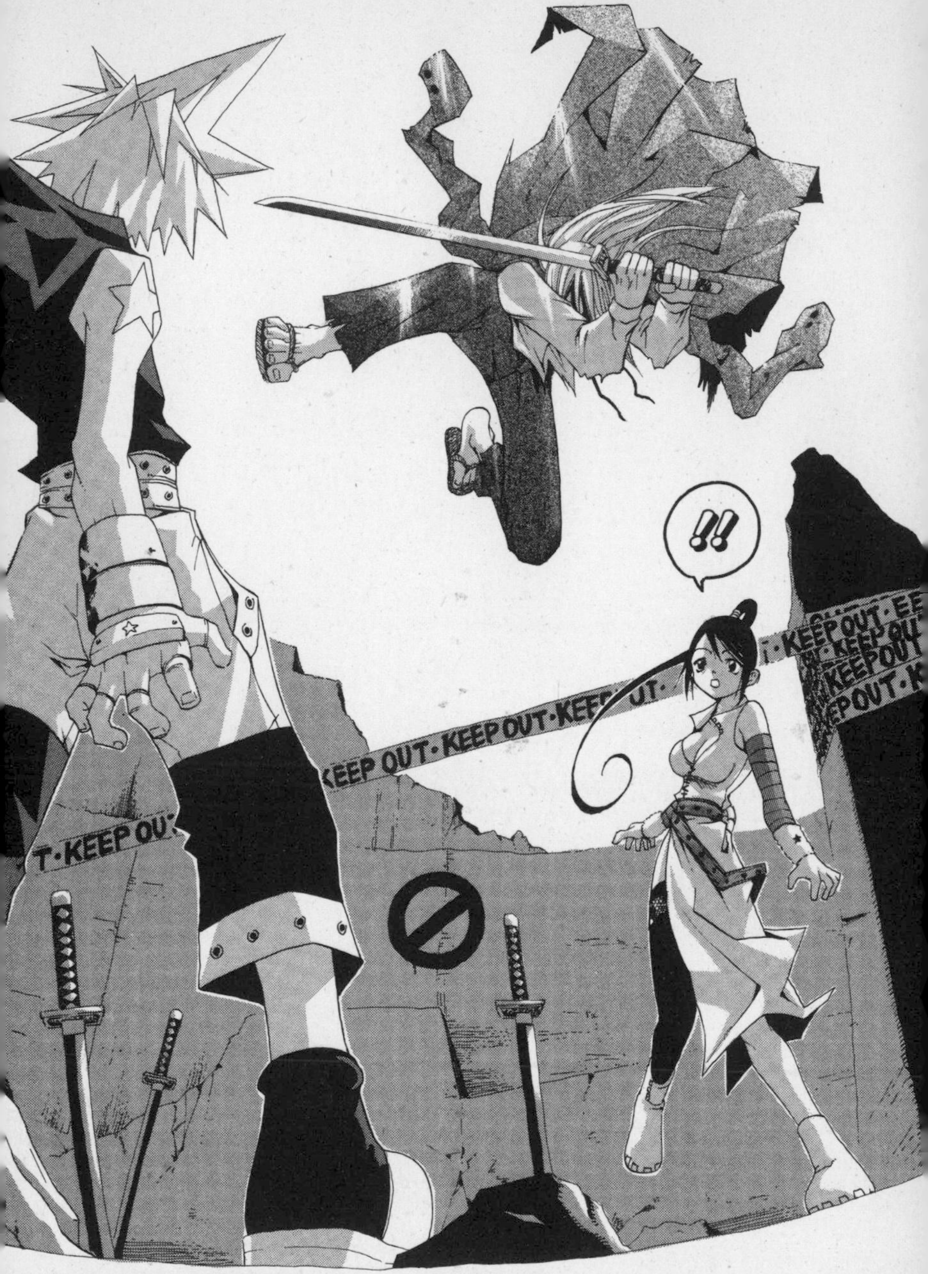

!!
i·KEEP OUT·EE
KEEPOUT·KEEPOUT·K
KEEP OUT·KEEP OUT·KEEP OUT·
T·KEEP OUT

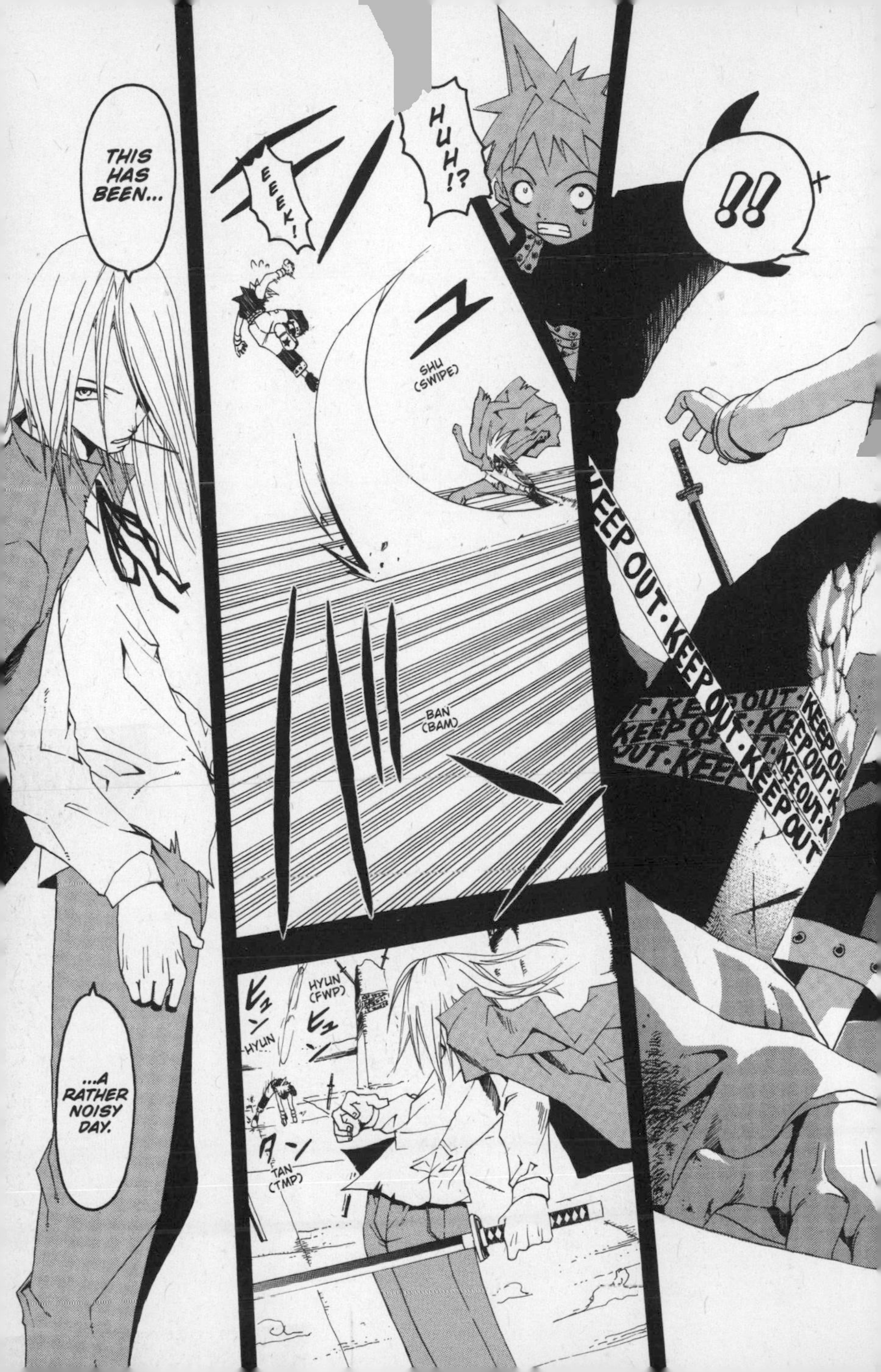

!!
HUH!?
EEEK!
SHU (SWIPE)
BAN (BAM)
KEEP OUT·KEEP OUT·KEEP OUT
HYUN (FWP)
HYUN
TAN (TMP)
THIS HAS BEEN...
...A RATHER NOISY DAY.

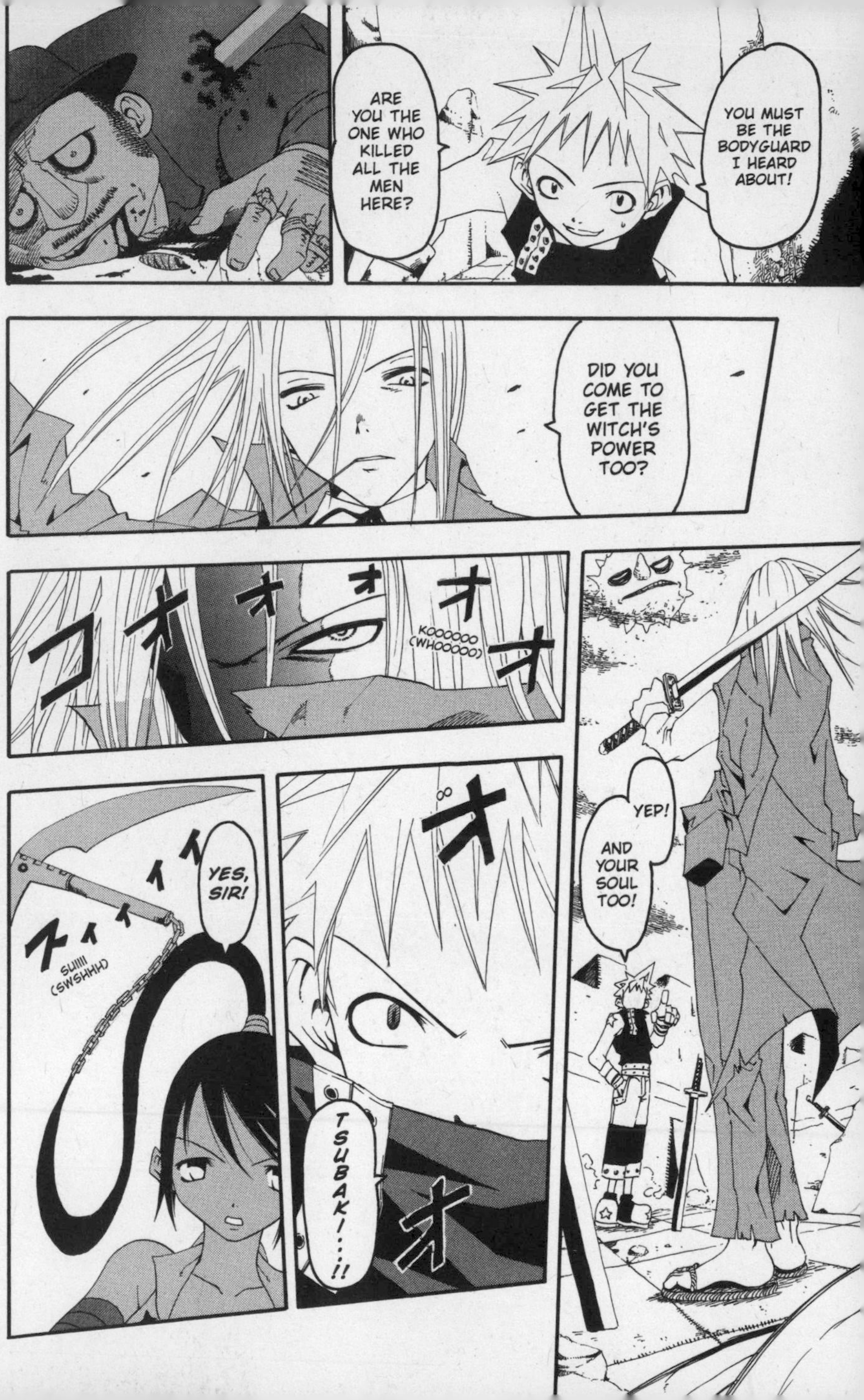
YOU MUST BE THE BODYGUARD I HEARD ABOUT!
ARE YOU THE ONE WHO KILLED ALL THE MEN HERE?
DID YOU COME TO GET THE WITCH'S POWER TOO?
YEP!
AND YOUR SOUL TOO!
コオオオオ
KOOOOOO (WHOOOOO)
オオ
TSUBAKI...!!
YES, SIR!
スィィィ
SUIIII (SWSHHH)

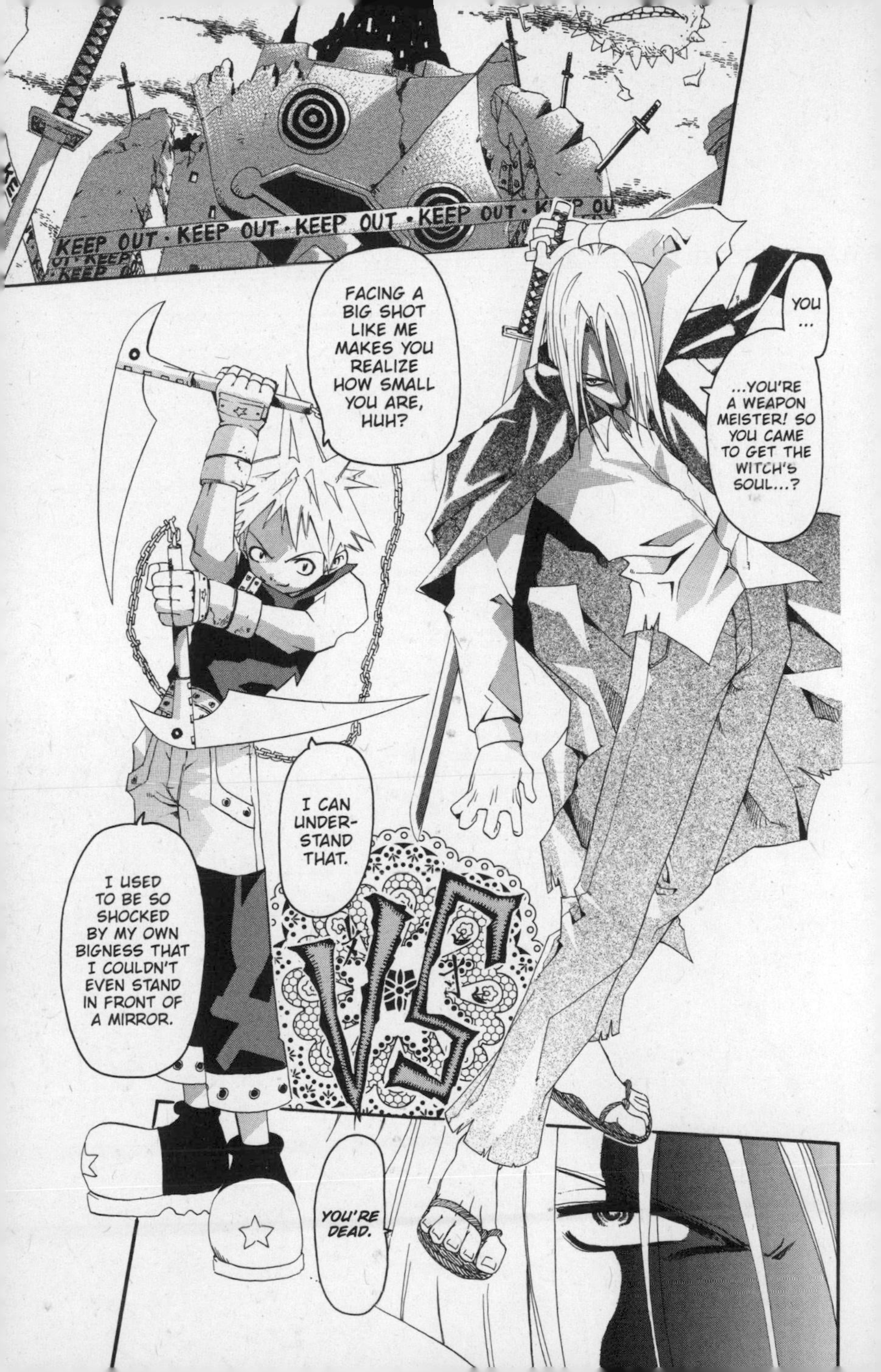
KEEP OUT · KEEP OUT · KEEP OUT · KEEP OUT
YOU ...
...YOU'RE A WEAPON MEISTER! SO YOU CAME TO GET THE WITCH'S SOUL...?
FACING A BIG SHOT LIKE ME MAKES YOU REALIZE HOW SMALL YOU ARE, HUH?
I CAN UNDER-STAND THAT.
I USED TO BE SO SHOCKED BY MY OWN BIGNESS THAT I COULDN'T EVEN STAND IN FRONT OF A MIRROR.
VS
YOU'RE DEAD.

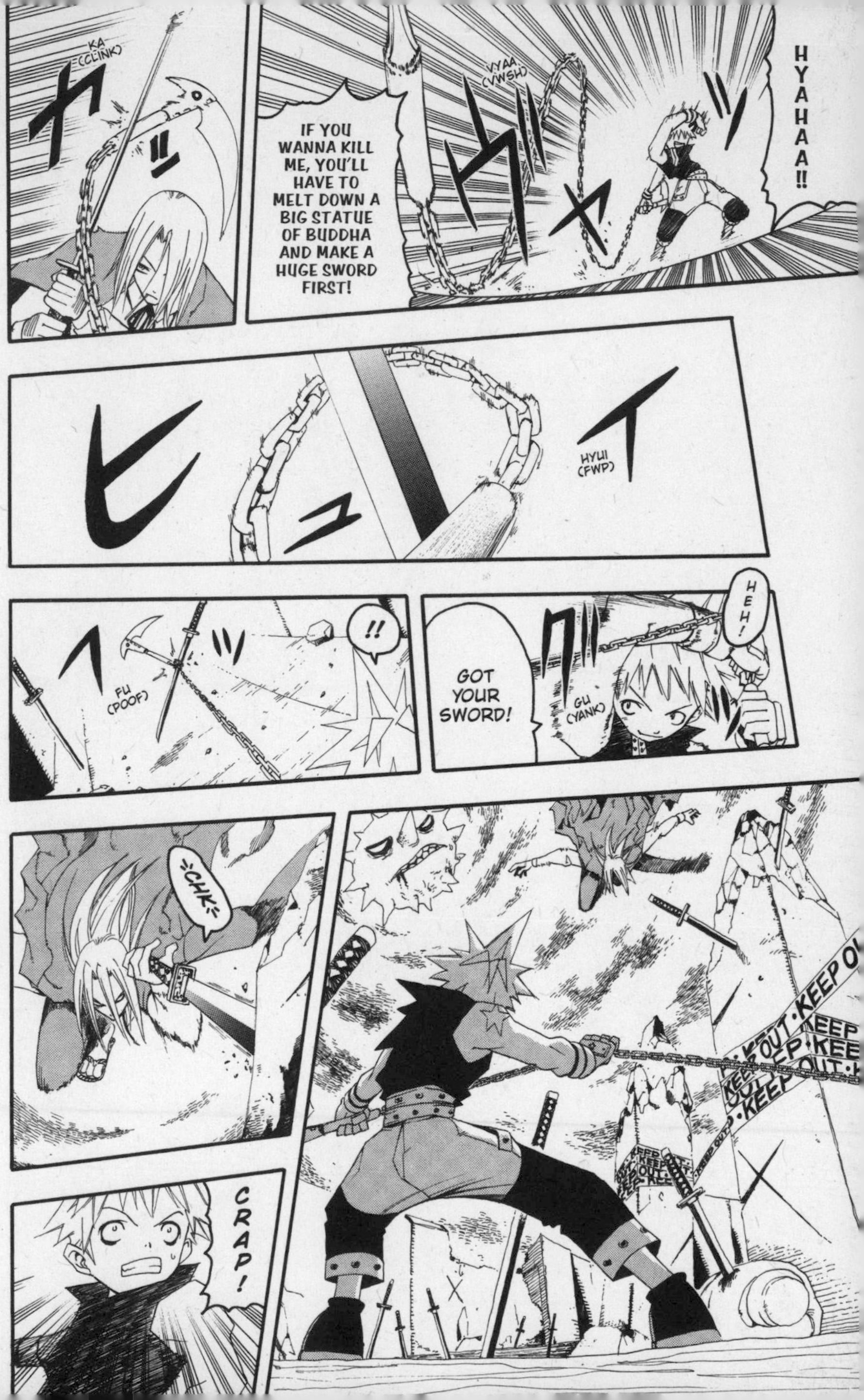
HYAHAA!!
VYAA (VWSH)
IF YOU WANNA KILL ME, YOU'LL HAVE TO MELT DOWN A BIG STATUE OF BUDDHA AND MAKE A HUGE SWORD FIRST!
KA (CLINK)
HYUI (FWP)
HEH!
GU (YANK)
GOT YOUR SWORD!
!!
FU (POOF)
KEEP OUT
CHK
CRAP!

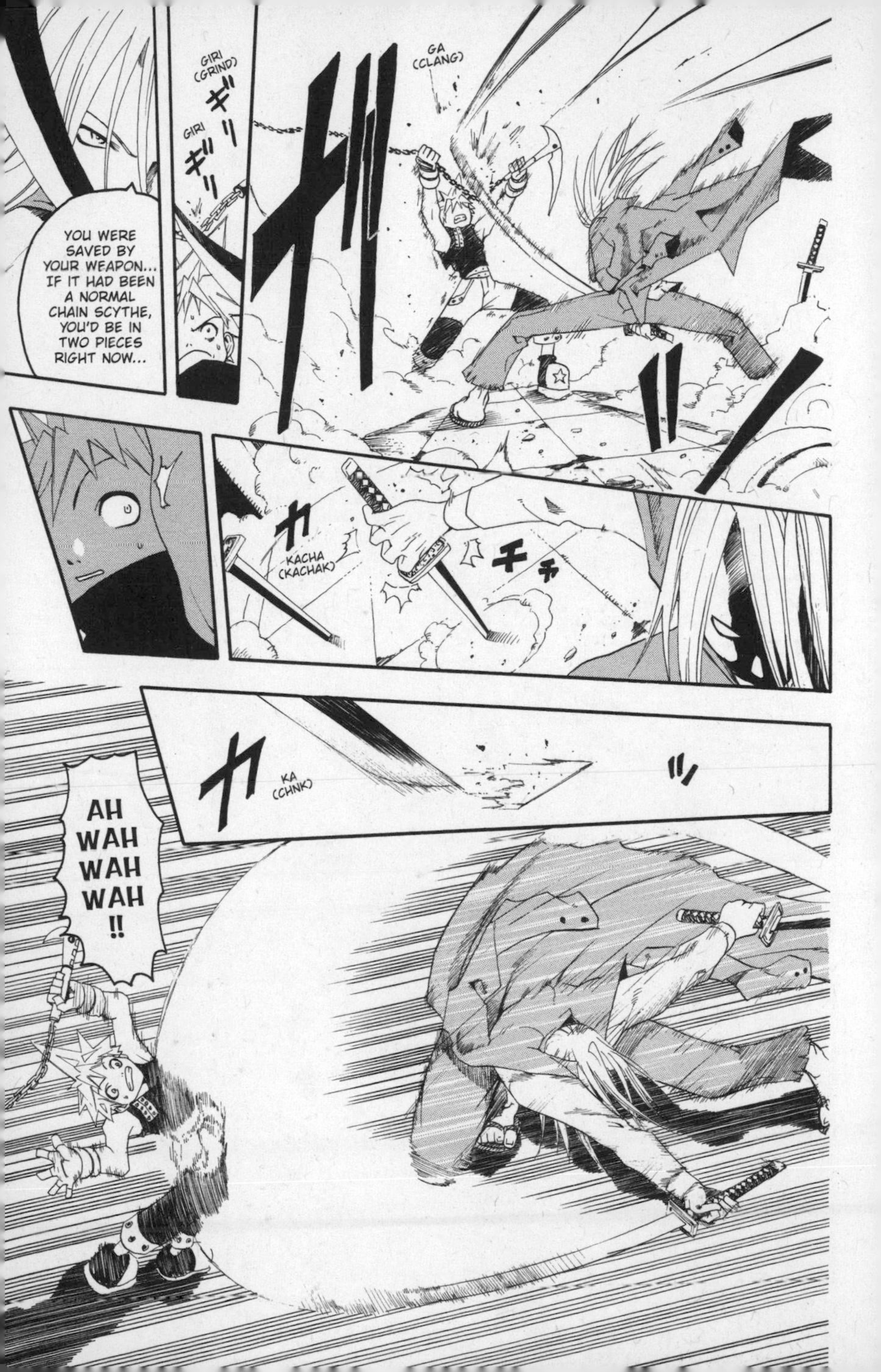
GA (CLANG)
GIRI (GRIND) ギリ
GIRI ギリ
YOU WERE SAVED BY YOUR WEAPON... IF IT HAD BEEN A NORMAL CHAIN SCYTHE, YOU'D BE IN TWO PIECES RIGHT NOW...
チャ
カ
KACHA (KACHAK)
カ
KA (CHNK)
AH WAH WAH WAH!!

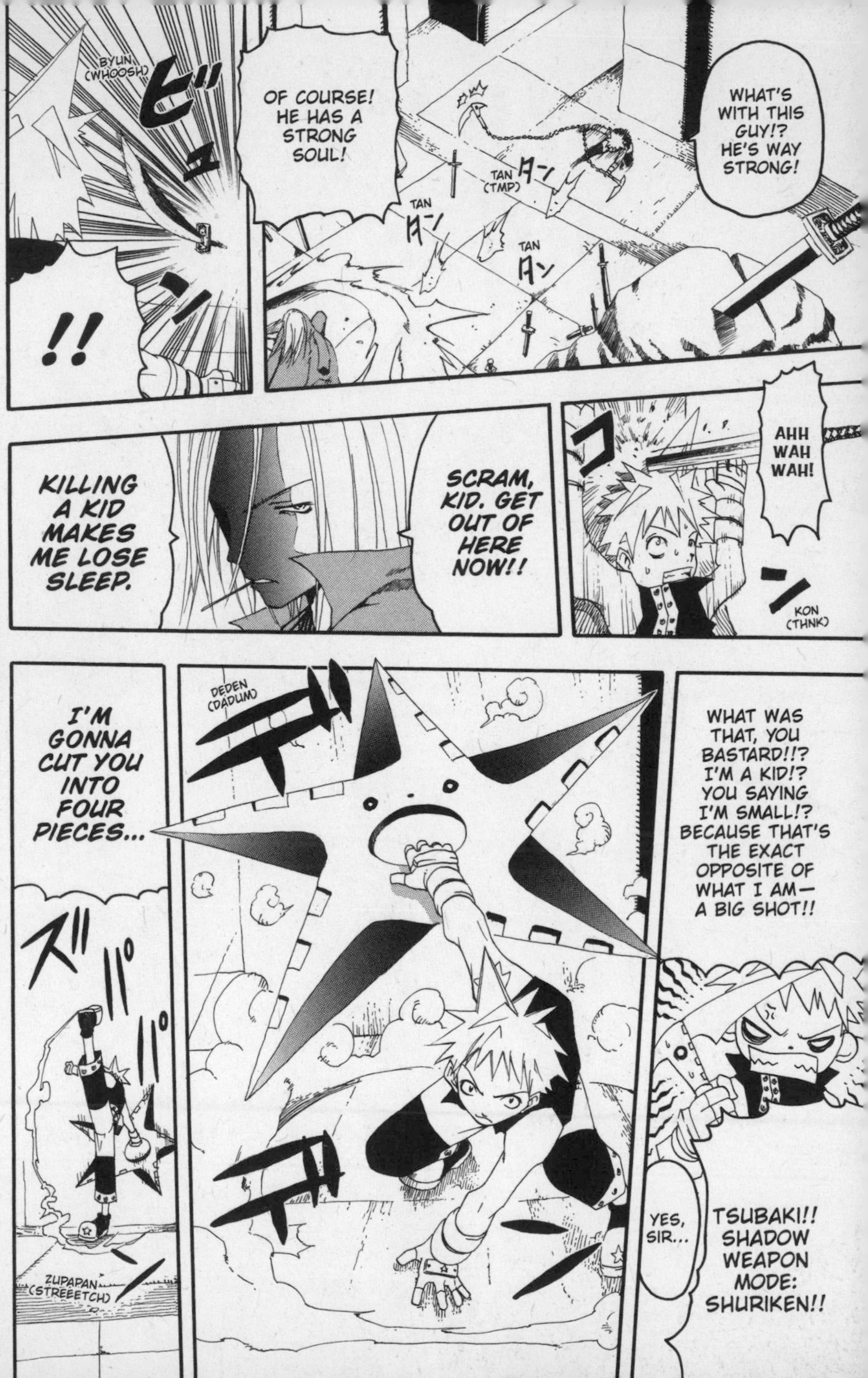
WHAT'S WITH THIS GUY!? HE'S WAY STRONG!
TAN (TMP)
TAN
TAN
OF COURSE! HE HAS A STRONG SOUL!
BYUN (WHOOSH)
!!
AHH WAH WAH!
KON (THNK)
SCRAM, KID. GET OUT OF HERE NOW!!
KILLING A KID MAKES ME LOSE SLEEP.
WHAT WAS THAT, YOU BASTARD!!? I'M A KID!? YOU SAYING I'M SMALL!? BECAUSE THAT'S THE EXACT OPPOSITE OF WHAT I AM— A BIG SHOT!!
TSUBAKI!! SHADOW WEAPON MODE: SHURIKEN!!
YES, SIR...
DEDEN (DADUM)
I'M GONNA CUT YOU INTO FOUR PIECES...
ZUPAPAN (STREEETCH)

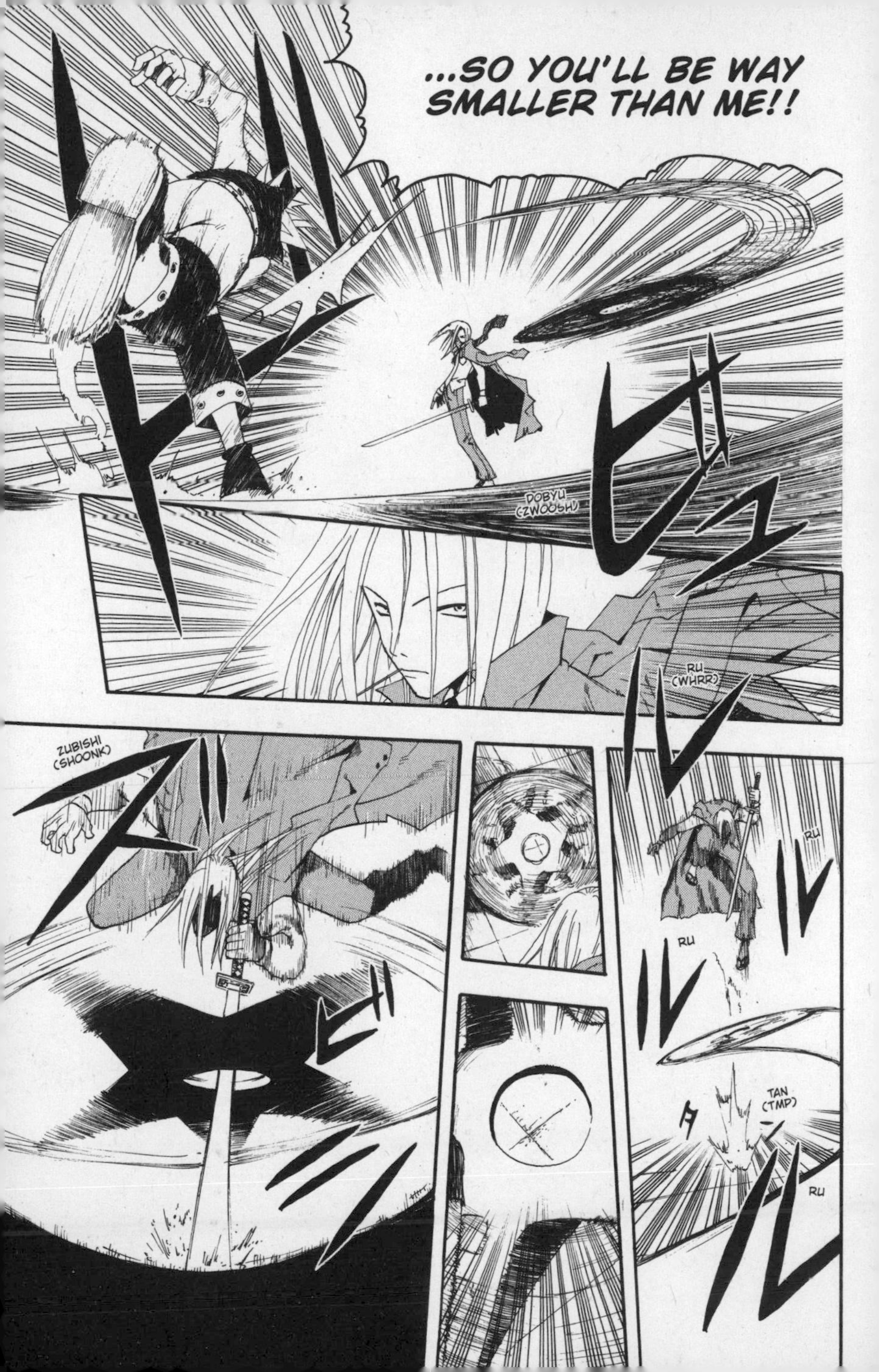
...SO YOU'LL BE WAY SMALLER THAN ME!!
DOBYU (ZWOOSH)
RU (WHRR)
RU
RU
TAN (TMP)
RU
ZUBISHI (SHOONK)

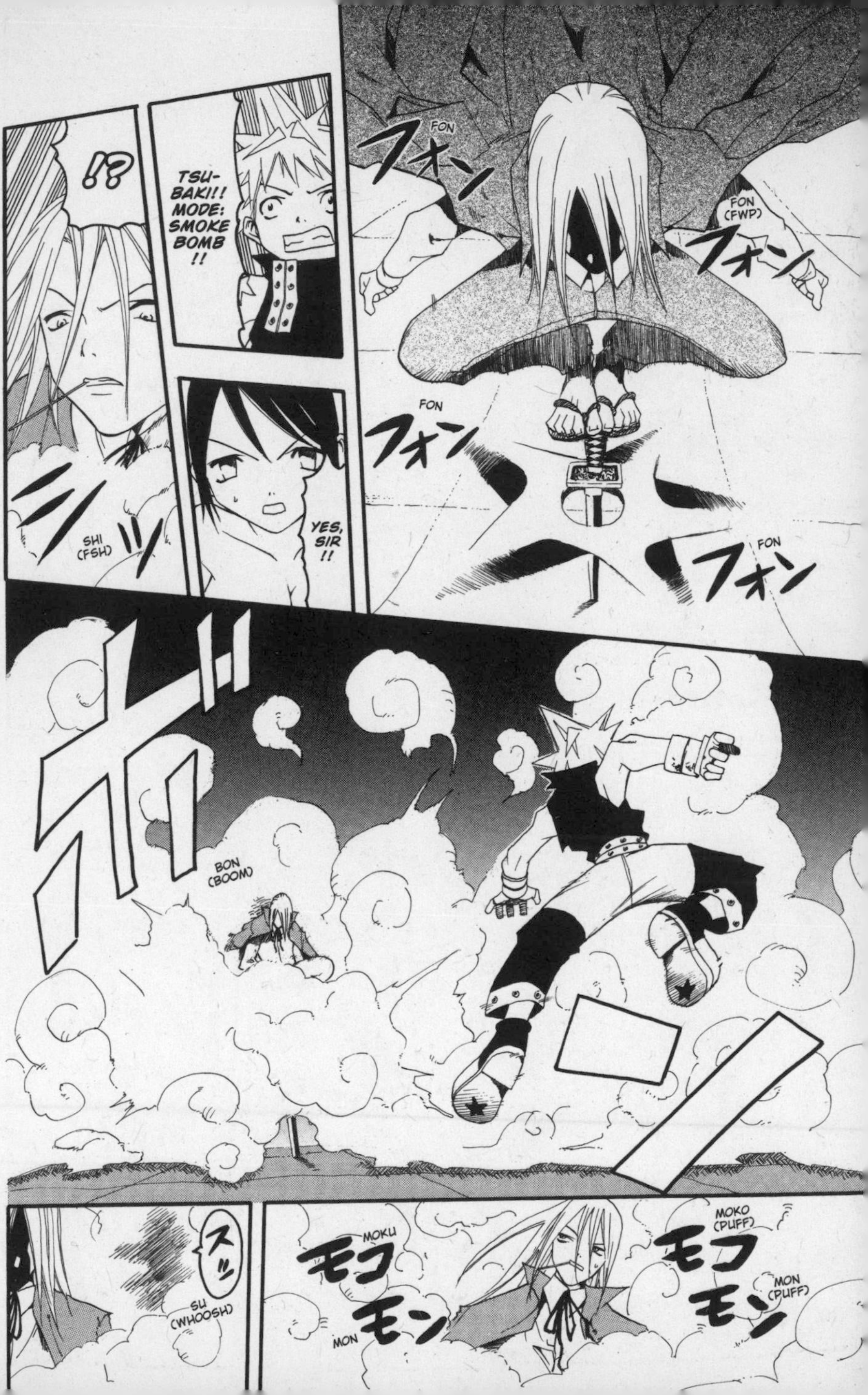

FON
フォン
FON (FWP)
フォン
FON
フォン
FON
フォン
TSU-BAKI!! MODE: SMOKE BOMB !!
YES, SIR !!
!?
SHI (FSH)
BON (BOOM)
MOKO (PUFF)
MON (PUFF)
MOKU
MON
SU (WHOOSH)

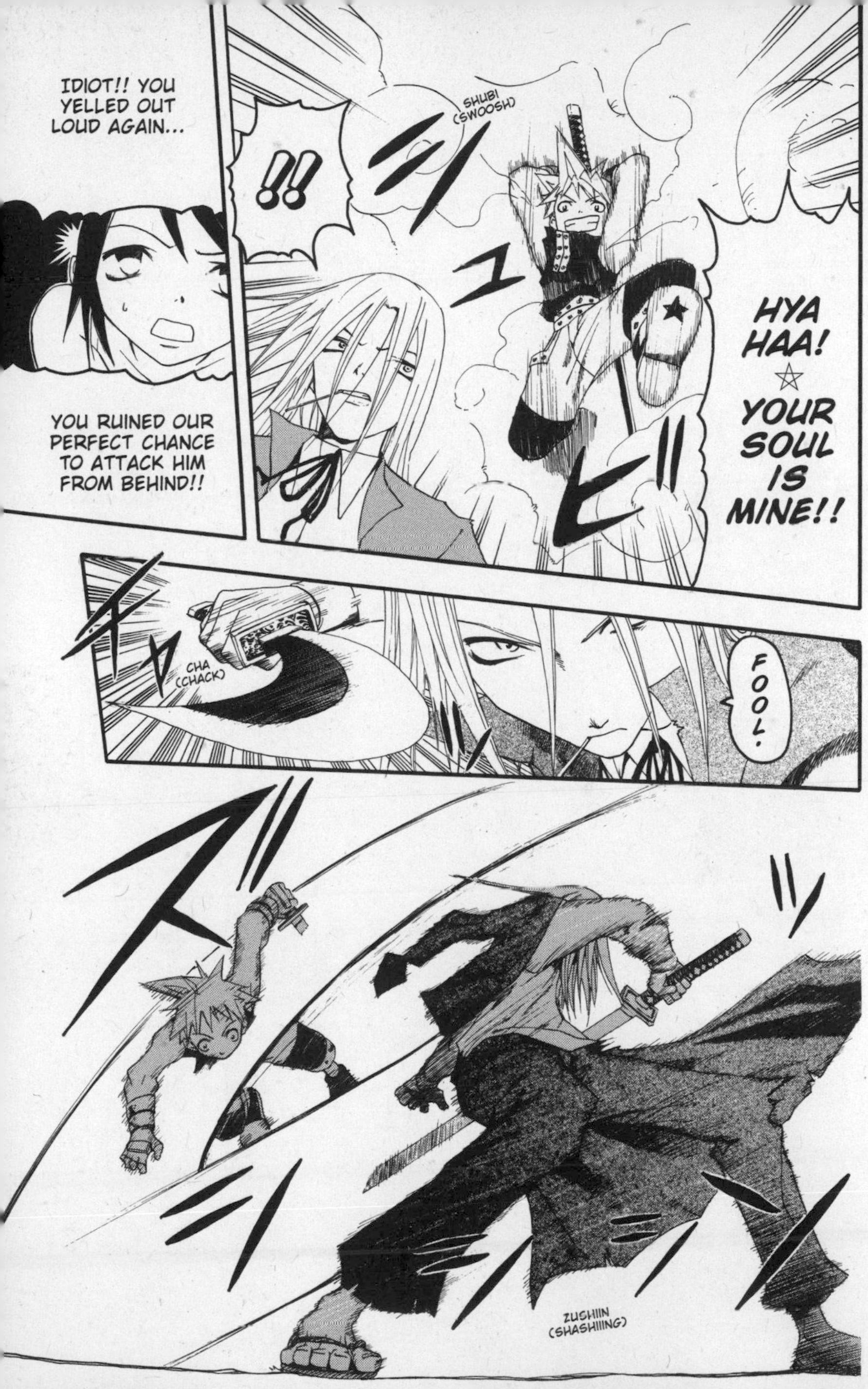
HYA HAA! ☆ YOUR SOUL IS MINE!!
SHUBI (SWOOSH)
!!
IDIOT!! YOU YELLED OUT LOUD AGAIN...
YOU RUINED OUR PERFECT CHANCE TO ATTACK HIM FROM BEHIND!!
FOOL.
CHA (CHACK)
ZUSHIIN (SHASHIIING)

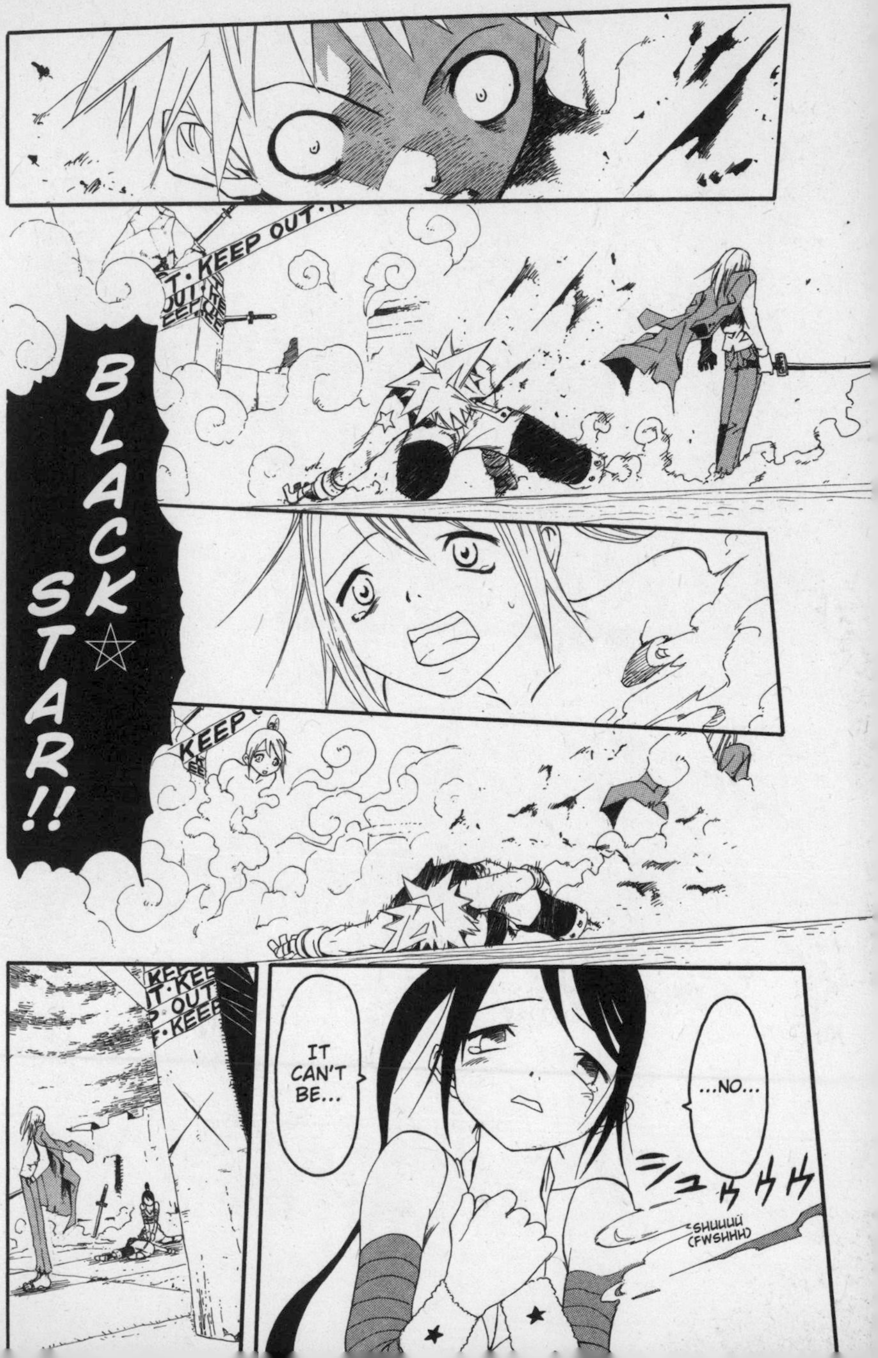
BLACK STAR!!
...NO...
IT CAN'T BE...
SHUUUU
(FWSHHH)

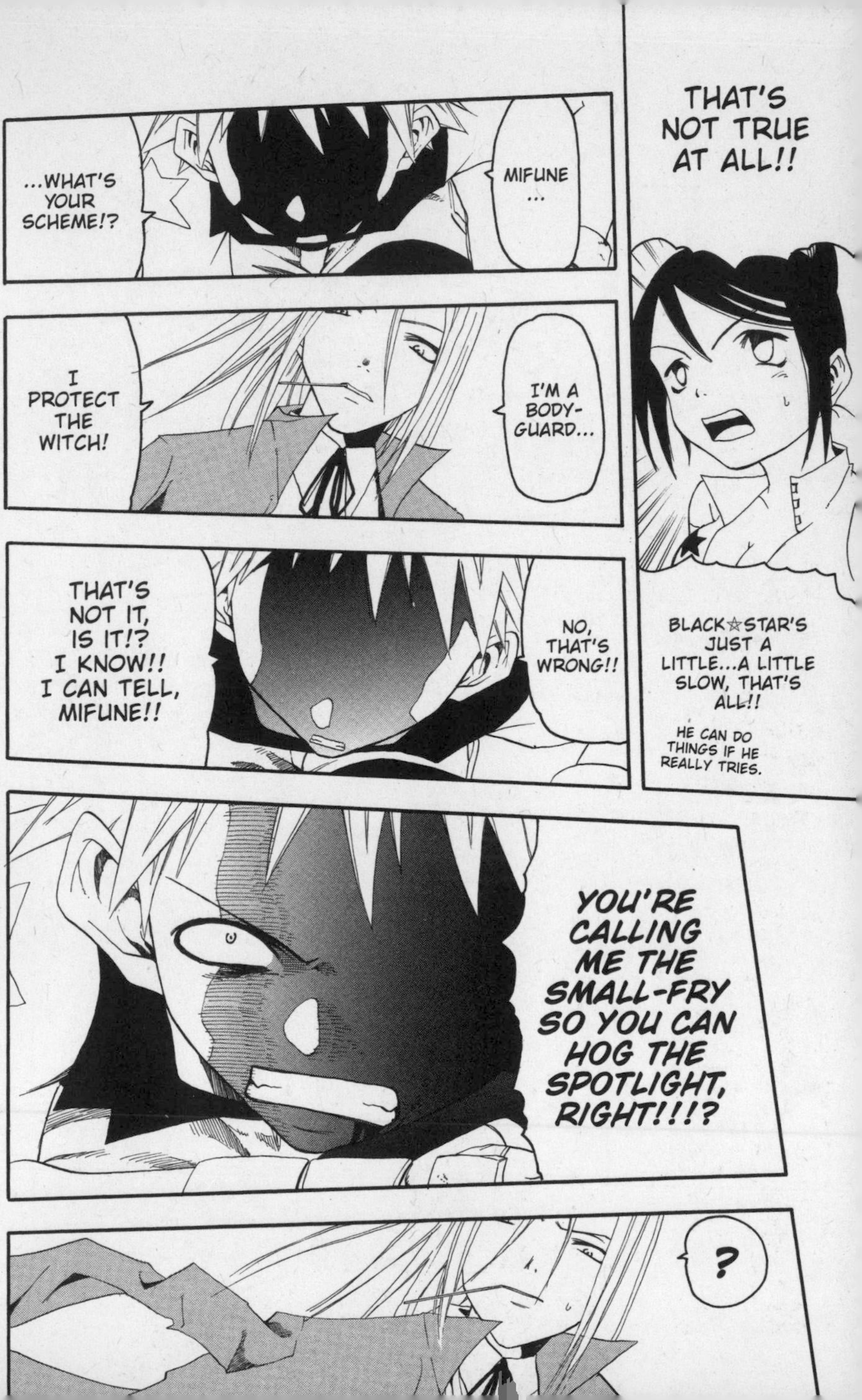
THAT'S NOT TRUE AT ALL!!
BLACK☆STAR'S JUST A LITTLE...A LITTLE SLOW, THAT'S ALL!!
HE CAN DO THINGS IF HE REALLY TRIES.
MIFUNE...
...WHAT'S YOUR SCHEME!?
I'M A BODY-GUARD...
I PROTECT THE WITCH!
NO, THAT'S WRONG!!
THAT'S NOT IT, IS IT!? I KNOW!! I CAN TELL, MIFUNE!!
YOU'RE CALLING ME THE SMALL-FRY SO YOU CAN HOG THE SPOTLIGHT, RIGHT!!!?
?

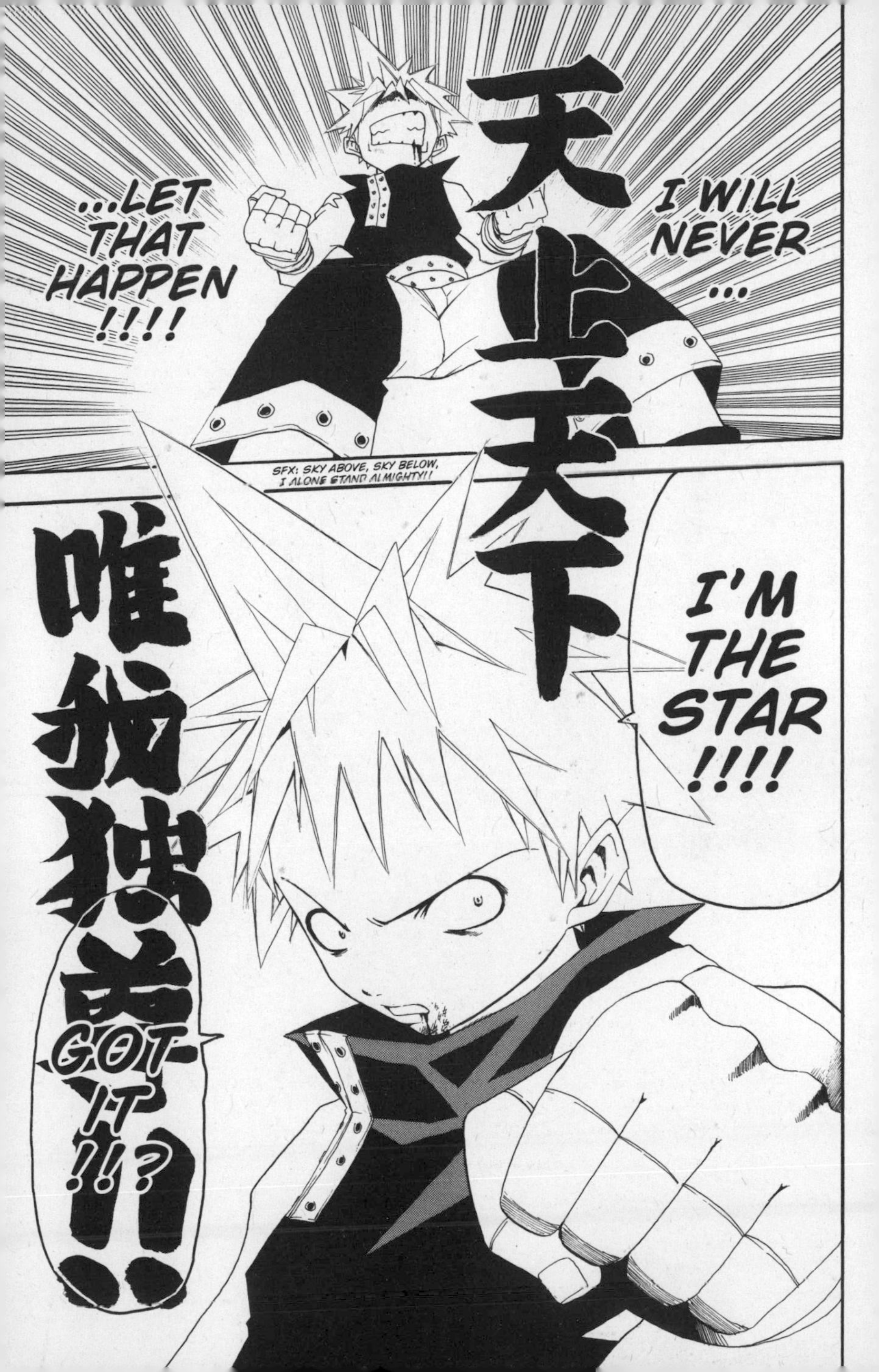
I WILL NEVER ...
...LET THAT HAPPEN !!!!
天上天下
SFX: SKY ABOVE, SKY BELOW, I ALONE STAND ALMIGHTY!!
唯我独尊
I'M THE STAR !!!!
GOT IT !!?

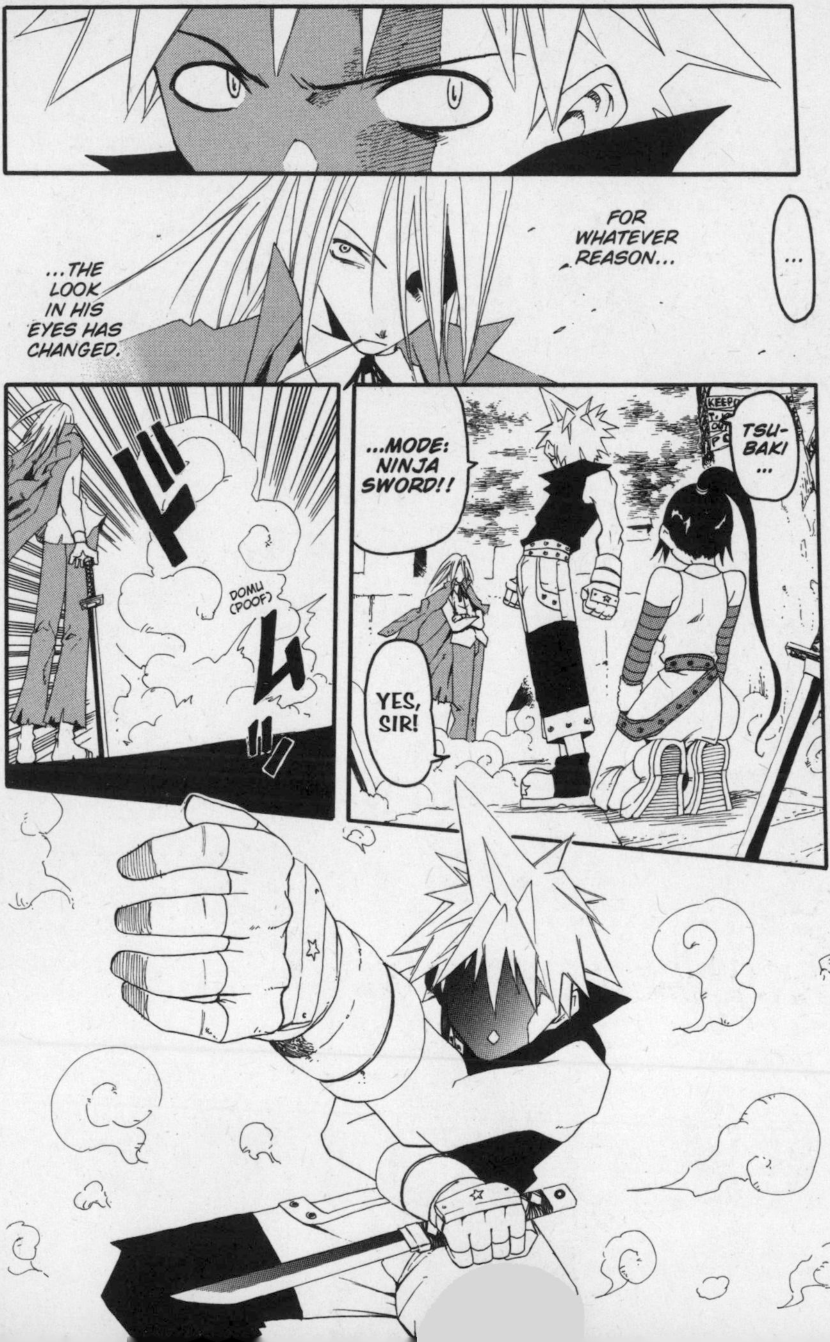
...
FOR WHATEVER REASON...
...THE LOOK IN HIS EYES HAS CHANGED.
TSU-BAKI...
...MODE: NINJA SWORD!!
YES, SIR!
DOMU (POOF)

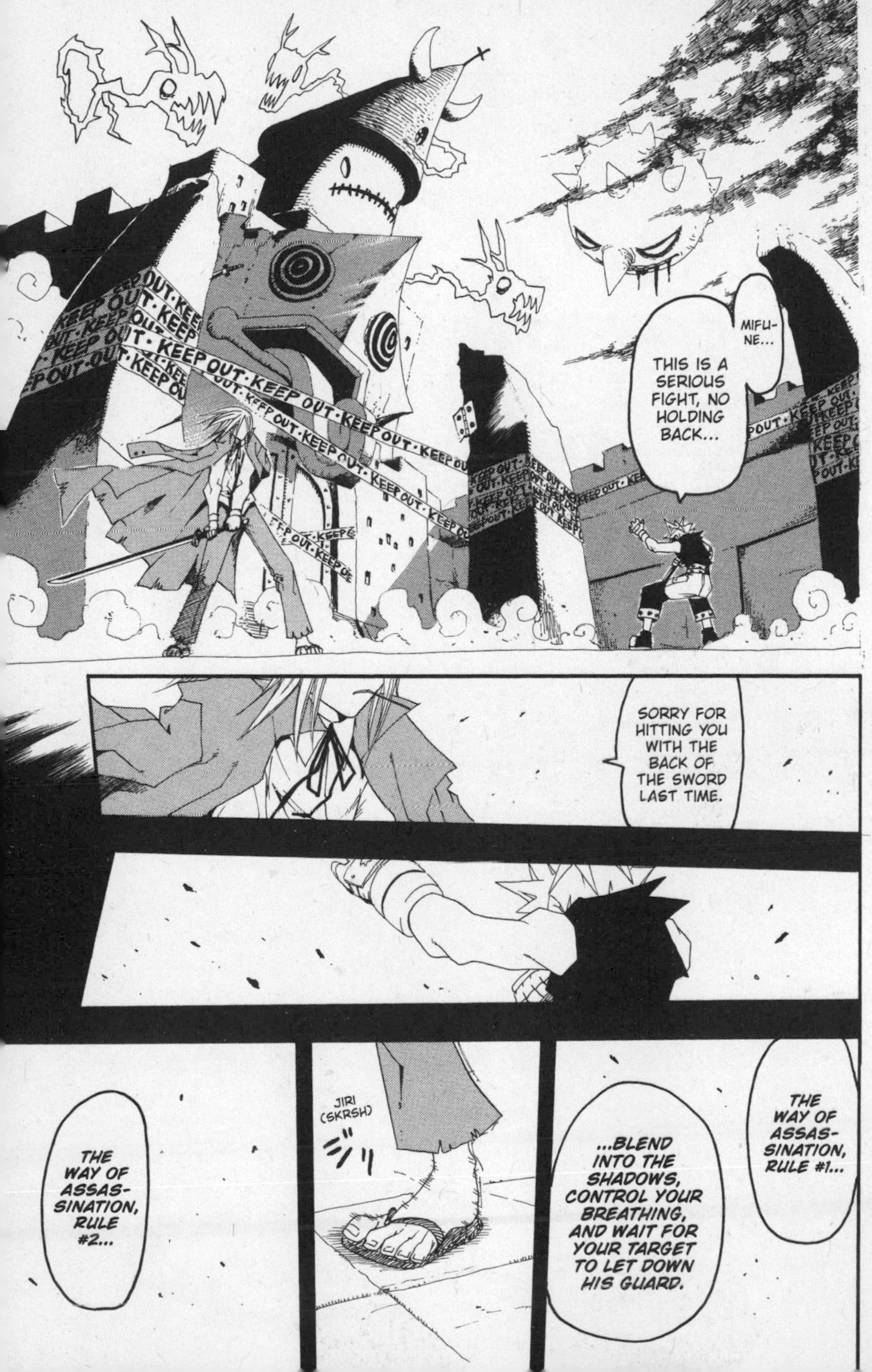
MIFUNE...
THIS IS A SERIOUS FIGHT, NO HOLDING BACK...
SORRY FOR HITTING YOU WITH THE BACK OF THE SWORD LAST TIME.
THE WAY OF ASSASSINATION, RULE #1...
...BLEND INTO THE SHADOWS, CONTROL YOUR BREATHING, AND WAIT FOR YOUR TARGET TO LET DOWN HIS GUARD.
JIRI (SKRSH)
THE WAY OF ASSASSINATION, RULE #2...

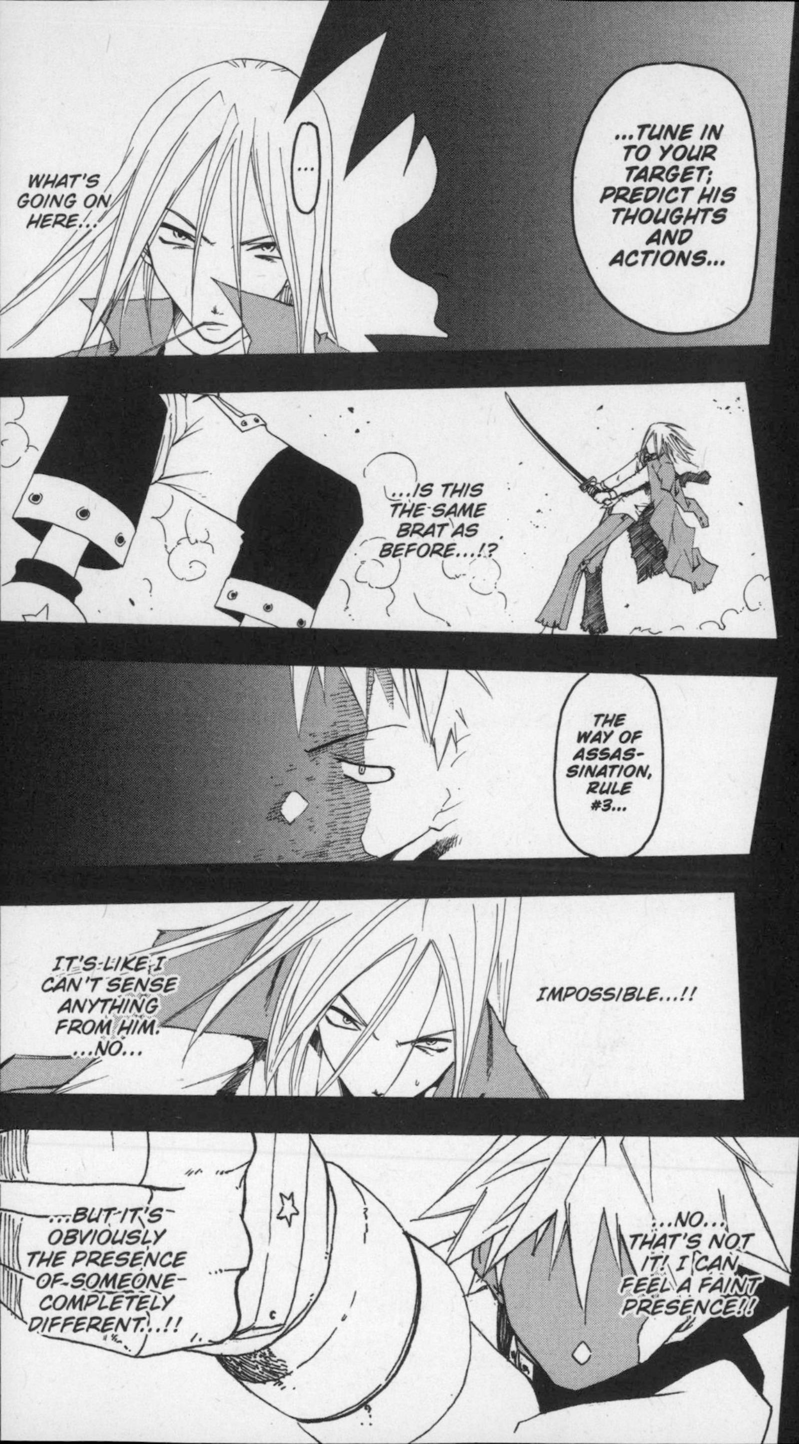
...TUNE IN TO YOUR TARGET; PREDICT HIS THOUGHTS AND ACTIONS...
...
WHAT'S GOING ON HERE...
...IS THIS THE SAME BRAT AS BEFORE...!?
THE WAY OF ASSAS-SINATION, RULE #3...
IMPOSSIBLE...!!
IT'S LIKE I CAN'T SENSE ANYTHING FROM HIM. ...NO...
...NO... THAT'S NOT IT! I CAN FEEL A FAINT PRESENCE!!
...BUT IT'S OBVIOUSLY THE PRESENCE OF SOMEONE COMPLETELY DIFFERENT...!!

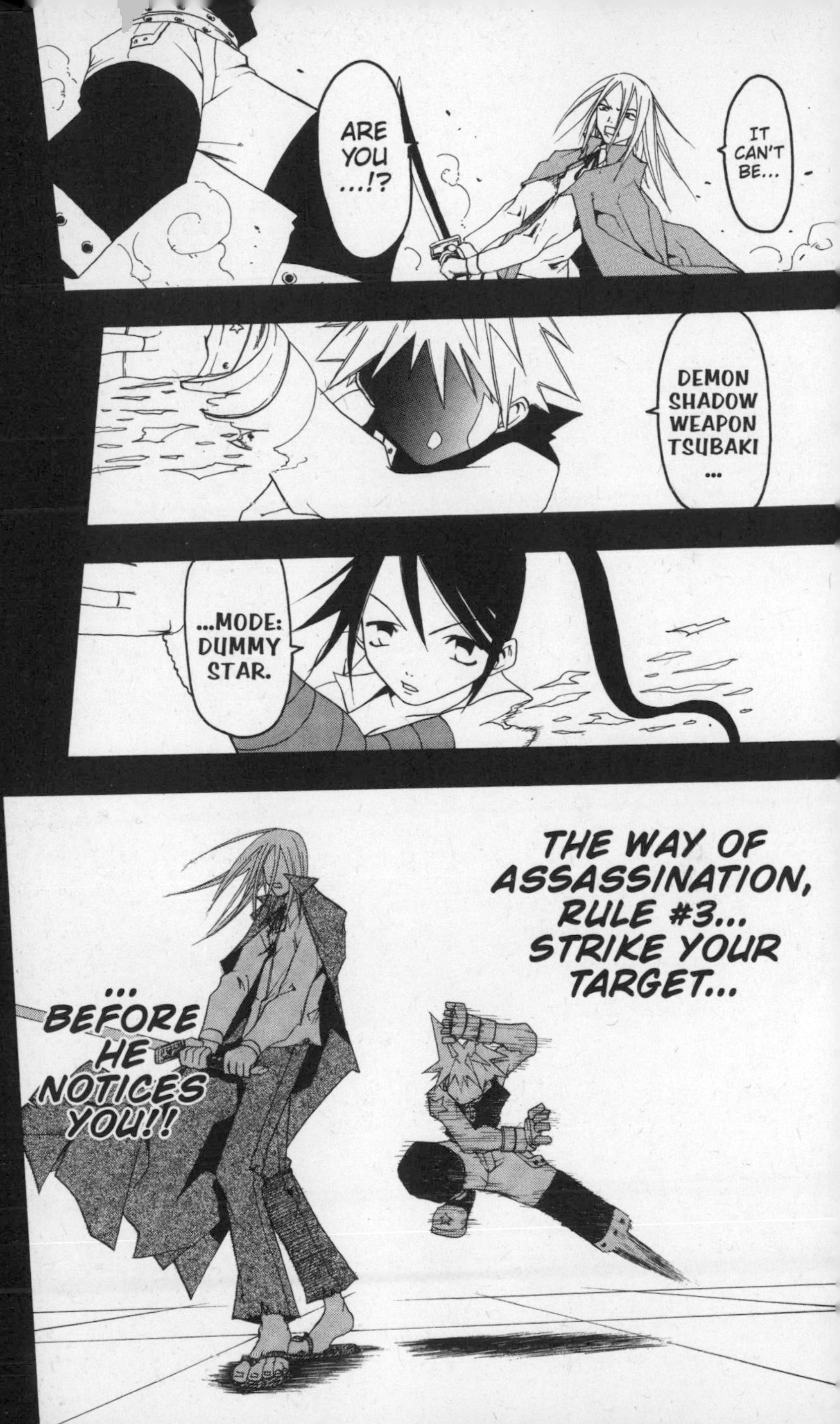
IT CAN'T BE...
ARE YOU ...!?
DEMON SHADOW WEAPON TSUBAKI ...
...MODE: DUMMY STAR.
THE WAY OF ASSASSINATION, RULE #3... STRIKE YOUR TARGET...
... BEFORE HE NOTICES YOU!!

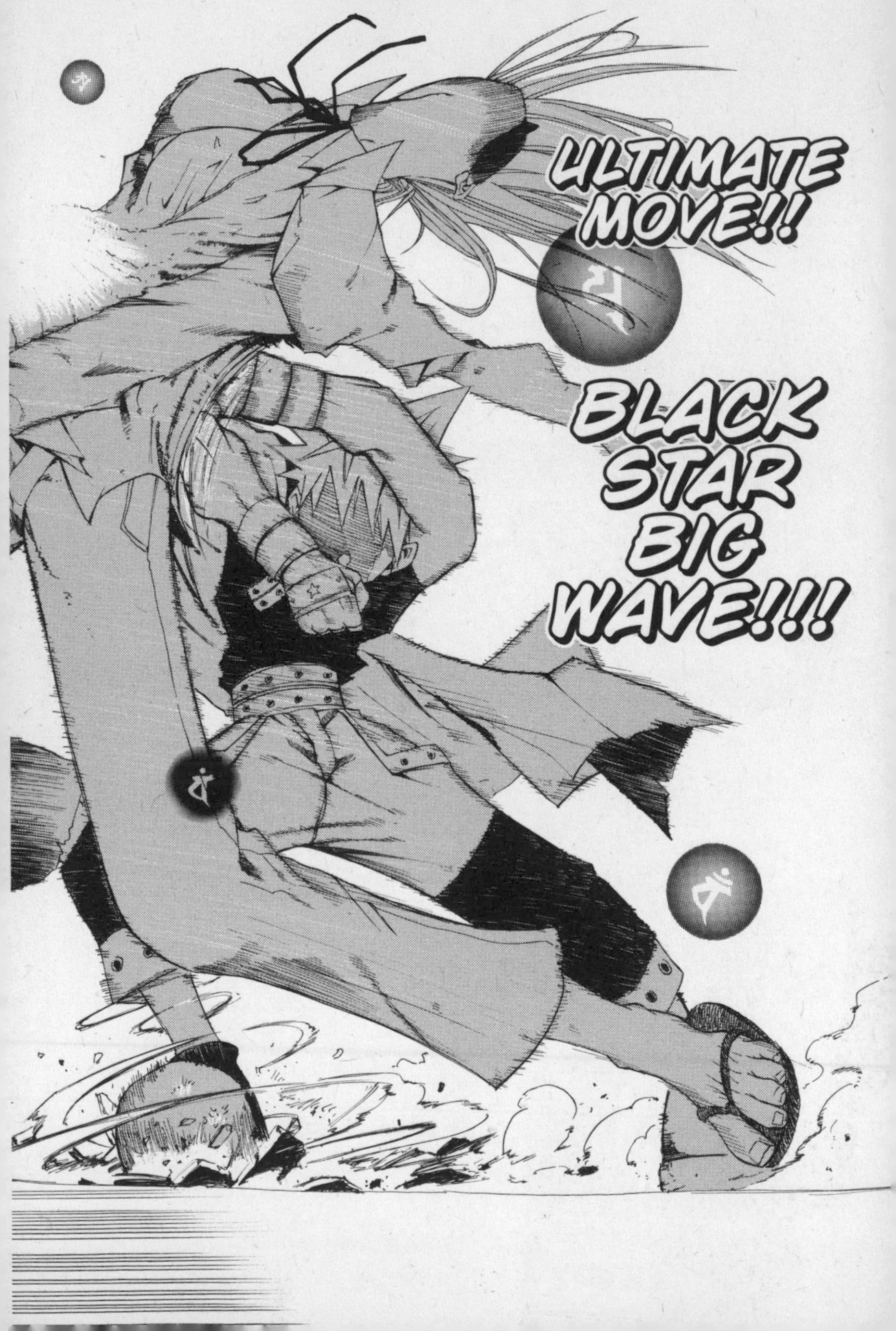
ULTIMATE MOVE!!
BLACK STAR BIG WAVE!!!

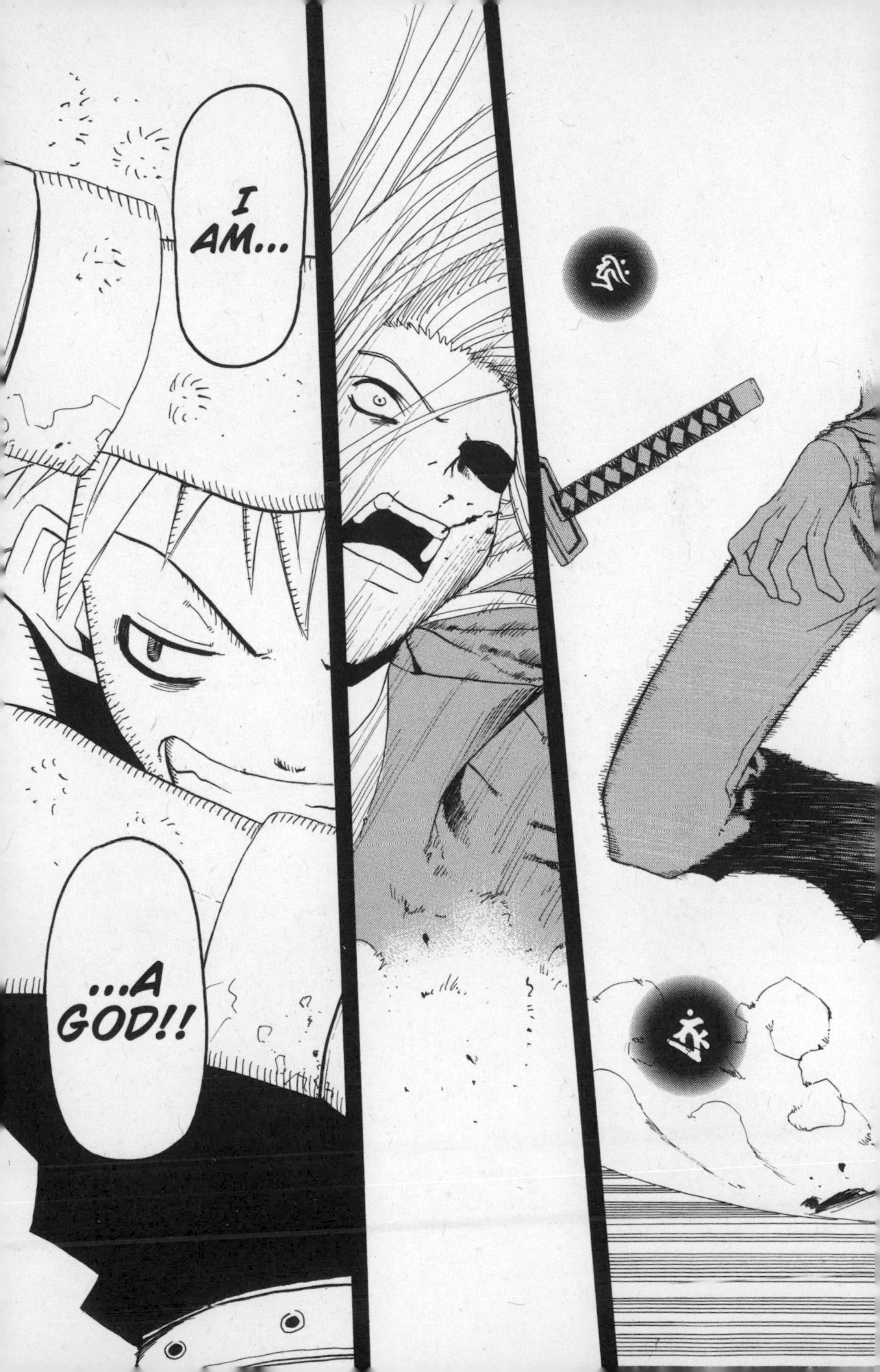
I AM...
...A GOD!!

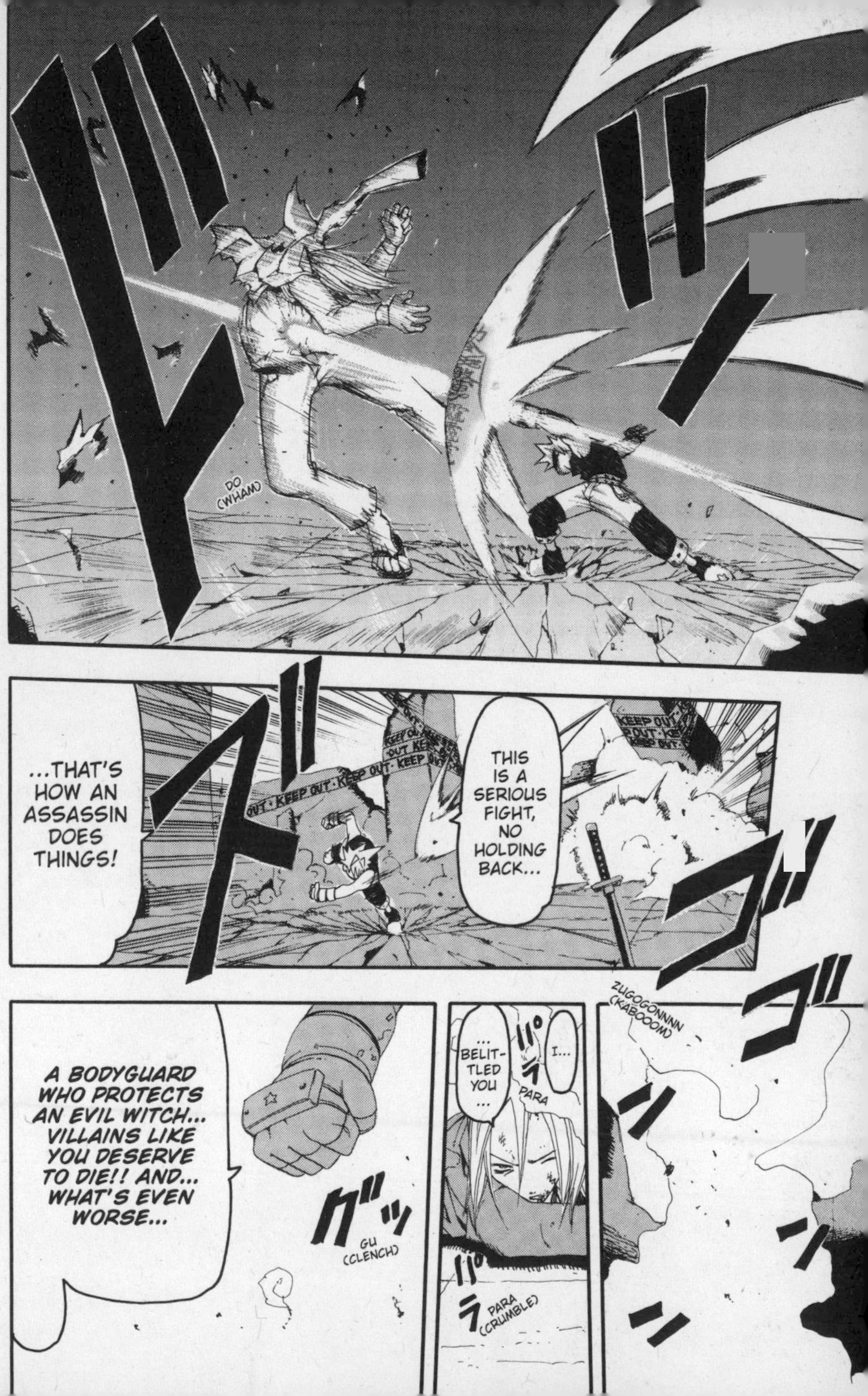
DO (WHAM)
THIS IS A SERIOUS FIGHT, NO HOLDING BACK...
...THAT'S HOW AN ASSASSIN DOES THINGS!
ZUGOGONNNN (KABOOOM)
I...
...BELITTLED YOU...
PARA
PARA (CRUMBLE)
A BODYGUARD WHO PROTECTS AN EVIL WITCH... VILLAINS LIKE YOU DESERVE TO DIE!! AND... WHAT'S EVEN WORSE...
GU (CLENCH)

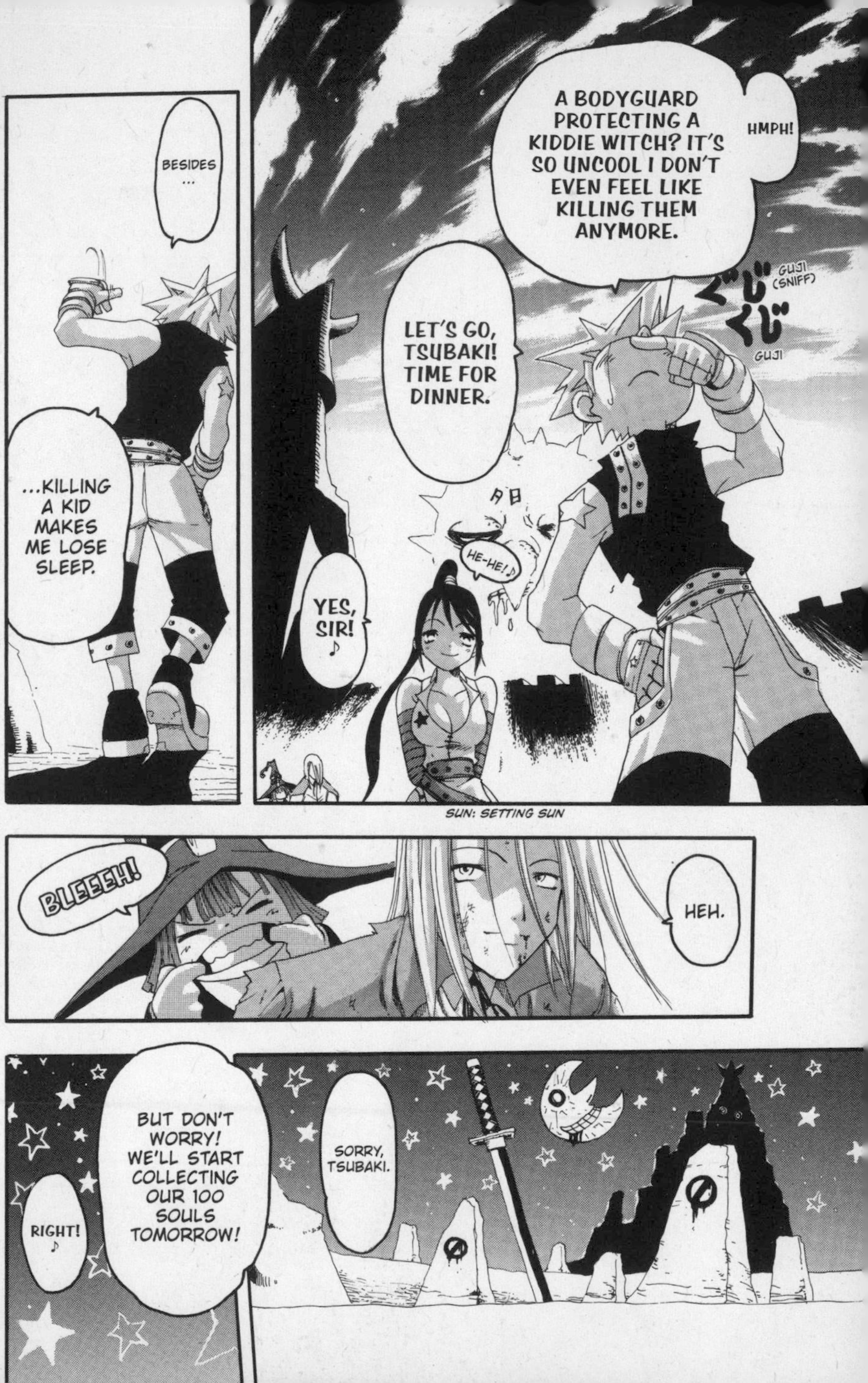
HMPH!
A BODYGUARD PROTECTING A KIDDIE WITCH? IT'S SO UNCOOL I DON'T EVEN FEEL LIKE KILLING THEM ANYMORE.
GUJI (SNIFF)
GUJI
LET'S GO, TSUBAKI! TIME FOR DINNER.
HE-HE! ♪
YES, SIR! ♪
BESIDES...
...KILLING A KID MAKES ME LOSE SLEEP.
SUN: SETTING SUN
HEH.
BLEEEH!
SORRY, TSUBAKI.
BUT DON'T WORRY! WE'LL START COLLECTING OUR 100 SOULS TOMORROW!
RIGHT! ♪

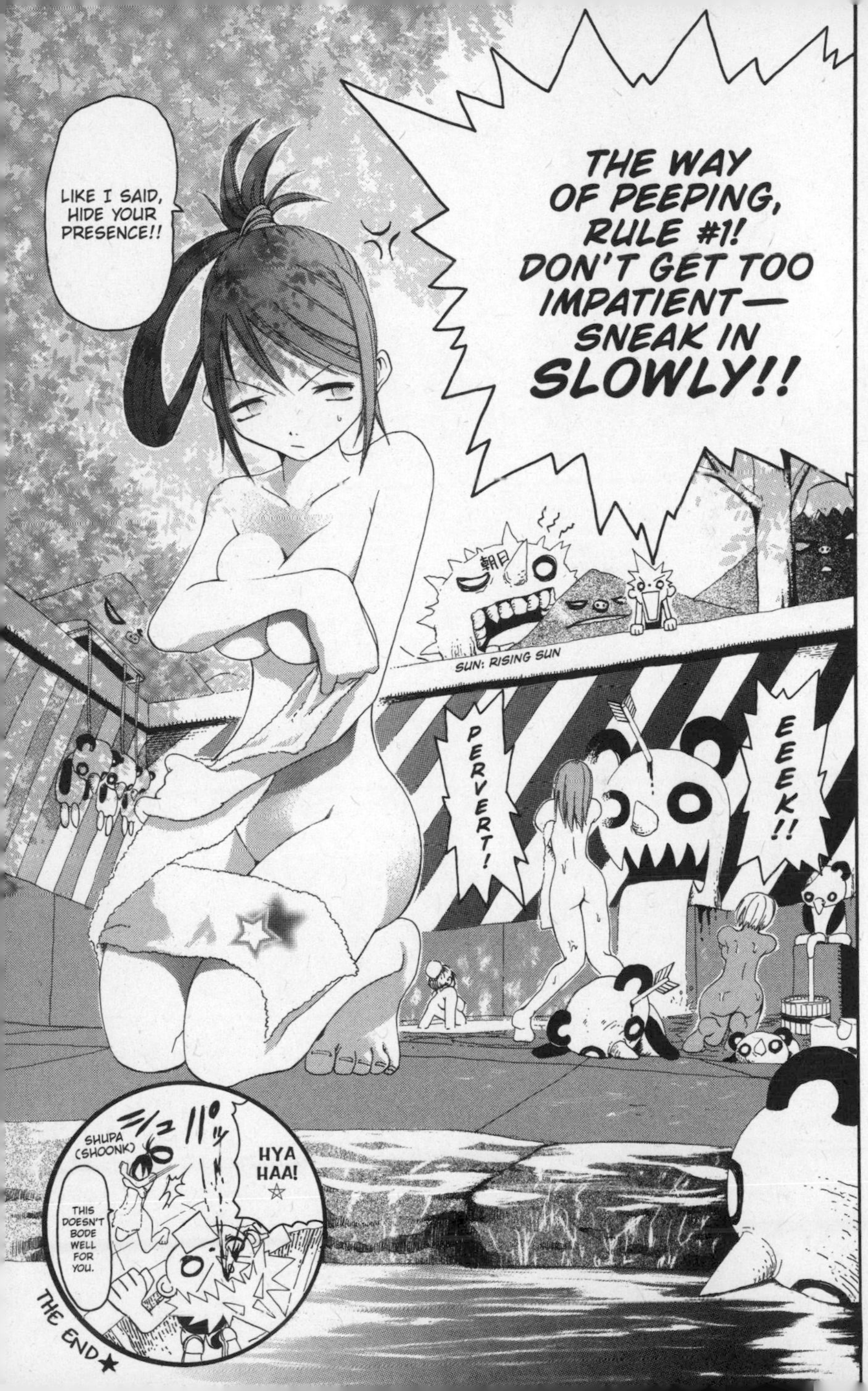
THE WAY OF PEEPING, RULE #1! DON'T GET TOO IMPATIENT—SNEAK IN SLOWLY!!
LIKE I SAID, HIDE YOUR PRESENCE!!
朝日
SUN: RISING SUN
EEEK!!
PERVERT!
HYA HAA! ☆
SHUPA (SHOONK)
THIS DOESN'T BODE WELL FOR YOU.
THE END★

SOUL EATER

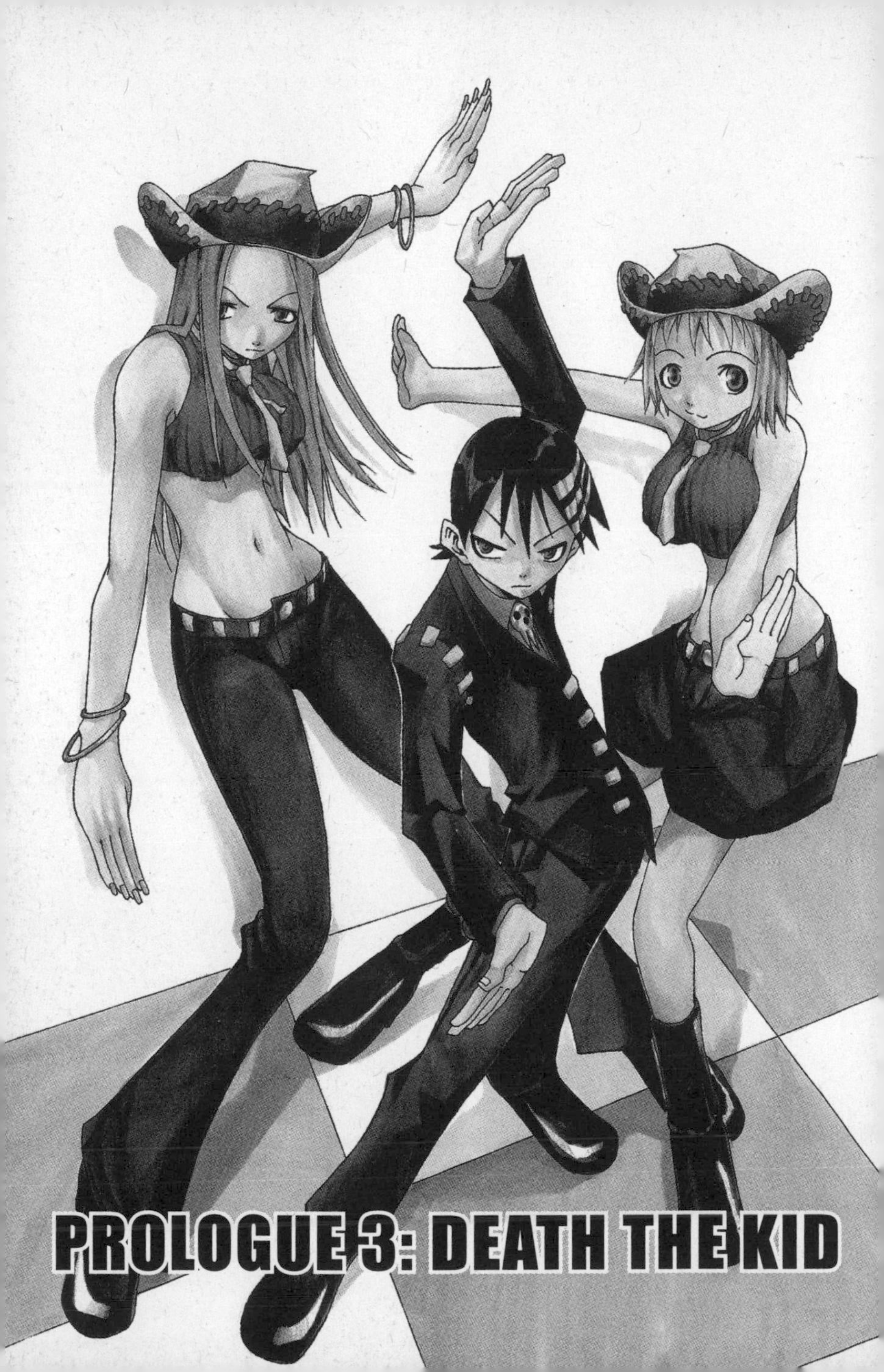

PROLOGUE 3: DEATH THE KID

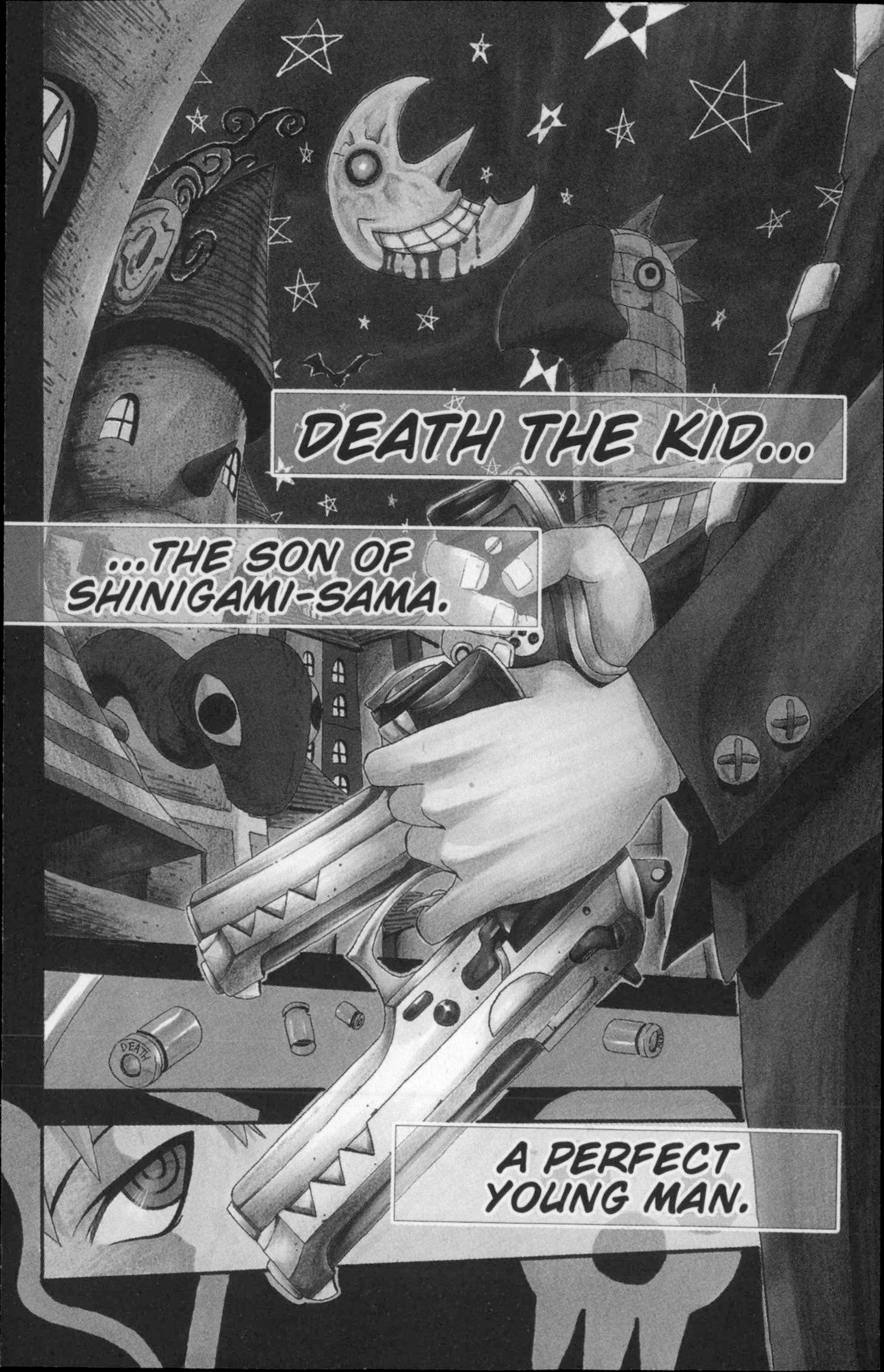
DEATH THE KID...
...THE SON OF SHINIGAMI-SAMA.
A PERFECT YOUNG MAN.
DEATH

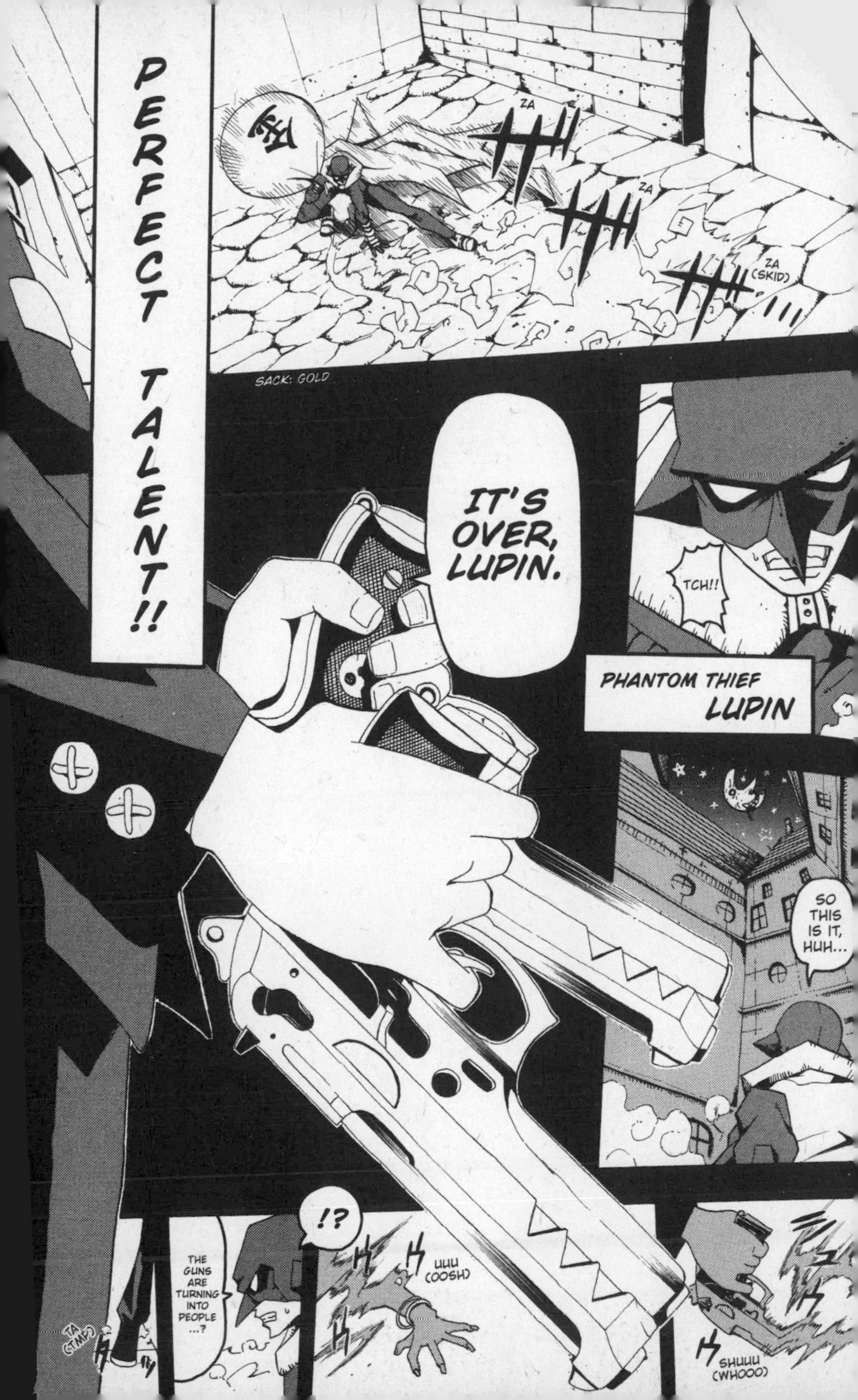
ZA
ZA
ZA (SKID)
SACK: GOLD
PERFECT TALENT!!
TCH!!
PHANTOM THIEF LUPIN
IT'S OVER, LUPIN.
SO THIS IS IT, HUH...
SHUUU (WHOOO)
UUU (OOSH)
!?
THE GUNS ARE TURNING INTO PEOPLE ...?
TA (TMP)

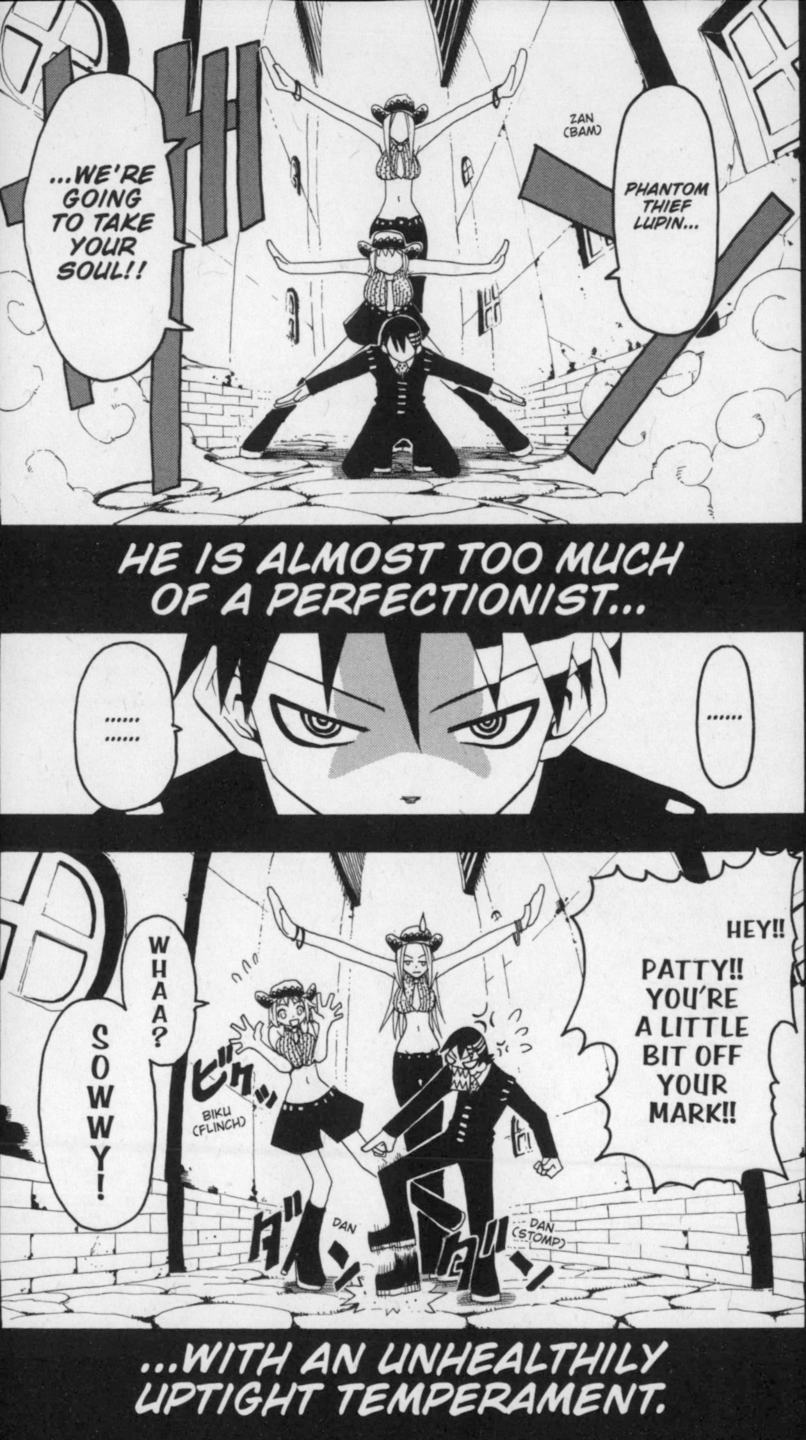
PHANTOM THIEF LUPIN...
ZAN (BAM)
...WE'RE GOING TO TAKE YOUR SOUL!!
HE IS ALMOST TOO MUCH OF A PERFECTIONIST...
......
....
HEY!!
PATTY!! YOU'RE A LITTLE BIT OFF YOUR MARK!!
DAN (STOMP)
DAN
BIKU (FLINCH)
WHAA?
SOWWY!
...WITH AN UNHEALTHILY UPTIGHT TEMPERAMENT.

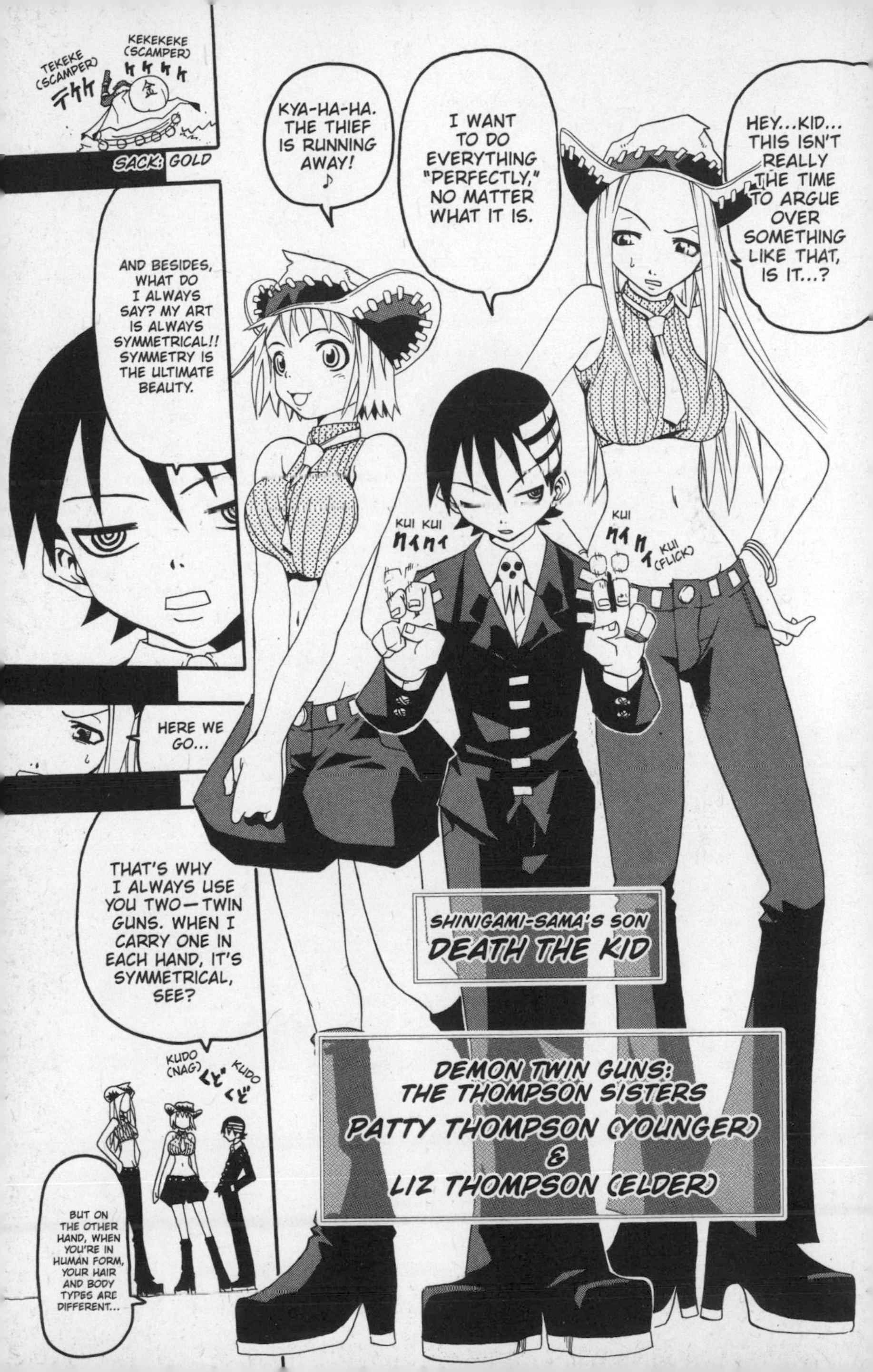
HEY...KID... THIS ISN'T REALLY THE TIME TO ARGUE OVER SOMETHING LIKE THAT, IS IT...?
I WANT TO DO EVERYTHING "PERFECTLY," NO MATTER WHAT IT IS.
KYA-HA-HA. THE THIEF IS RUNNING AWAY! ♪
KUI KUI (FLICK)
KUI KUI
SHINIGAMI-SAMA'S SON
DEATH THE KID
DEMON TWIN GUNS: THE THOMPSON SISTERS
PATTY THOMPSON (YOUNGER) & LIZ THOMPSON (ELDER)
KEKEKEKE (SCAMPER)
TEKEKE (SCAMPER)
SACK: GOLD
AND BESIDES, WHAT DO I ALWAYS SAY? MY ART IS ALWAYS SYMMETRICAL!! SYMMETRY IS THE ULTIMATE BEAUTY.
HERE WE GO...
THAT'S WHY I ALWAYS USE YOU TWO—TWIN GUNS. WHEN I CARRY ONE IN EACH HAND, IT'S SYMMETRICAL, SEE?
KUDO
KUDO (NAG)
BUT ON THE OTHER HAND, WHEN YOU'RE IN HUMAN FORM, YOUR HAIR AND BODY TYPES ARE DIFFERENT...

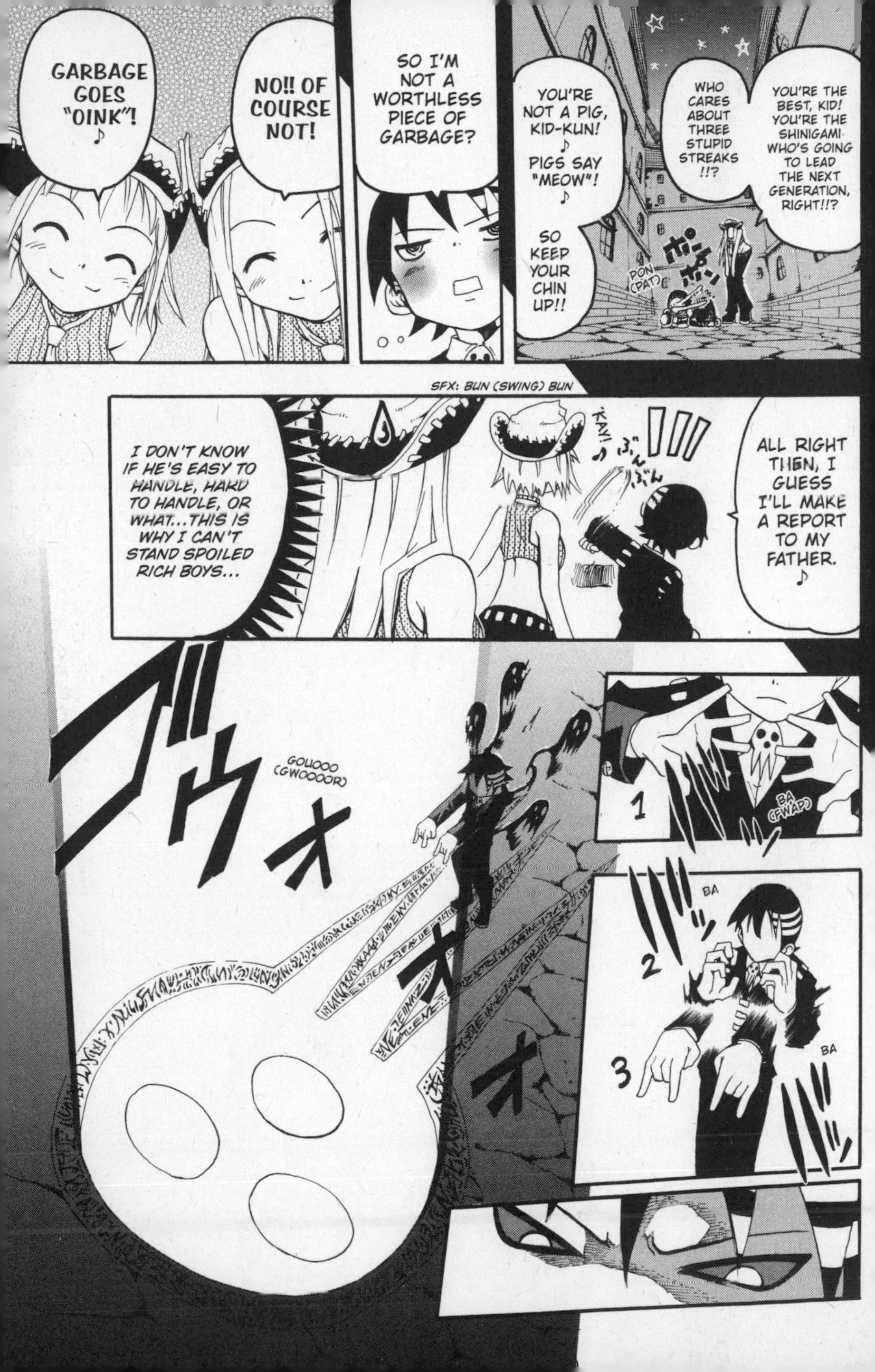
YOU'RE THE BEST, KID! YOU'RE THE SHINIGAMI WHO'S GOING TO LEAD THE NEXT GENERATION, RIGHT!!?
WHO CARES ABOUT THREE STUPID STREAKS !!?
YOU'RE NOT A PIG, KID-KUN! ♪ PIGS SAY "MEOW"! ♪
SO KEEP YOUR CHIN UP!!
PON (PAT)
SO I'M NOT A WORTHLESS PIECE OF GARBAGE?
NO!! OF COURSE NOT!
GARBAGE GOES "OINK"! ♪
SFX: BUN (SWING) BUN
ALL RIGHT THEN, I GUESS I'LL MAKE A REPORT TO MY FATHER. ♪
KAY! ♪
I DON'T KNOW IF HE'S EASY TO HANDLE, HARD TO HANDLE, OR WHAT...THIS IS WHY I CAN'T STAND SPOILED RICH BOYS...
1
BA (FWAP)
BA
2
3
BA
GOUOOO (GWOOOOR)

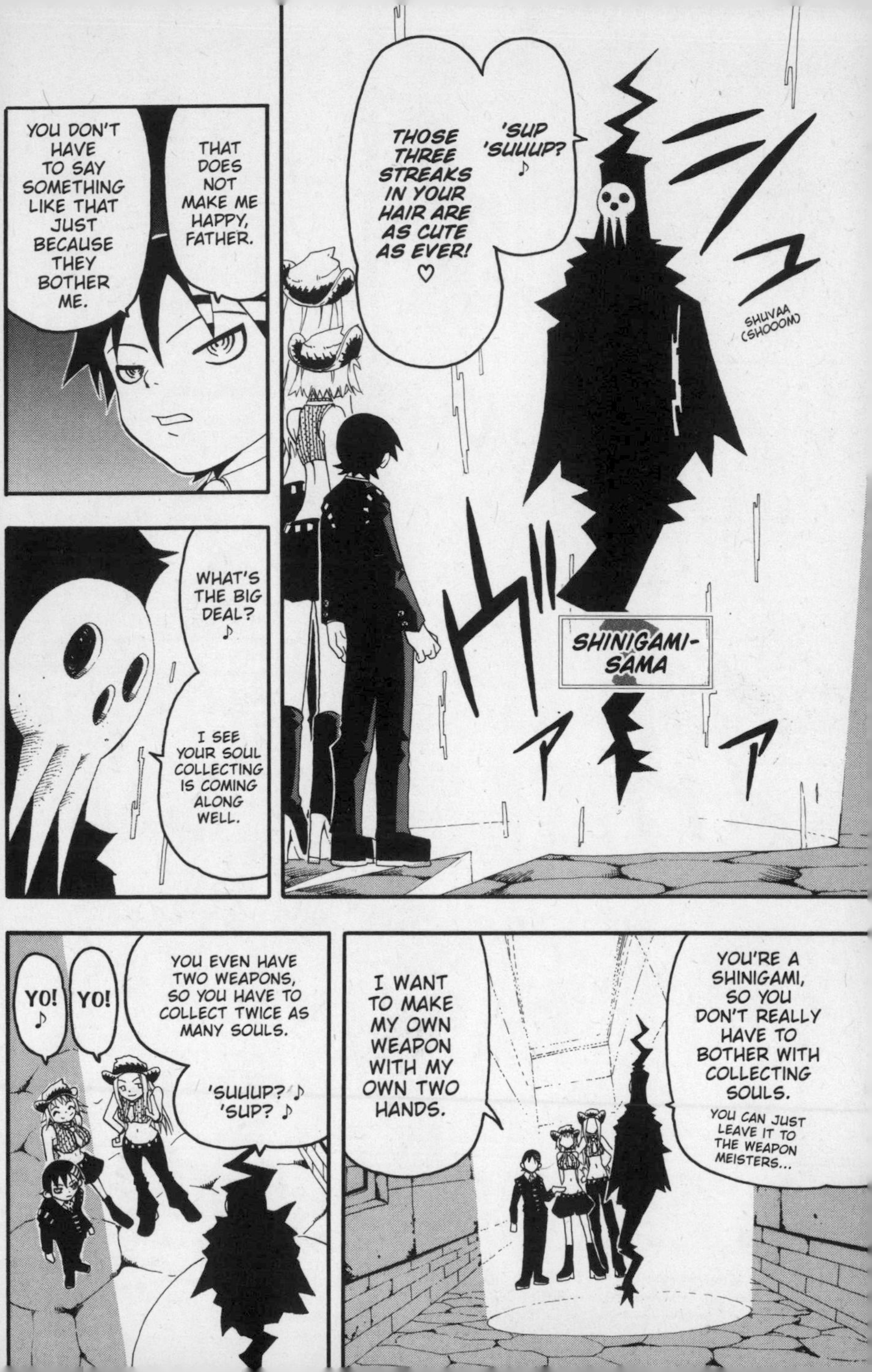
'SUP 'SUUUP? ♪
THOSE THREE STREAKS IN YOUR HAIR ARE AS CUTE AS EVER! ♡
SHUVAA (SHOOOM)
SHINIGAMI-SAMA
THAT DOES NOT MAKE ME HAPPY, FATHER.
YOU DON'T HAVE TO SAY SOMETHING LIKE THAT JUST BECAUSE THEY BOTHER ME.
WHAT'S THE BIG DEAL? ♪
I SEE YOUR SOUL COLLECTING IS COMING ALONG WELL.
YOU'RE A SHINIGAMI, SO YOU DON'T REALLY HAVE TO BOTHER WITH COLLECTING SOULS.
YOU CAN JUST LEAVE IT TO THE WEAPON MEISTERS...
I WANT TO MAKE MY OWN WEAPON WITH MY OWN TWO HANDS.
YOU EVEN HAVE TWO WEAPONS, SO YOU HAVE TO COLLECT TWICE AS MANY SOULS.
'SUUUP? ♪ 'SUP? ♪
YO!
YO! ♪

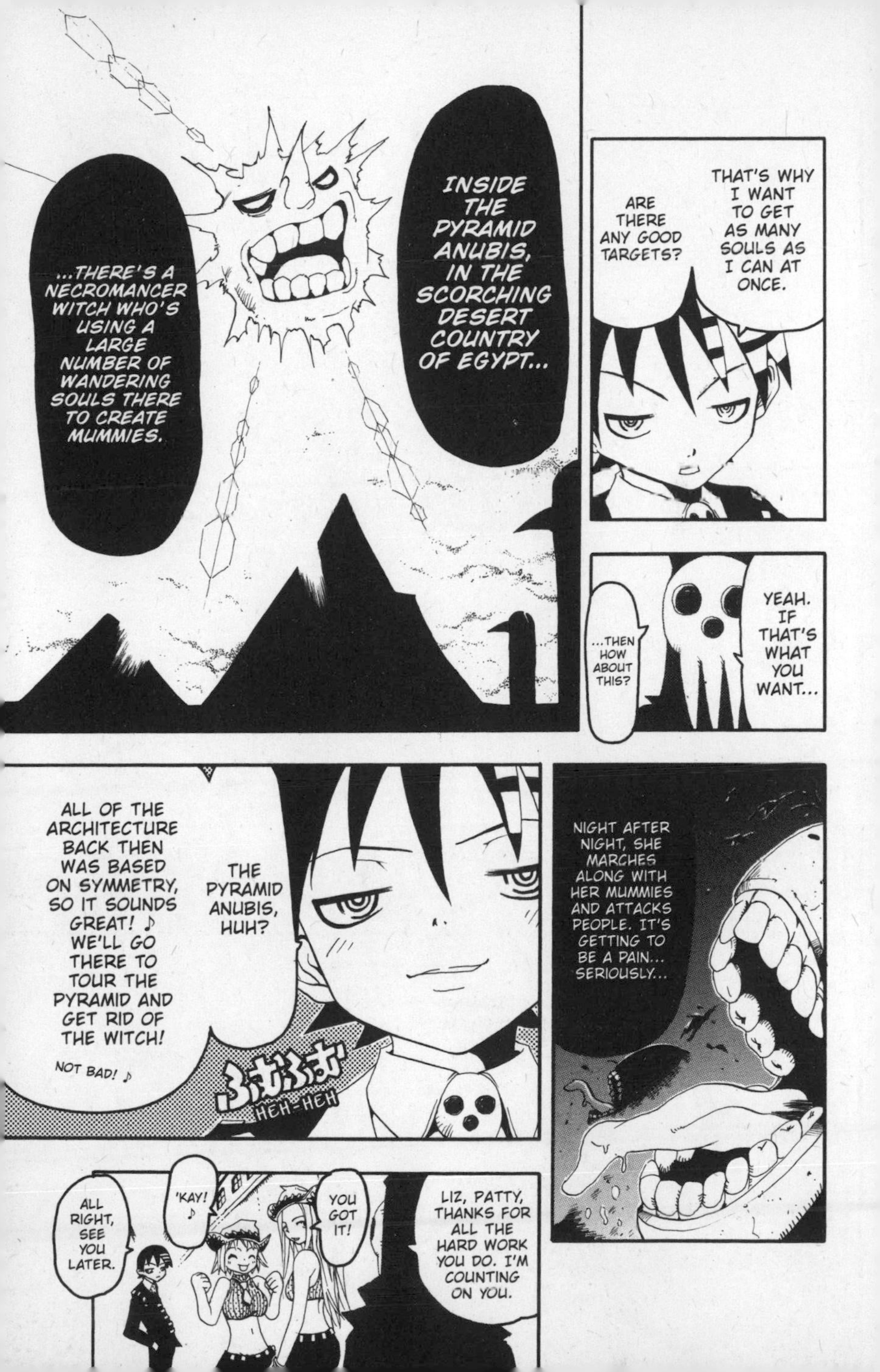
THAT'S WHY I WANT TO GET AS MANY SOULS AS I CAN AT ONCE.
ARE THERE ANY GOOD TARGETS?
YEAH. IF THAT'S WHAT YOU WANT...
...THEN HOW ABOUT THIS?
INSIDE THE PYRAMID ANUBIS, IN THE SCORCHING DESERT COUNTRY OF EGYPT...
...THERE'S A NECROMANCER WITCH WHO'S USING A LARGE NUMBER OF WANDERING SOULS THERE TO CREATE MUMMIES.
NIGHT AFTER NIGHT, SHE MARCHES ALONG WITH HER MUMMIES AND ATTACKS PEOPLE. IT'S GETTING TO BE A PAIN... SERIOUSLY...
THE PYRAMID ANUBIS, HUH?
ALL OF THE ARCHITECTURE BACK THEN WAS BASED ON SYMMETRY, SO IT SOUNDS GREAT! ♪ WE'LL GO THERE TO TOUR THE PYRAMID AND GET RID OF THE WITCH!
NOT BAD! ♪
ふむふむ
HEH-HEH
LIZ, PATTY, THANKS FOR ALL THE HARD WORK YOU DO. I'M COUNTING ON YOU.
YOU GOT IT!
'KAY! ♪
ALL RIGHT, SEE YOU LATER.

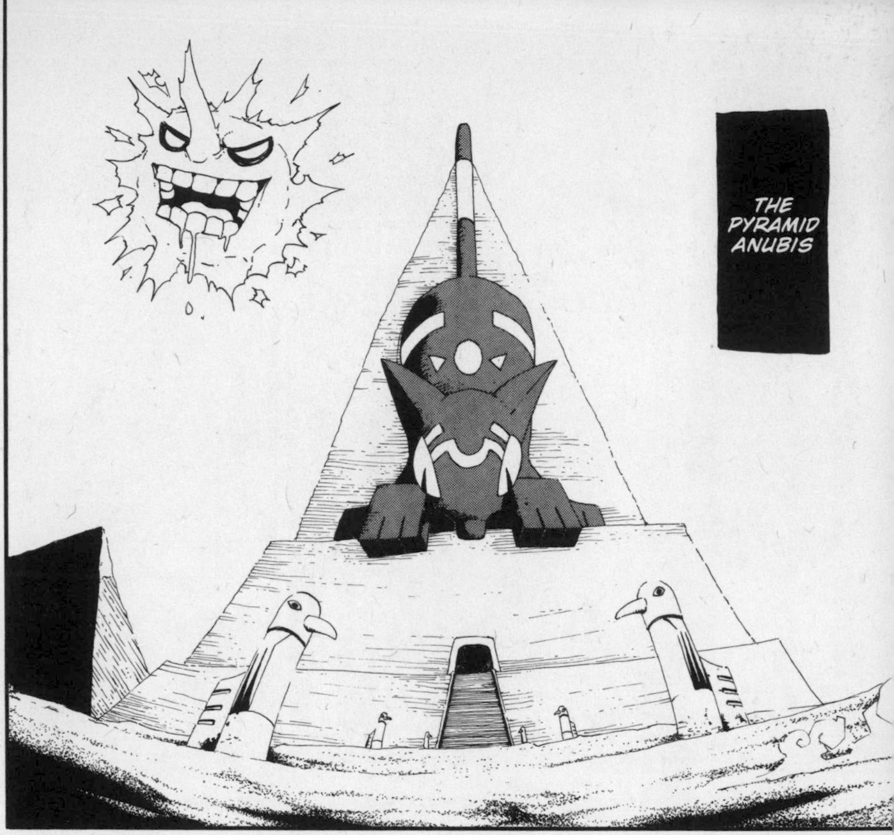
THE PYRAMID ANUBIS

SFX: GASHAN (GASHCK)

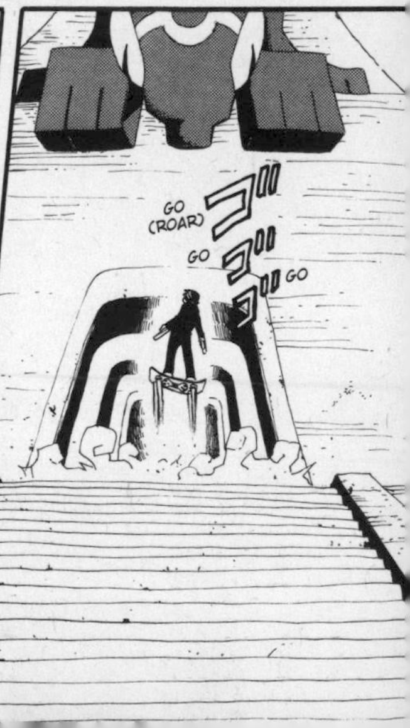
GO (ROAR)
GO
GO

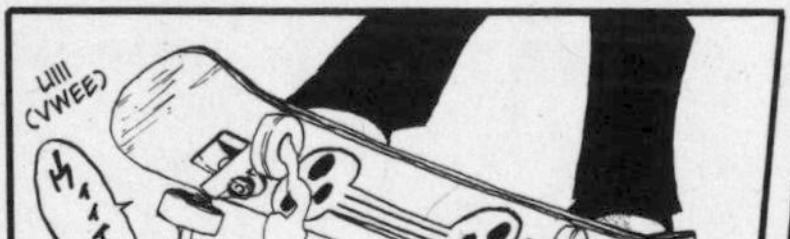
UIII (VWEE)

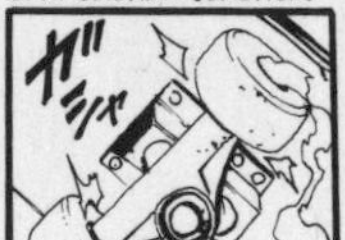

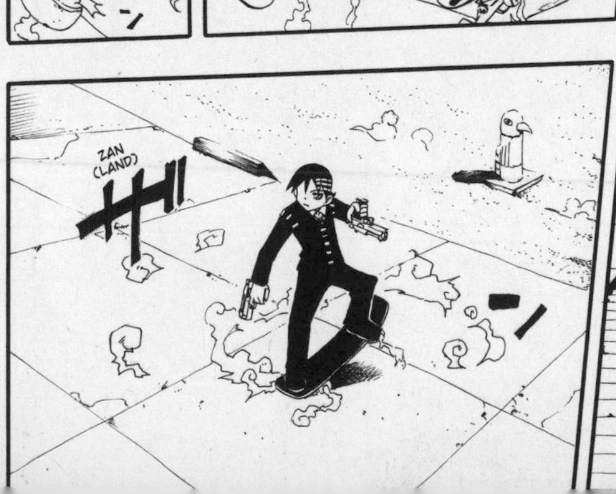
ZAN (LAND)

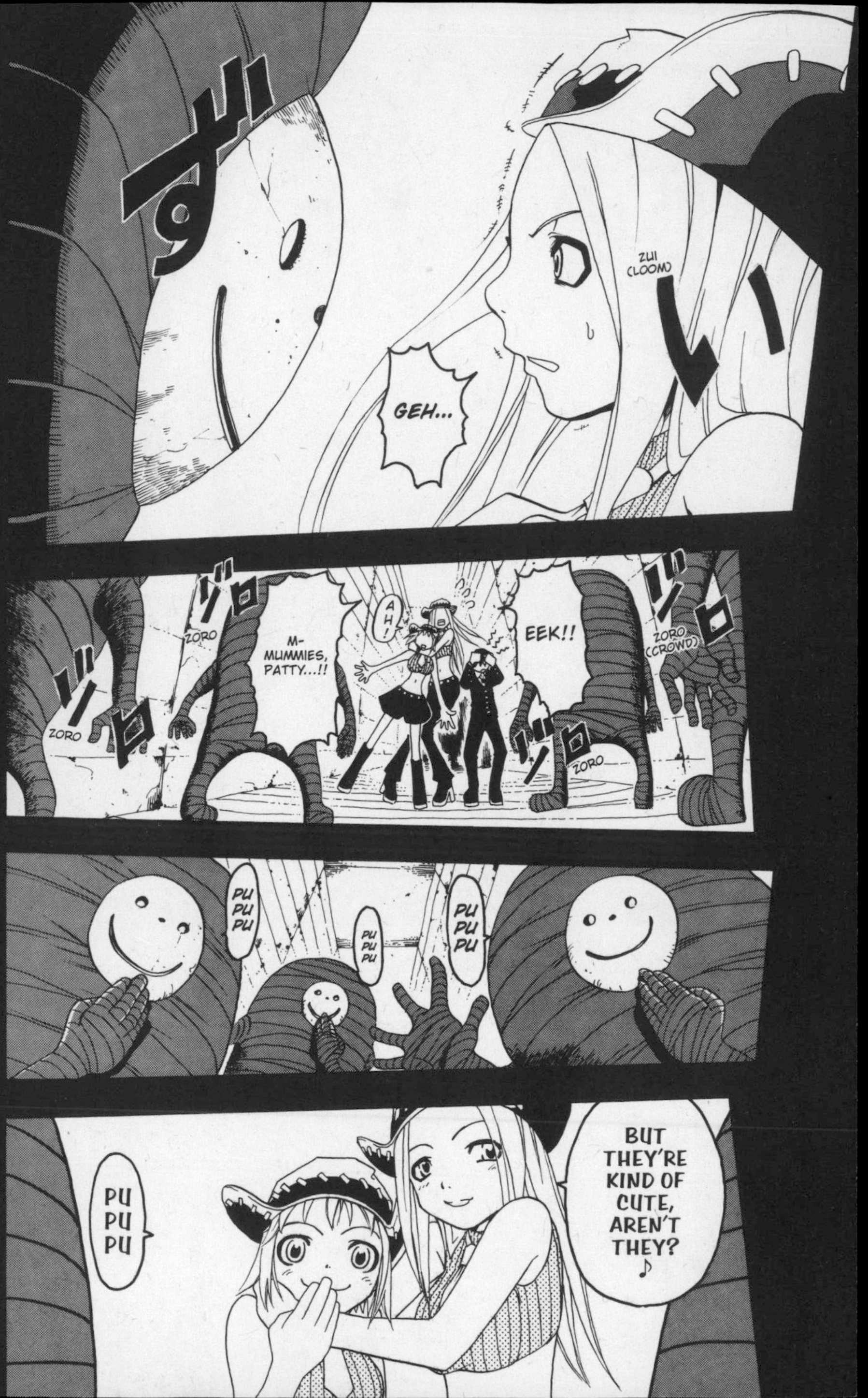
ZUI (LOOM)
GEH...
ZORO (CROWD)
EEK!!
AH!
ZORO
M-MUMMIES, PATTY...!!
ZORO
ZORO
PU PU PU
PU PU PU
PU PU PU
BUT THEY'RE KIND OF CUTE, AREN'T THEY? ♪
PU PU PU

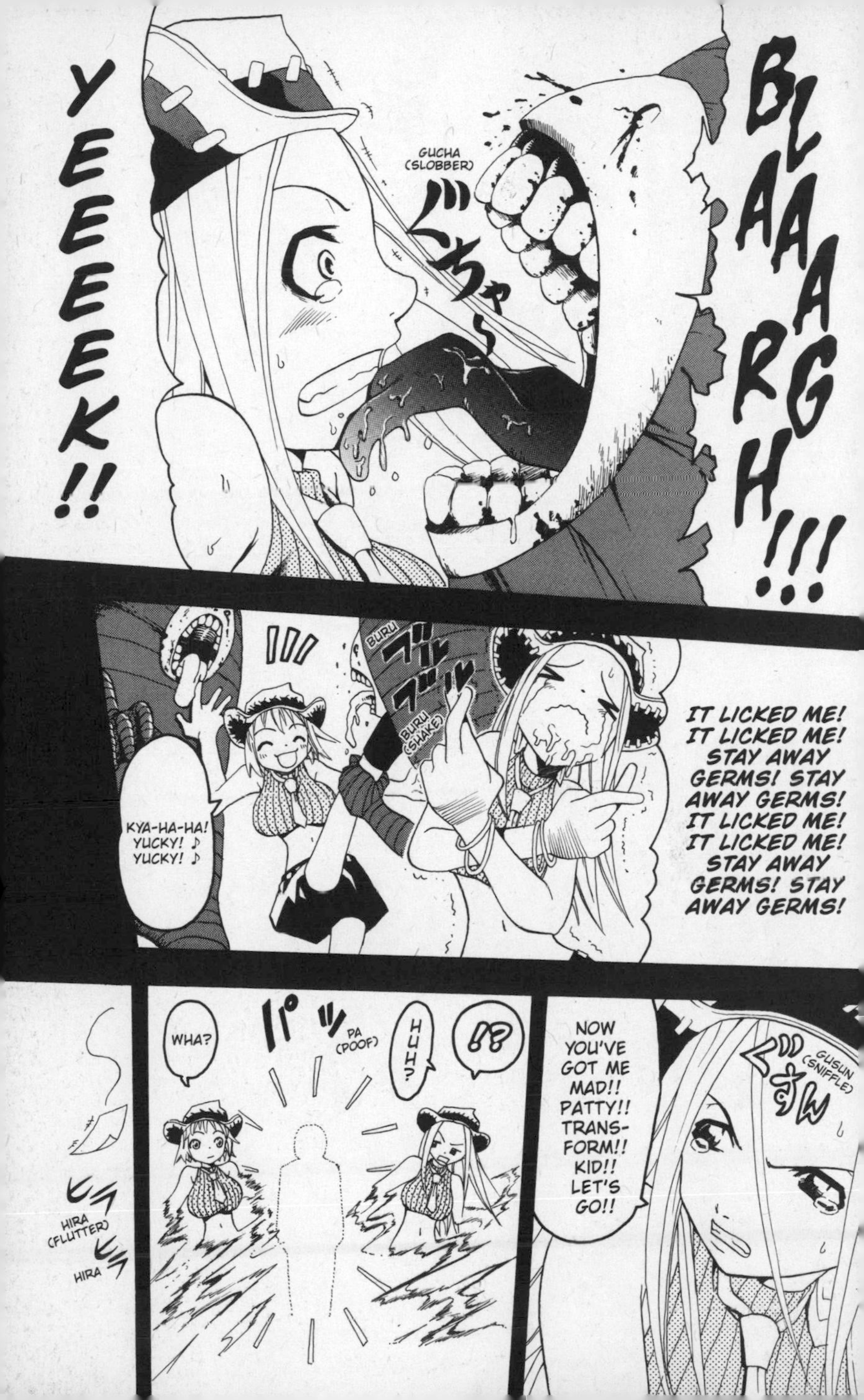

BLAAAARGH!!!
GUCHA (SLOBBER)
YEEEEK!!
IT LICKED ME! IT LICKED ME! STAY AWAY GERMS! STAY AWAY GERMS! IT LICKED ME! IT LICKED ME! STAY AWAY GERMS! STAY AWAY GERMS!
BURU BURU (SHAKE)
!!!
KYA-HA-HA! YUCKY! ♪ YUCKY! ♪
GUSUN (SNIFFLE)
NOW YOU'VE GOT ME MAD!! PATTY!! TRANS-FORM!! KID!! LET'S GO!!
!?
HUH?
PA (POOF)
WHA?
HIRA (FLUTTER)
HIRA

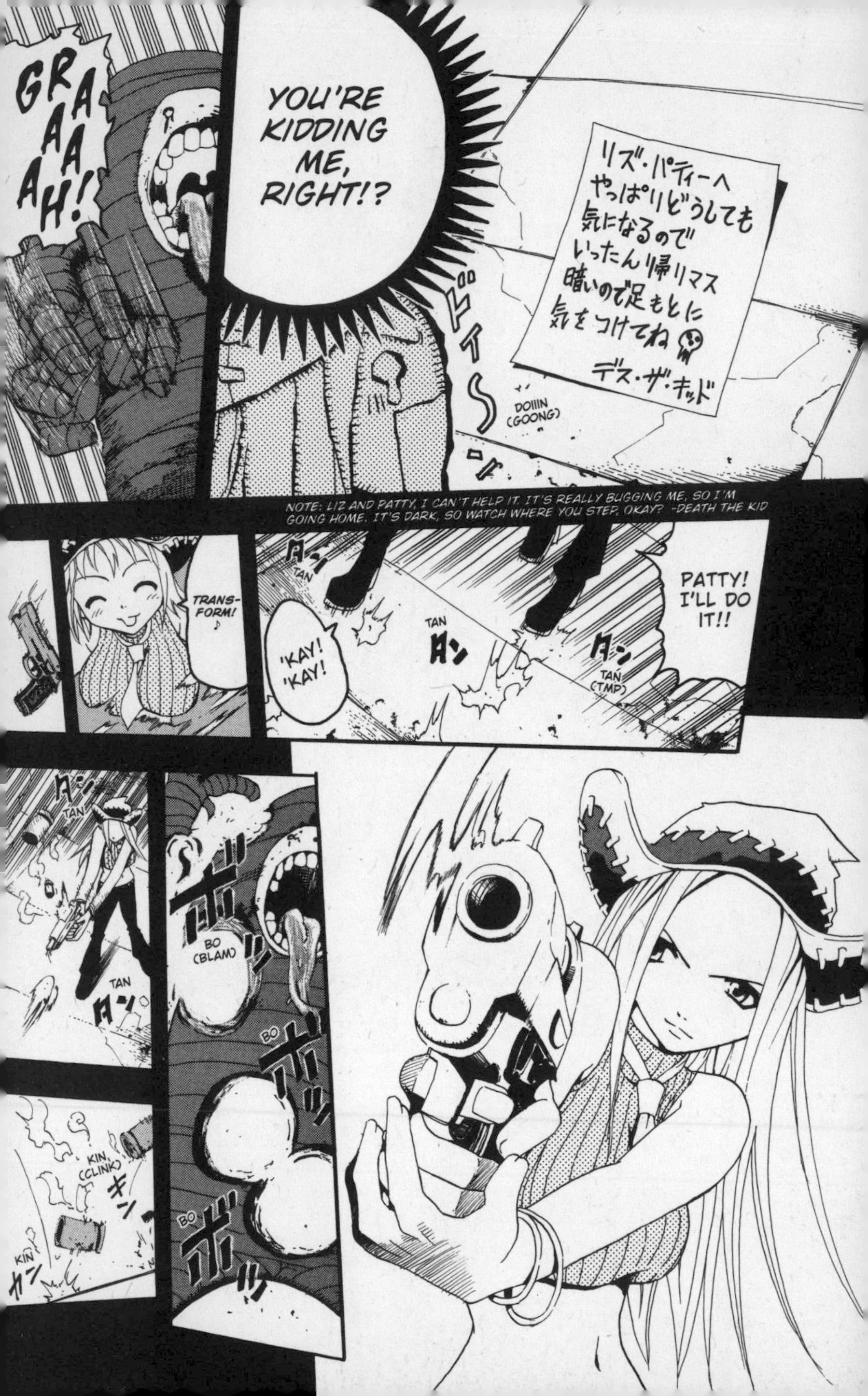
リズ・パティーへ
やっぱりどうしても
気になるので
いったん帰りマス
暗いので足もとに
気をつけてね
デス・ザ・キッド
DOIIIN (GOONG)
YOU'RE KIDDING ME, RIGHT!?
GRAAAAH!
NOTE: LIZ AND PATTY, I CAN'T HELP IT. IT'S REALLY BUGGING ME, SO I'M GOING HOME. IT'S DARK, SO WATCH WHERE YOU STEP, OKAY? -DEATH THE KID
PATTY! I'LL DO IT!!
TAN (TMP)
TAN
TAN
'KAY! 'KAY!
TRANS-FORM! ♪
BO (BLAM)
BO
BO
TAN
TAN
KIN (CLINK)
KIN

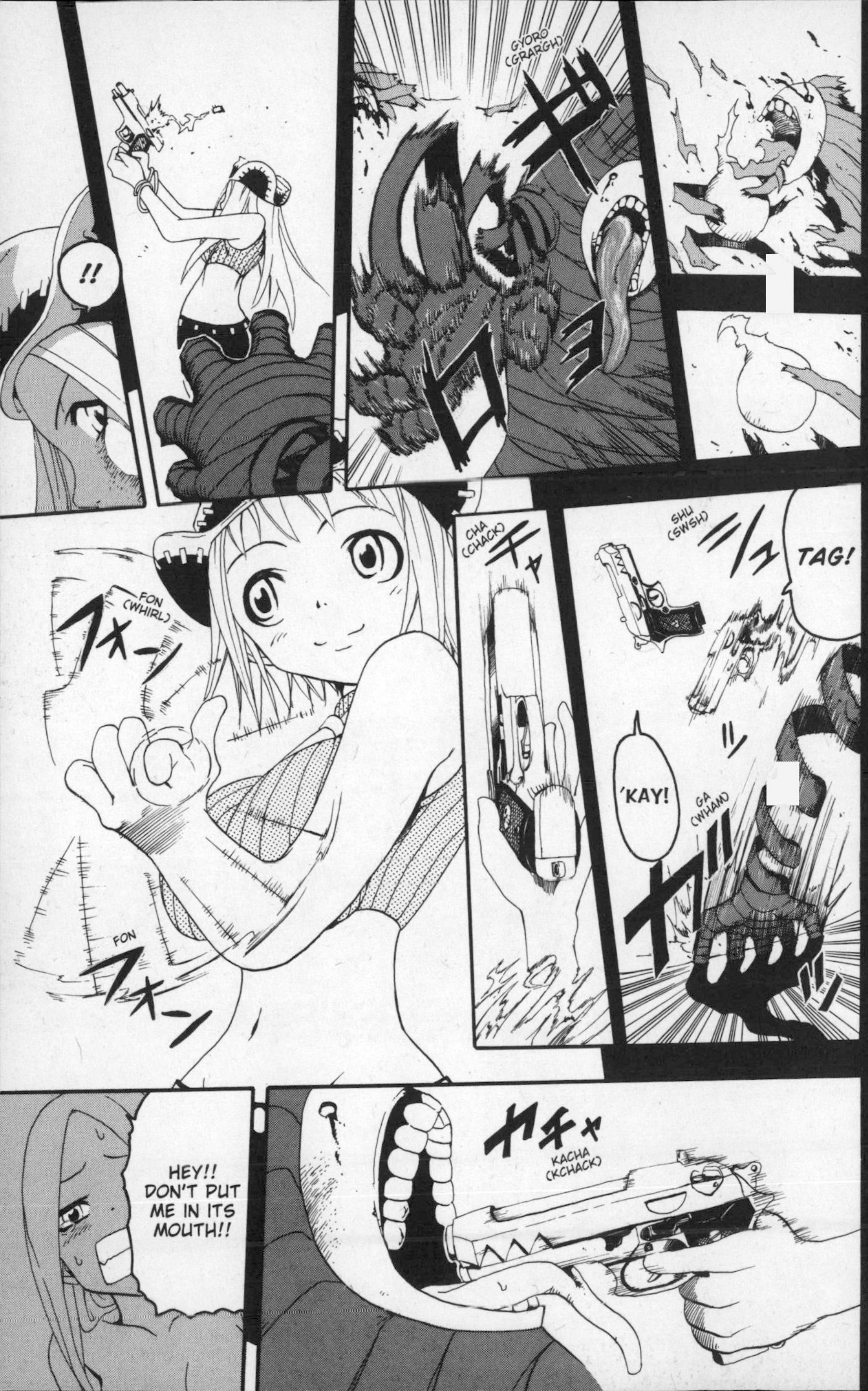
GYORO (GRARGH)
!!
TAG!
SHU (SWSH)
'KAY!
GA (WHAM)
CHA (CHACK)
FON (WHIRL)
FON
KACHA (KCHACK)
HEY!! DON'T PUT ME IN ITS MOUTH!!

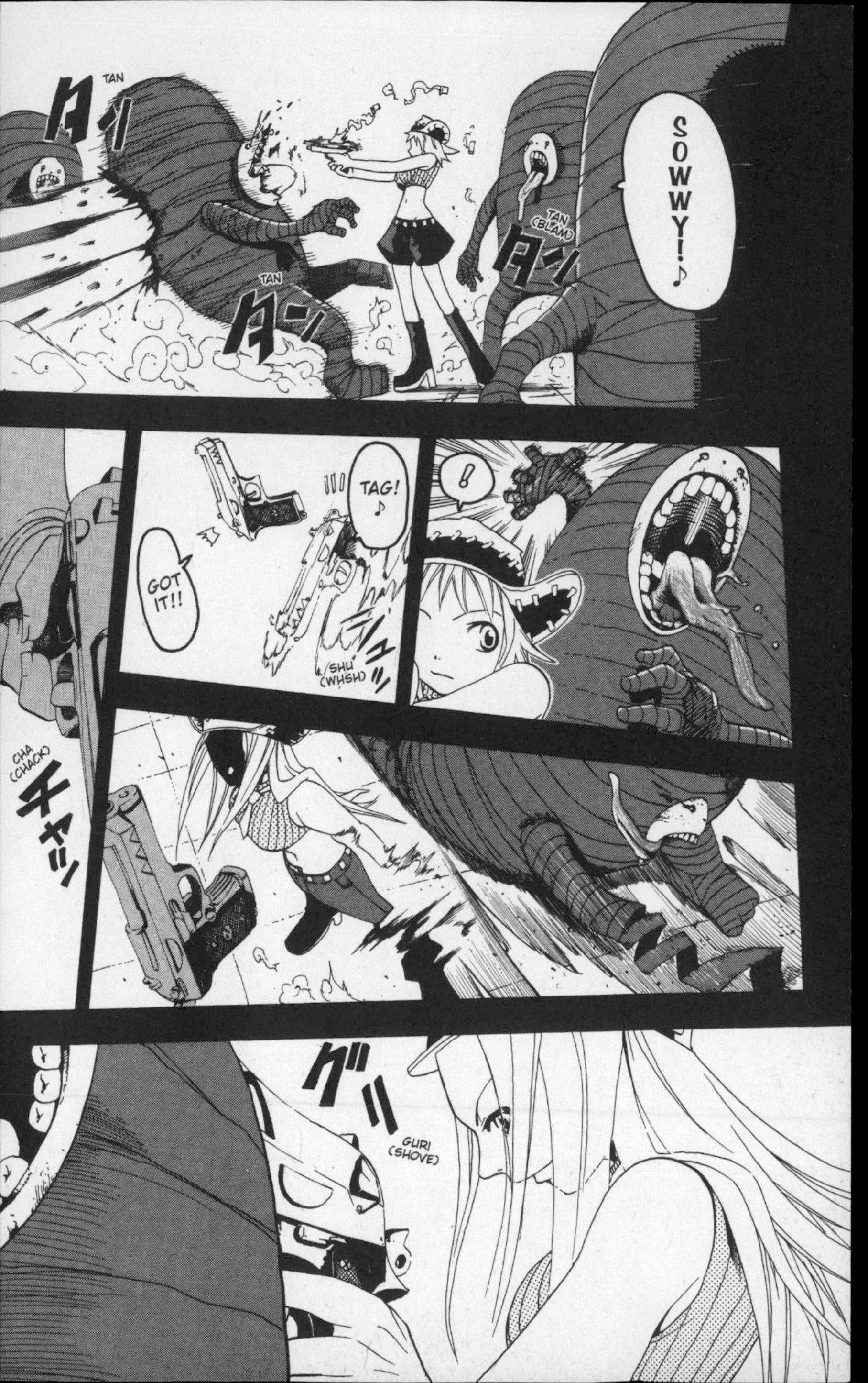
SOWWY!!♪
TAN (BLAM)
TAN
TAN
!
TAG! ♪
GOT IT!!
SHU (WHSH)
CHA (CHACK)
GURI (SHOVE)

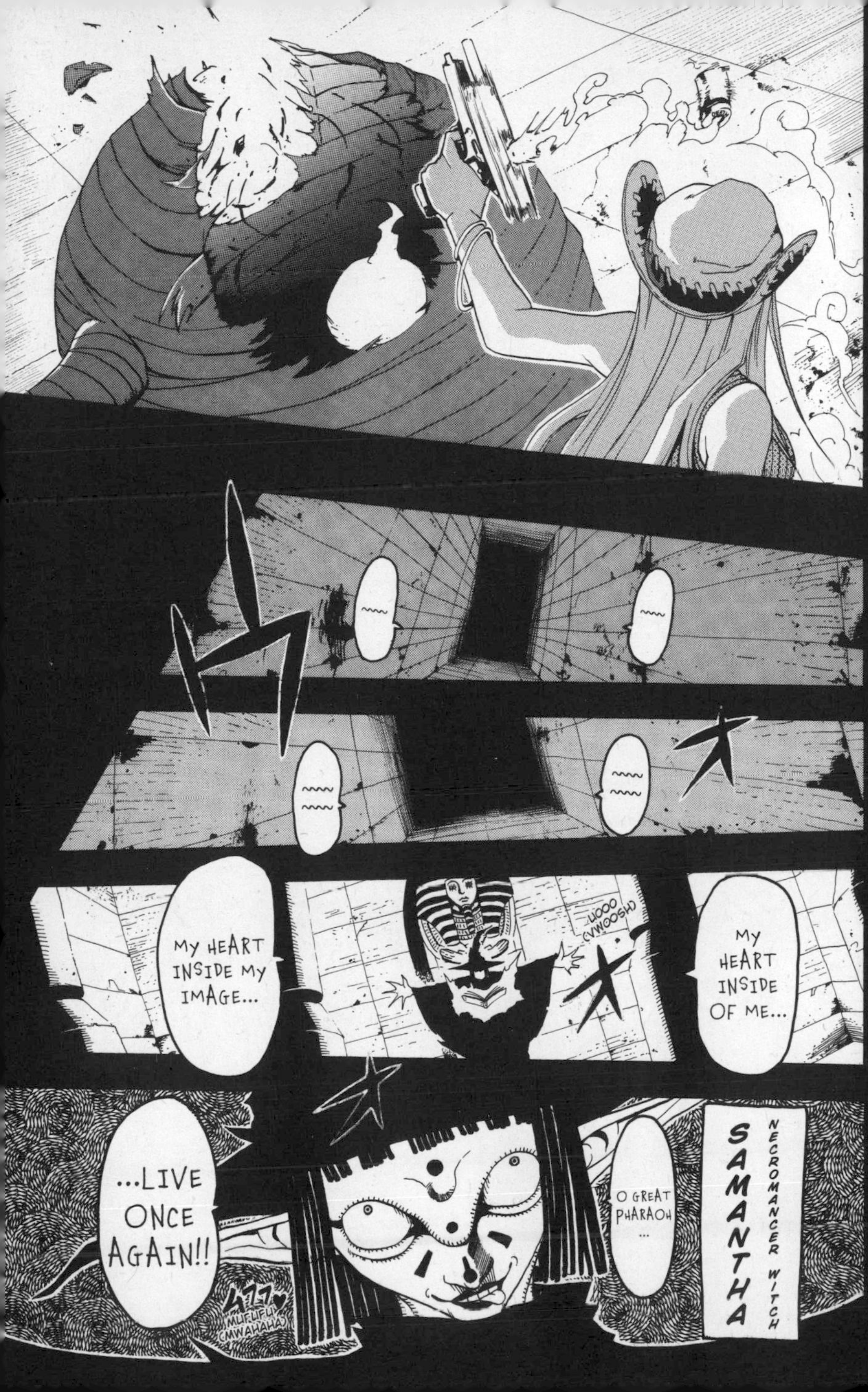
My HEART INSIDE OF ME...
(VWOOSH)
MY HEART INSIDE MY IMAGE...
SAMANTHA NECROMANCER WITCH
O GREAT PHARAOH ...
...LIVE ONCE AGAIN!!
MUFUFU (MWAHAHA)

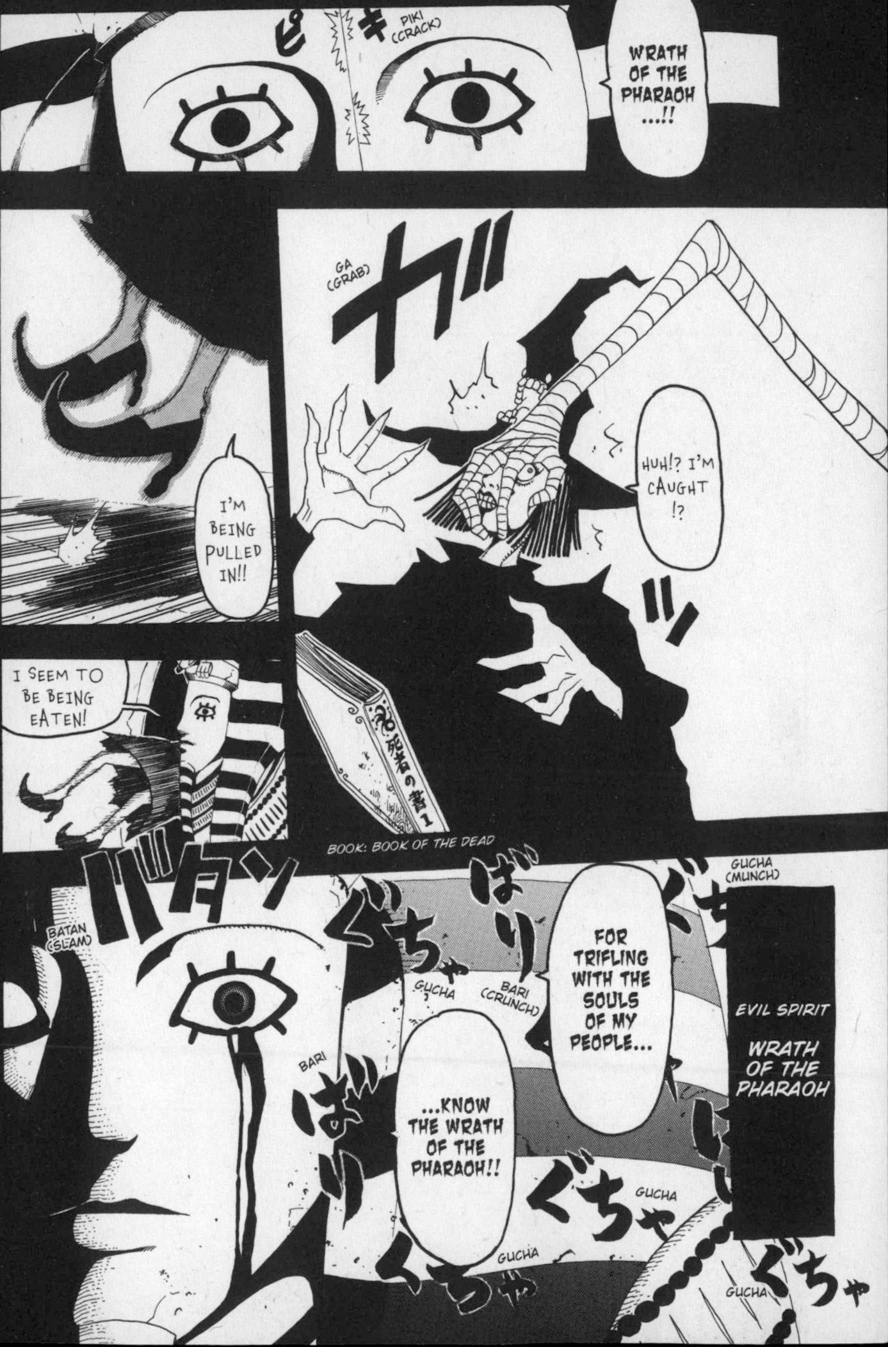
PIKI (CRACK)
WRATH OF THE PHARAOH ....!!
GA (GRAB)
HUH!? I'M CAUGHT !?
I'M BEING PULLED IN!!
I SEEM TO BE BEING EATEN!
BOOK: BOOK OF THE DEAD
死者の書1
GUCHA (MUNCH)
EVIL SPIRIT
WRATH OF THE PHARAOH
FOR TRIFLING WITH THE SOULS OF MY PEOPLE...
BARI (CRUNCH)
GUCHA
BATAN (SLAM)
...KNOW THE WRATH OF THE PHARAOH!!
BARI
GUCHA
GUCHA
GUCHA

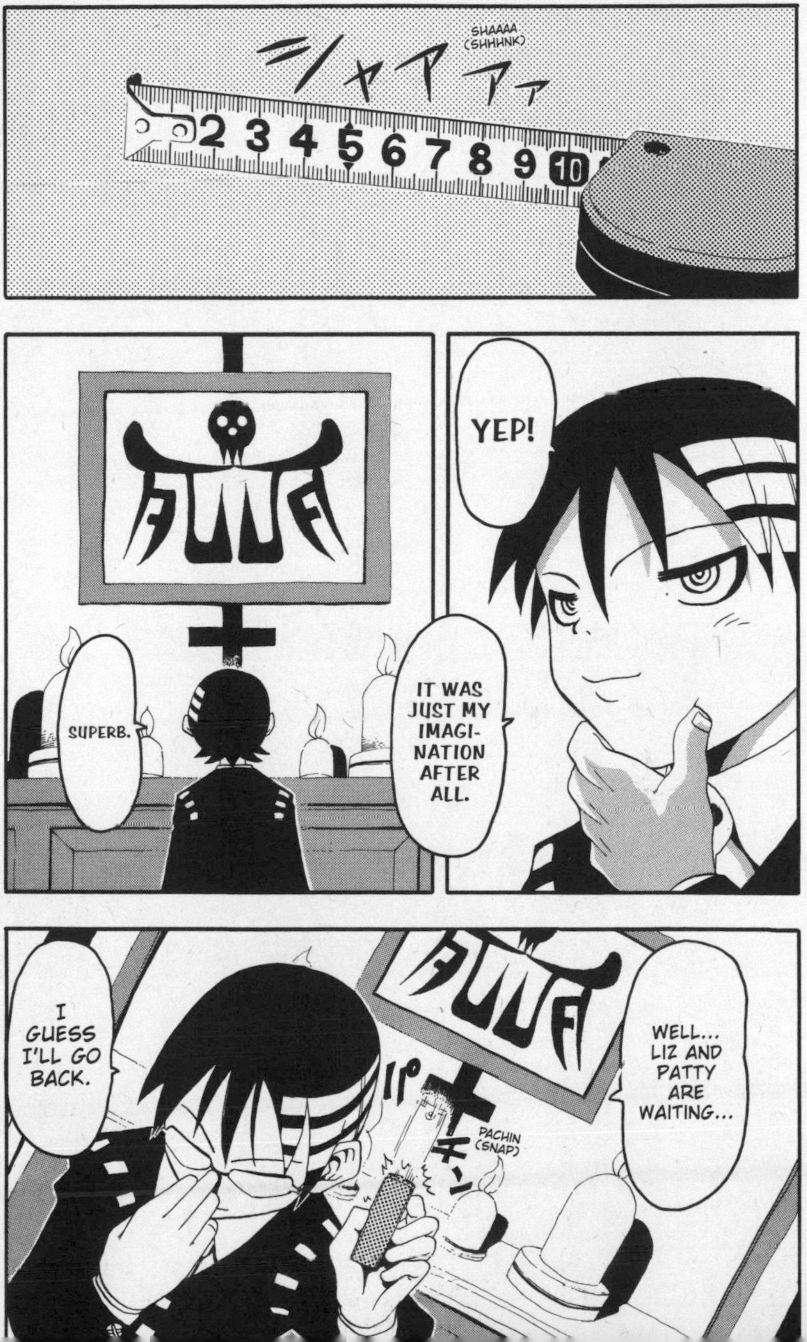

SHAAAA (SHHHNK)
YEP!
IT WAS JUST MY IMAGINATION AFTER ALL.
SUPERB.
WELL... LIZ AND PATTY ARE WAITING...
I GUESS I'LL GO BACK.
PACHIN (SNAP)

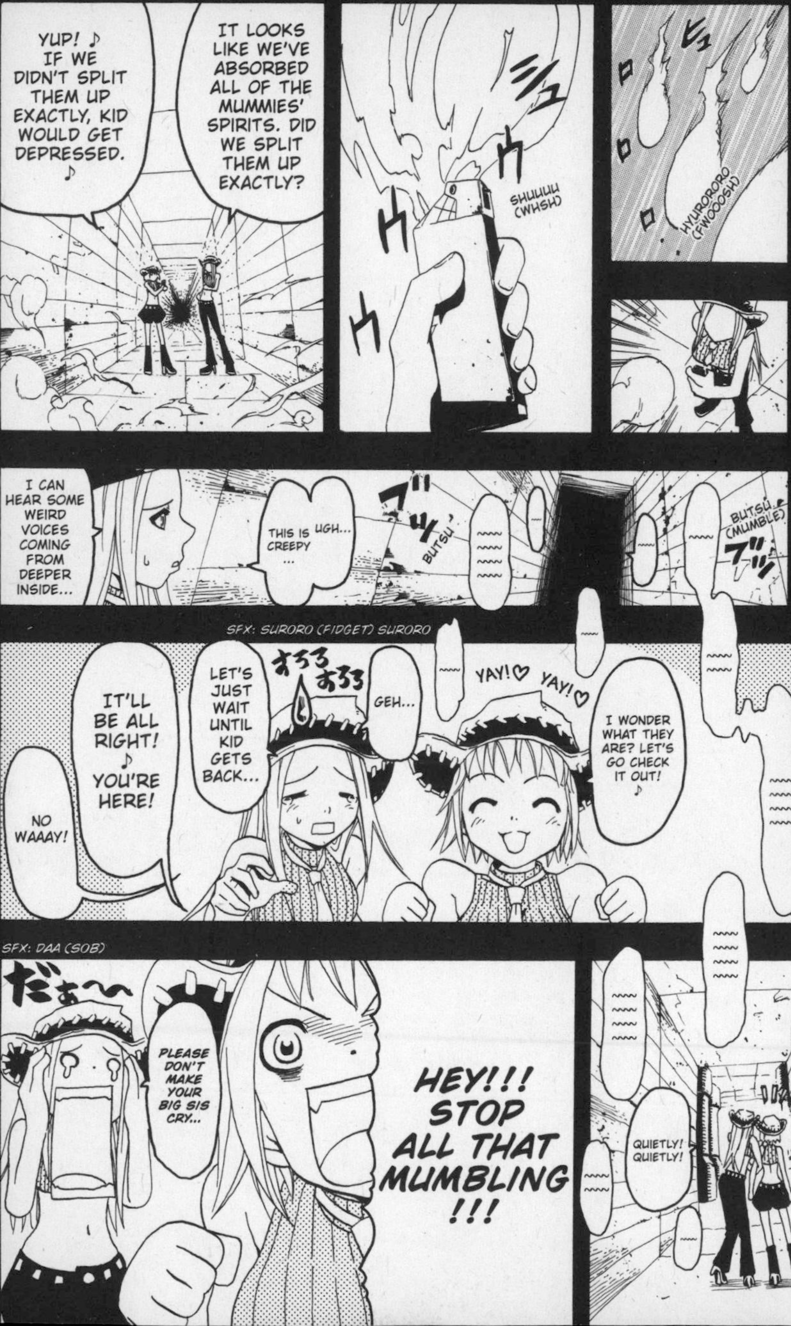
HYURORORO (FWOOOSH)
SHUUUU (WHSH)
IT LOOKS LIKE WE'VE ABSORBED ALL OF THE MUMMIES' SPIRITS. DID WE SPLIT THEM UP EXACTLY?
YUP! ♪ IF WE DIDN'T SPLIT THEM UP EXACTLY, KID WOULD GET DEPRESSED. ♪
BUTSU (MUMBLE)
BUTSU
UGH... THIS IS CREEPY...
I CAN HEAR SOME WEIRD VOICES COMING FROM DEEPER INSIDE...
SFX: SURORO (FIDGET) SURORO
I WONDER WHAT THEY ARE? LET'S GO CHECK IT OUT! ♪
YAY!♡ YAY!♡
GEH...
LET'S JUST WAIT UNTIL KID GETS BACK...
IT'LL BE ALL RIGHT! ♪ YOU'RE HERE!
NO WAAAY!
IT'S COMING FROM THIS DIREC-TION. ♪
QUIETLY! QUIETLY!
HEY!!! STOP ALL THAT MUMBLING!!!
PLEASE DON'T MAKE YOUR BIG SIS CRY...
SFX: DAA (SOB)

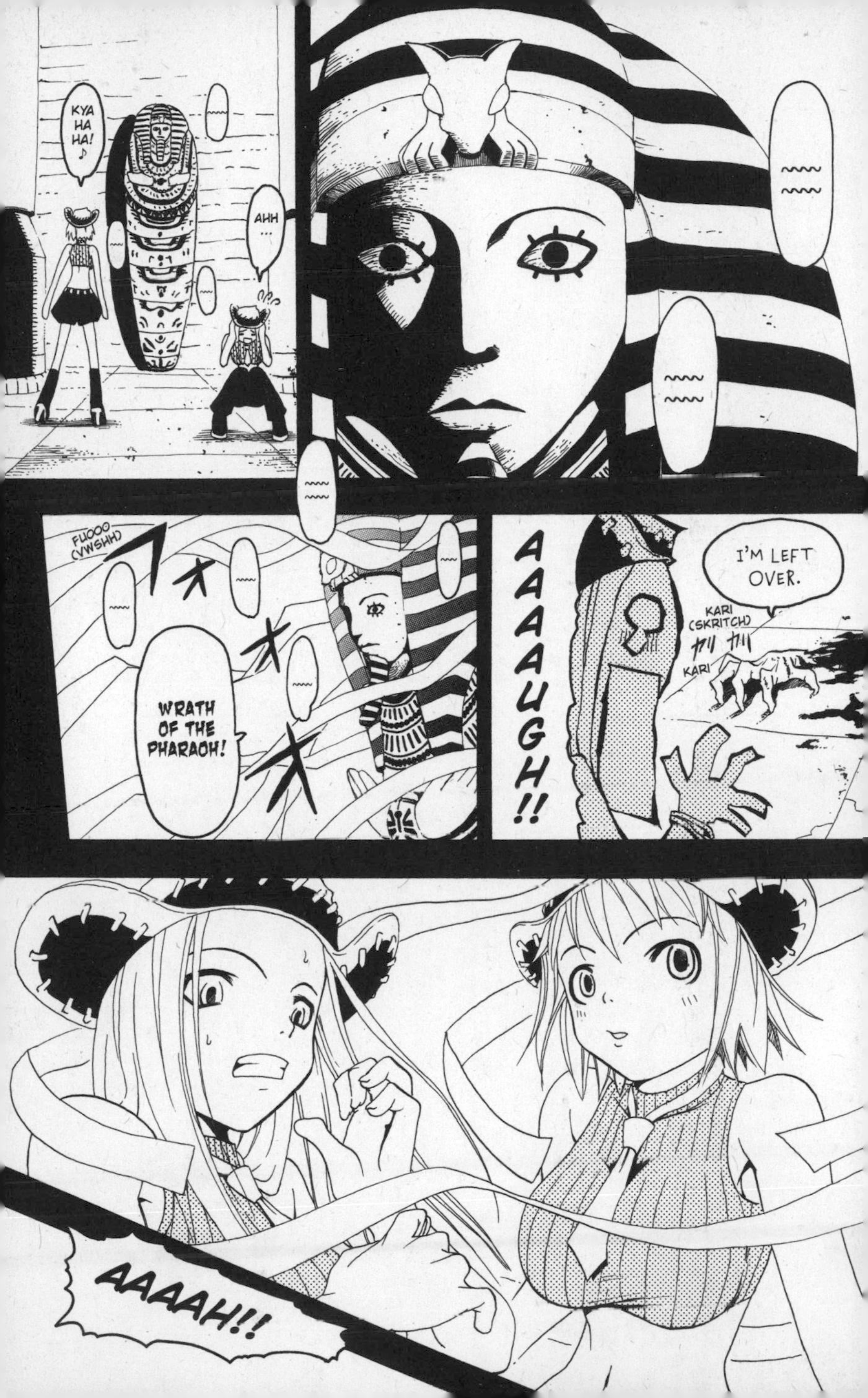
AHH ...
KYA HA HA! ♪
I'M LEFT OVER.
KARI (SKRITCH)
カリ カリ
KARI
AAAAAUGH!!
FUOOO (VWSHH)
WRATH OF THE PHARAOH!
AAAAH!!

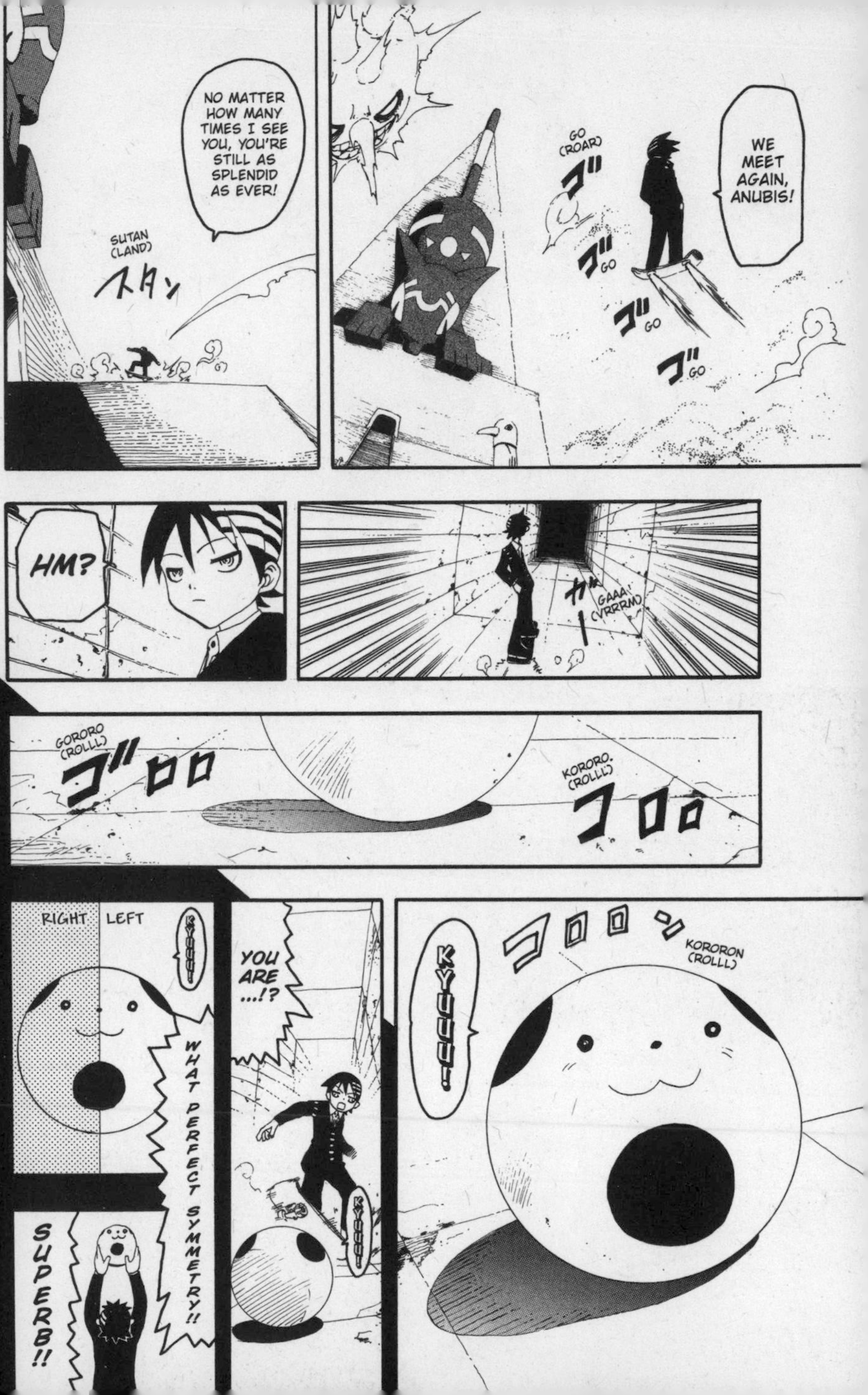
GO (ROAR)
ゴ
WE MEET AGAIN, ANUBIS!
ゴ GO
ゴ GO
ゴ GO
NO MATTER HOW MANY TIMES I SEE YOU, YOU'RE STILL AS SPLENDID AS EVER!
SUTAN (LAND)
スタン
GAAA (VRRRM)
ガー
HM?
KORORO. (ROLLL)
コロロ
GORORO (ROLLL)
ゴロロ
コロロン
KORORON (ROLLL)
KYUUU!
YOU ARE ...!?
KYUUU!
WHAT PERFECT SYMMETRY!!
RIGHT
LEFT
KYUUU!
SUPERB!!

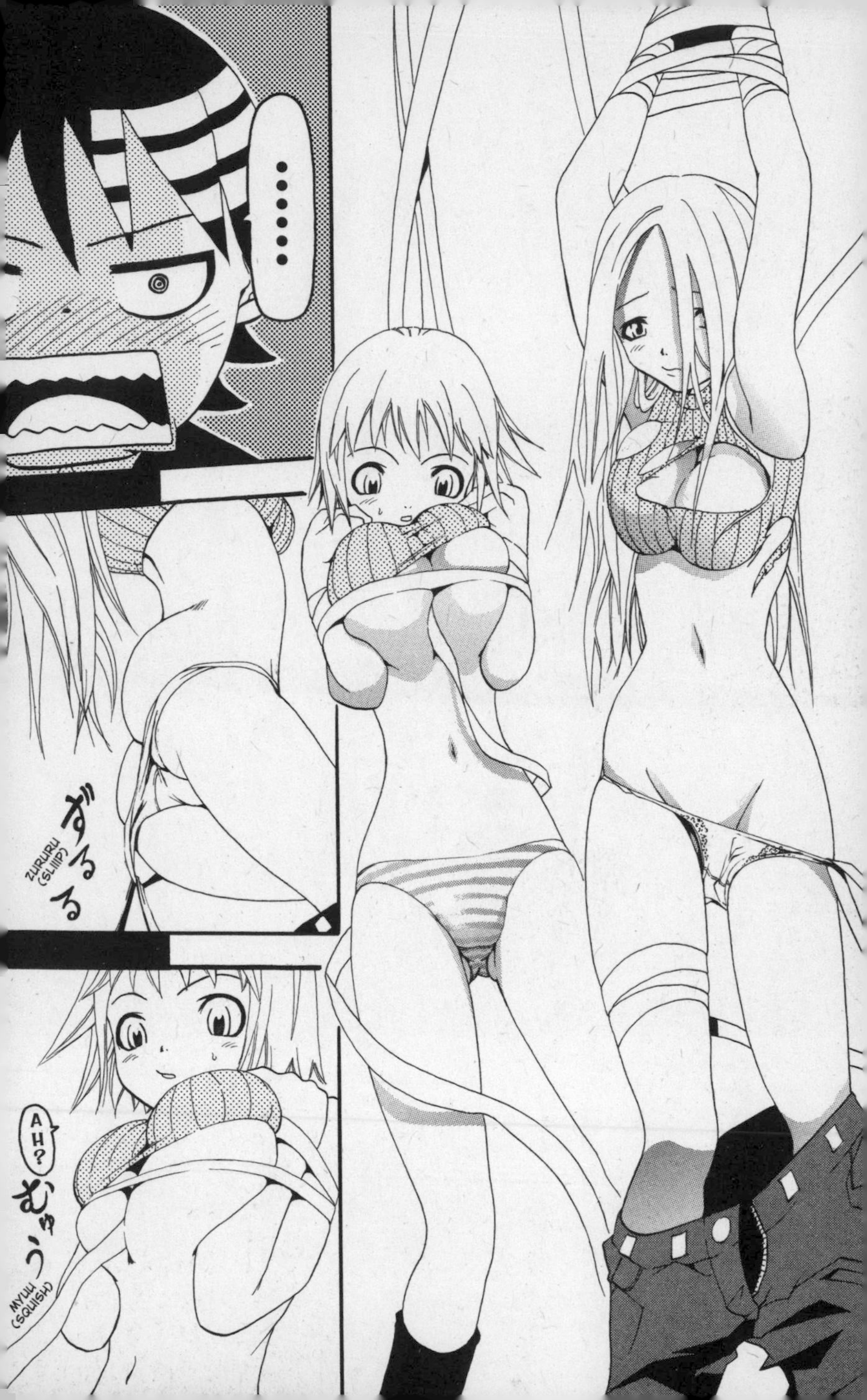
......
ずるる
ZURURU (SLIIIP)
AH?
むゅう
MYUU (SQUISH)

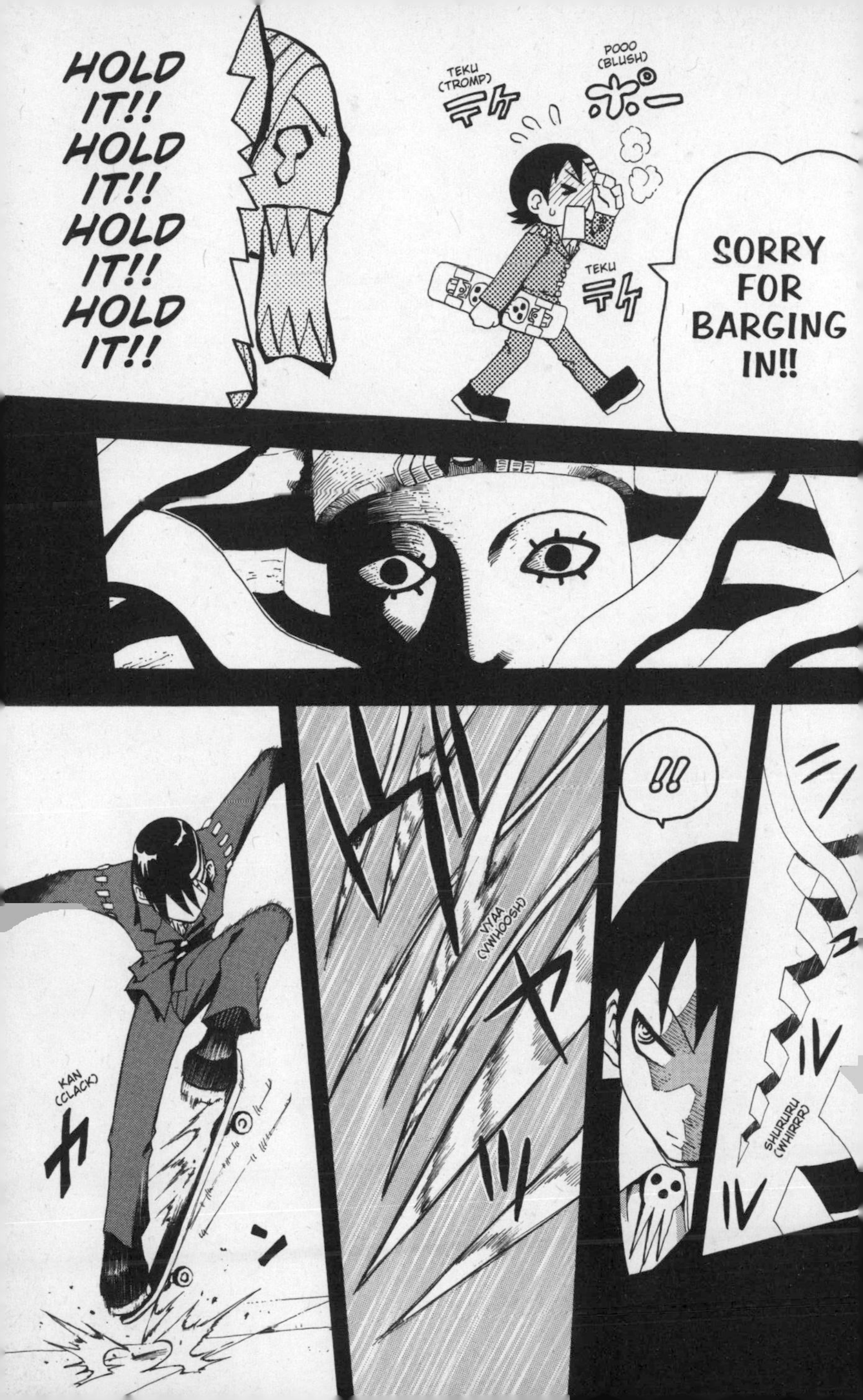
POOO (BLUSH)
TEKU (TROMP)
SORRY FOR BARGING IN!!
TEKU
HOLD IT!! HOLD IT!! HOLD IT!! HOLD IT!!
!!
SHURURU (WHIRRR)
VYAA (VWHOOSH)
KAN (CLACK)

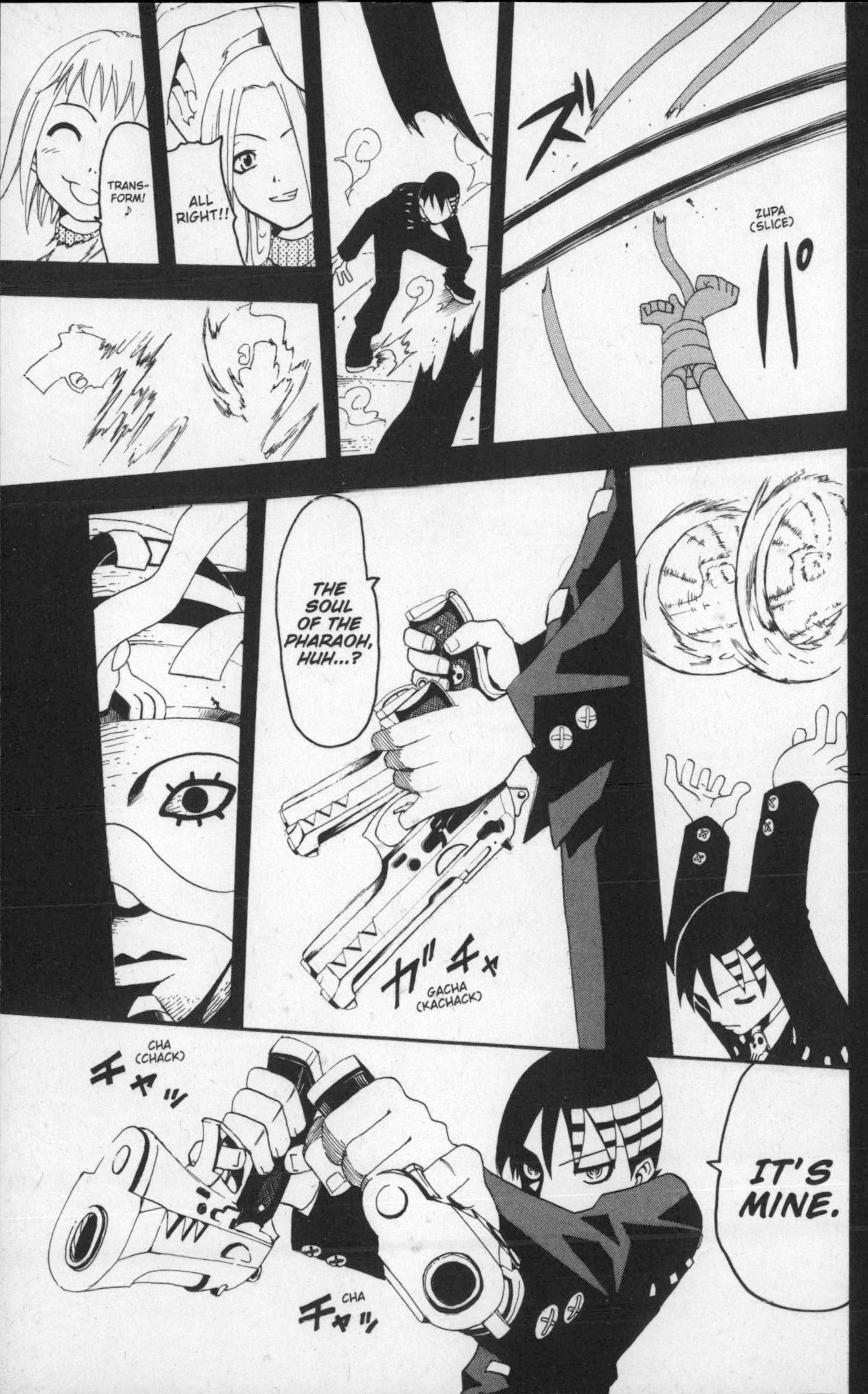
ズ
ZUPA (SLICE)
パ
ALL RIGHT!!
TRANS-FORM! ♪
THE SOUL OF THE PHARAOH, HUH...?
ガチャ
GACHA (KACHACK)
IT'S MINE.
CHA (CHACK)
チャッ
CHA
チャッ

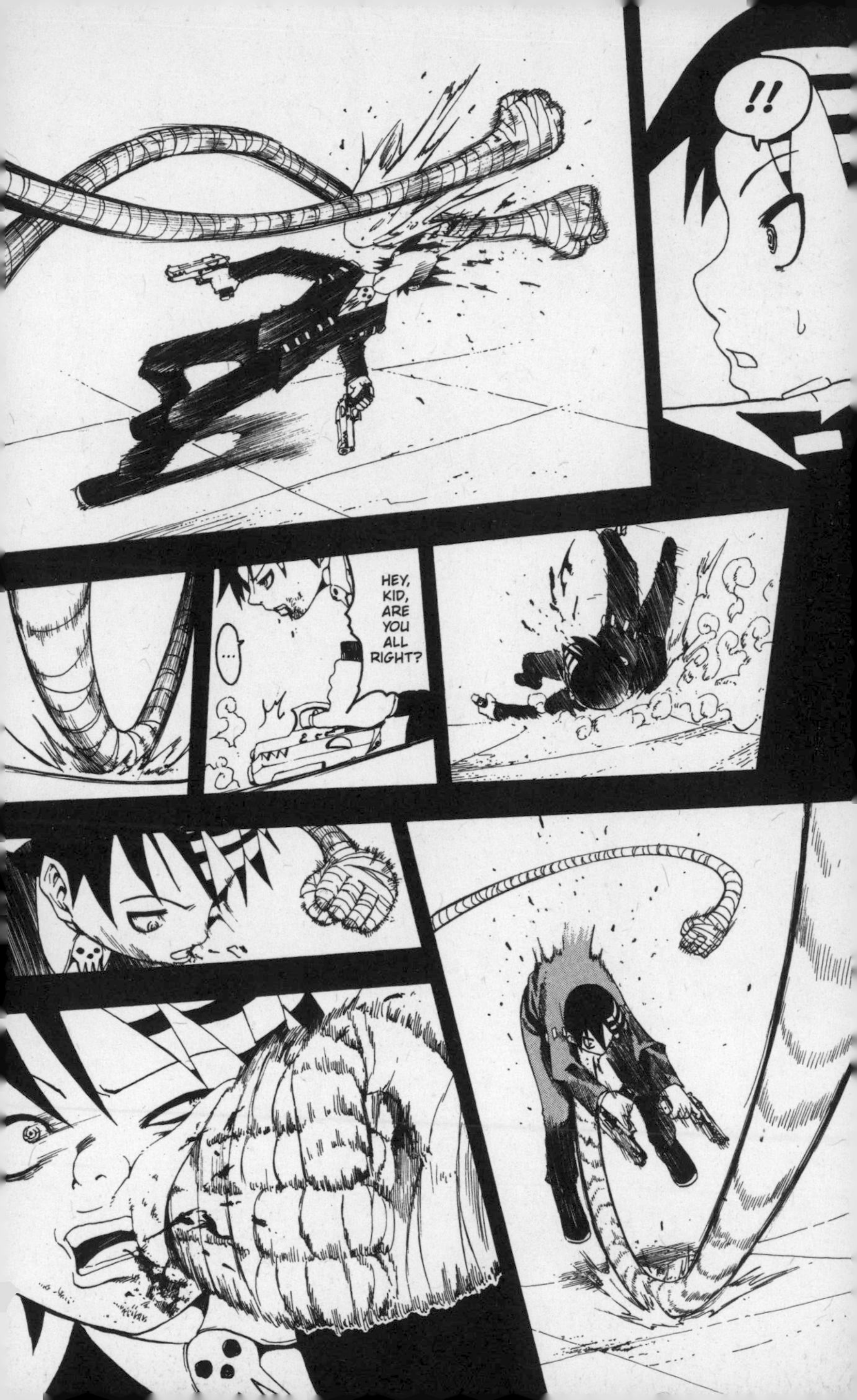
!!
HEY, KID, ARE YOU ALL RIGHT?
...

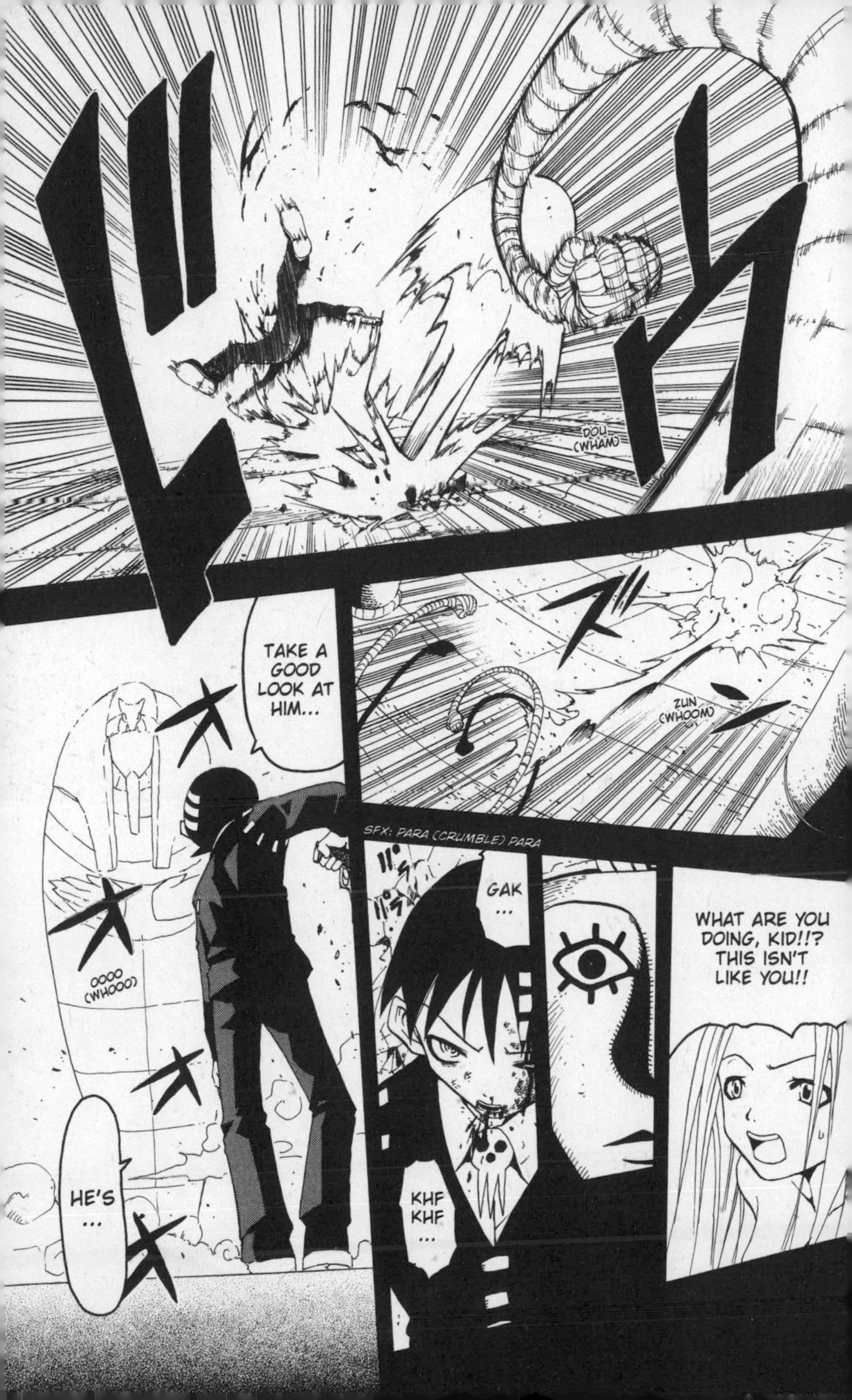
DOU (WHAM)
ZUN (WHOOM)
WHAT ARE YOU DOING, KID!!? THIS ISN'T LIKE YOU!!
SFX: PARA (CRUMBLE) PARA
GAK ...
KHF KHF ...
TAKE A GOOD LOOK AT HIM...
OOOO (WHOOO)
HE'S ...

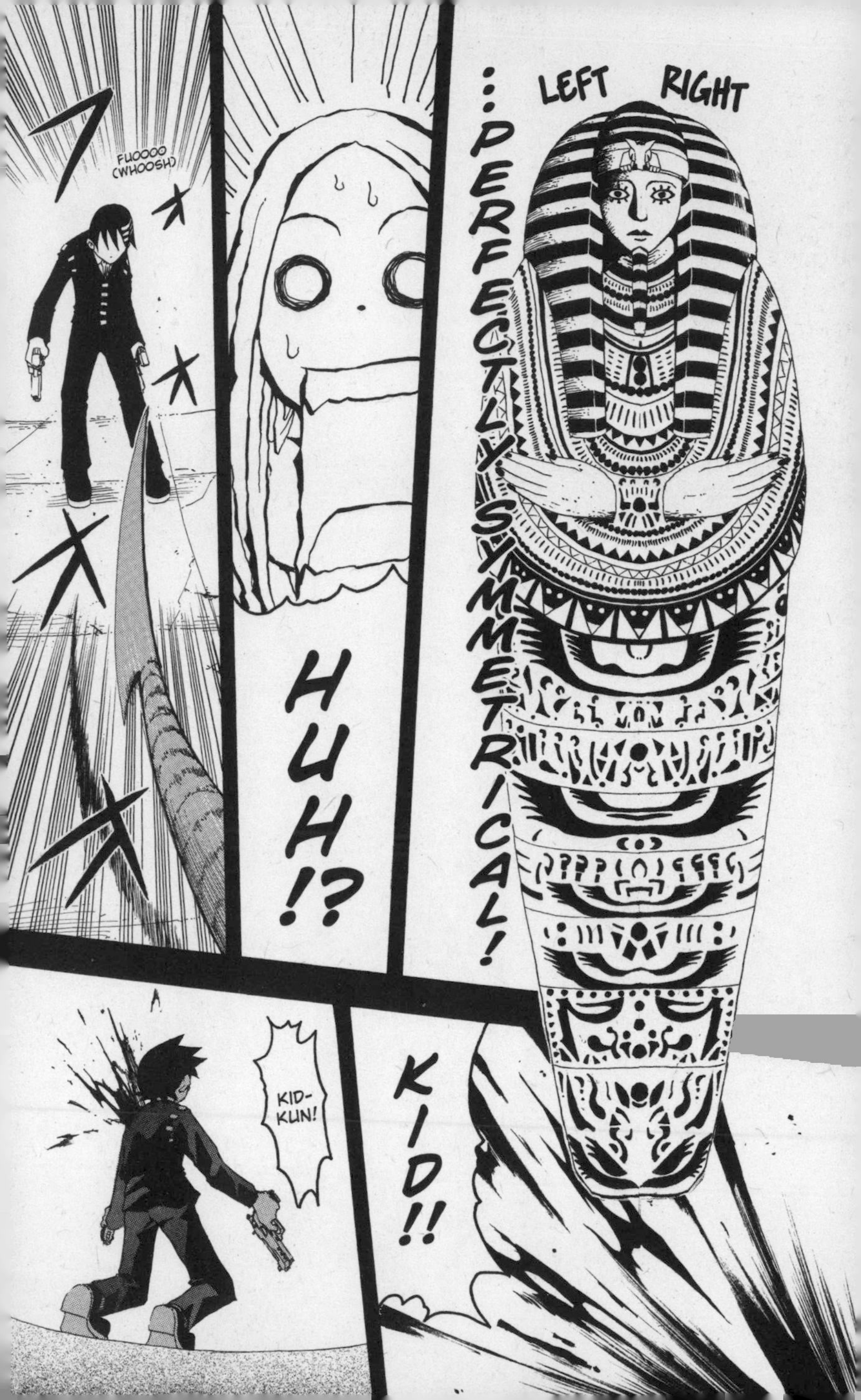
LEFT RIGHT
...PERFECTLY SYMMETRICAL!
HUH!?
FUOOOO (WHOOSH)
KID!!
KID-KUN!

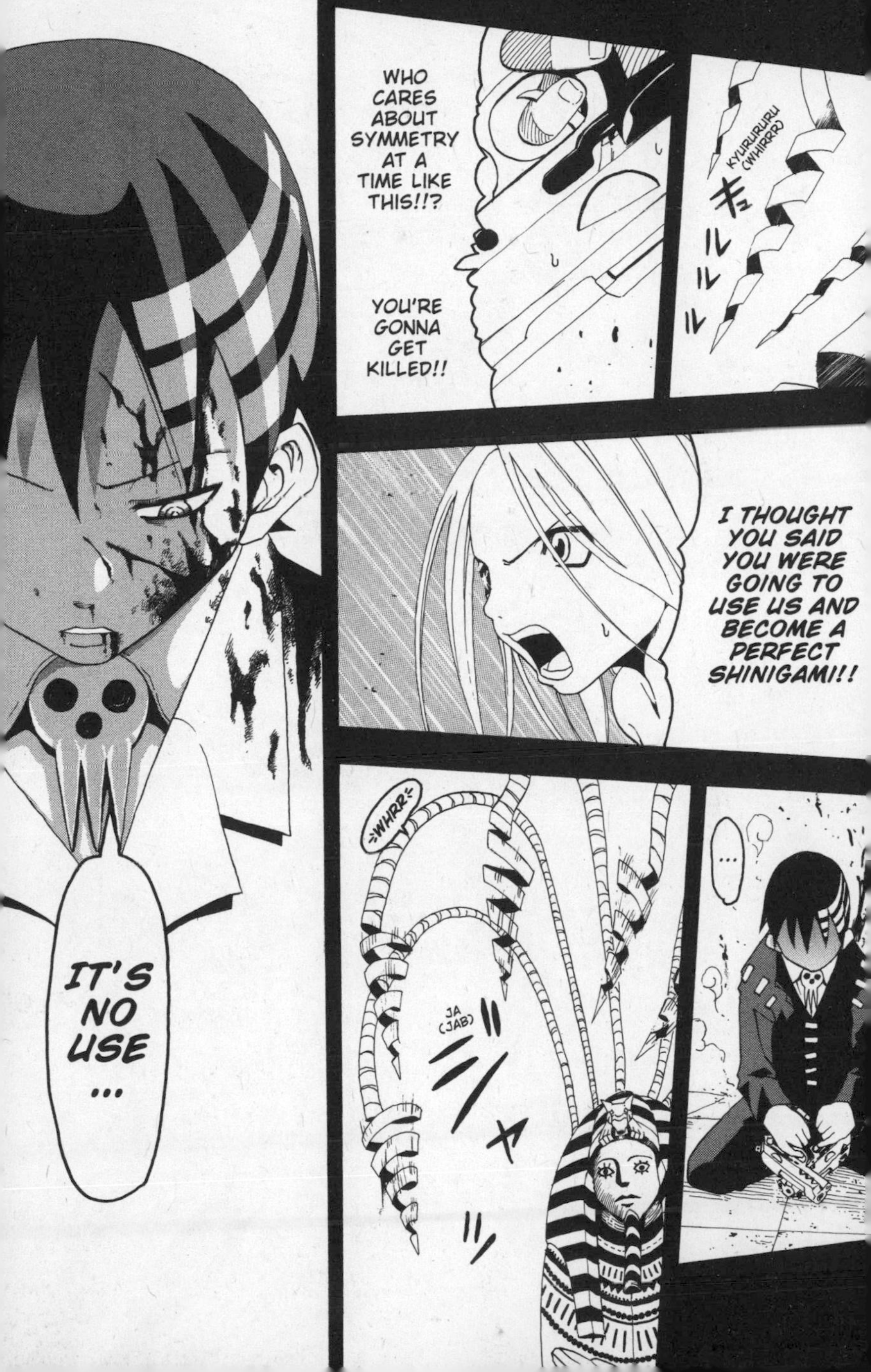
KYURURURU (WHIRRR)
キュルルル
WHO CARES ABOUT SYMMETRY AT A TIME LIKE THIS!!?
YOU'RE GONNA GET KILLED!!
I THOUGHT YOU SAID YOU WERE GOING TO USE US AND BECOME A PERFECT SHINIGAMI!!
...
WHRR
JA (JAB)
IT'S NO USE ...

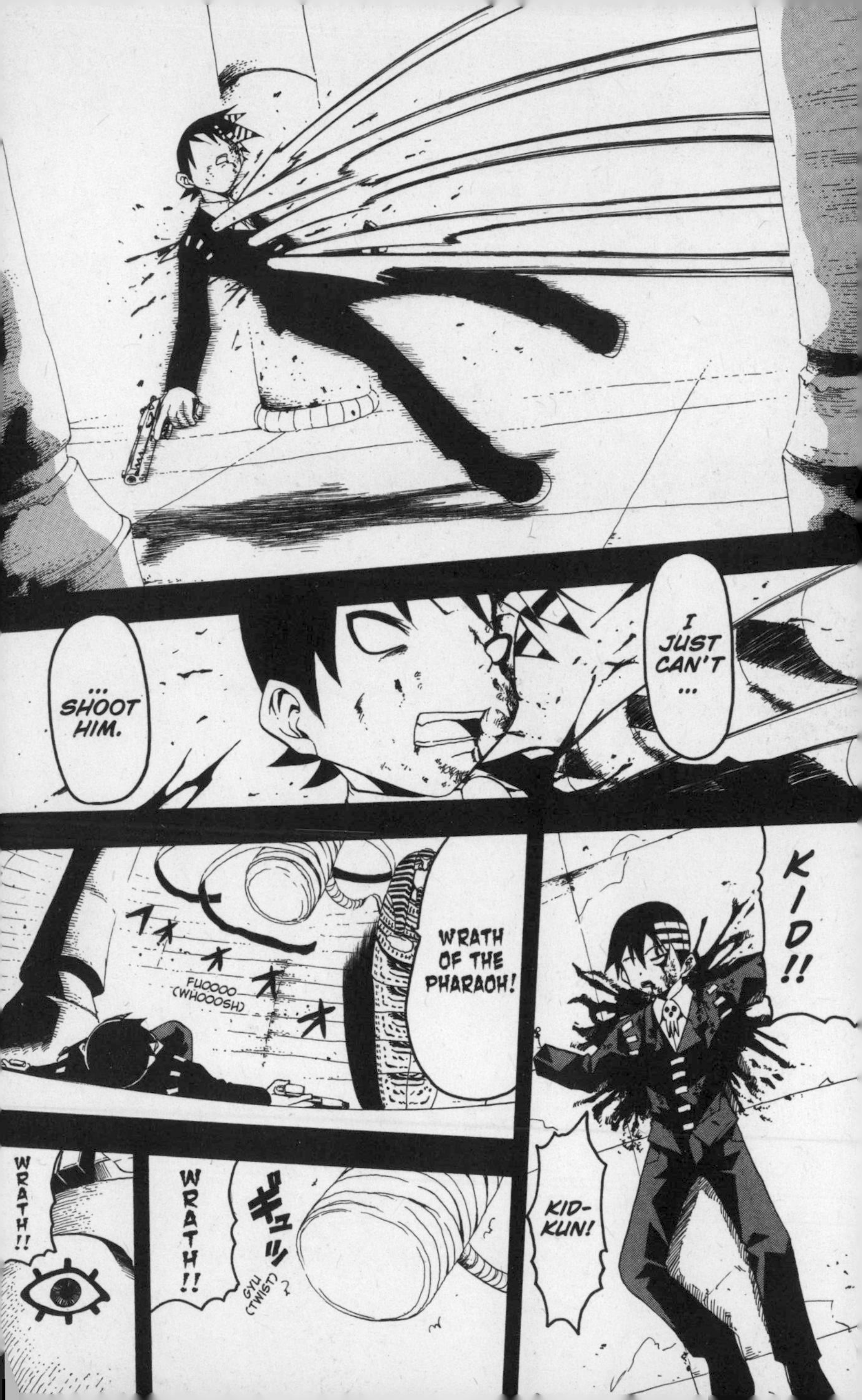
I JUST CAN'T ...
... SHOOT HIM.
KID!!
KID-KUN!
WRATH OF THE PHARAOH!
FUOOOO (WHOOOSH)
WRATH!!
ギュッ
GYU (TWIST)
WRATH!!

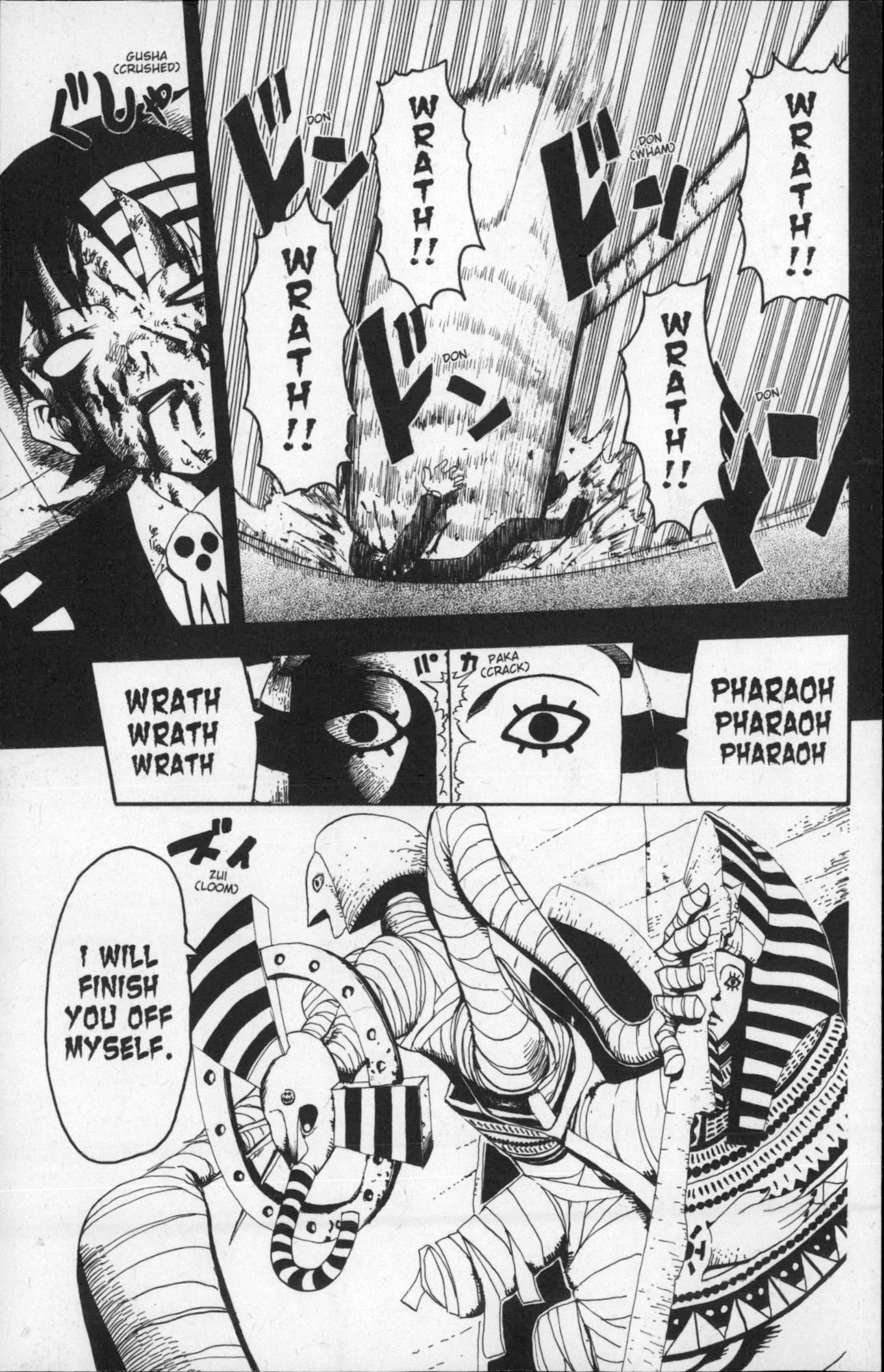

WRATH!!
DON (WHAM)
WRATH!!
DON
WRATH!!
DON
DON
WRATH!!
GUSHA (CRUSHED)
PHARAOH PHARAOH PHARAOH
PAKA (CRACK)
WRATH WRATH WRATH
ZUI (LOOM)
I WILL FINISH YOU OFF MYSELF.

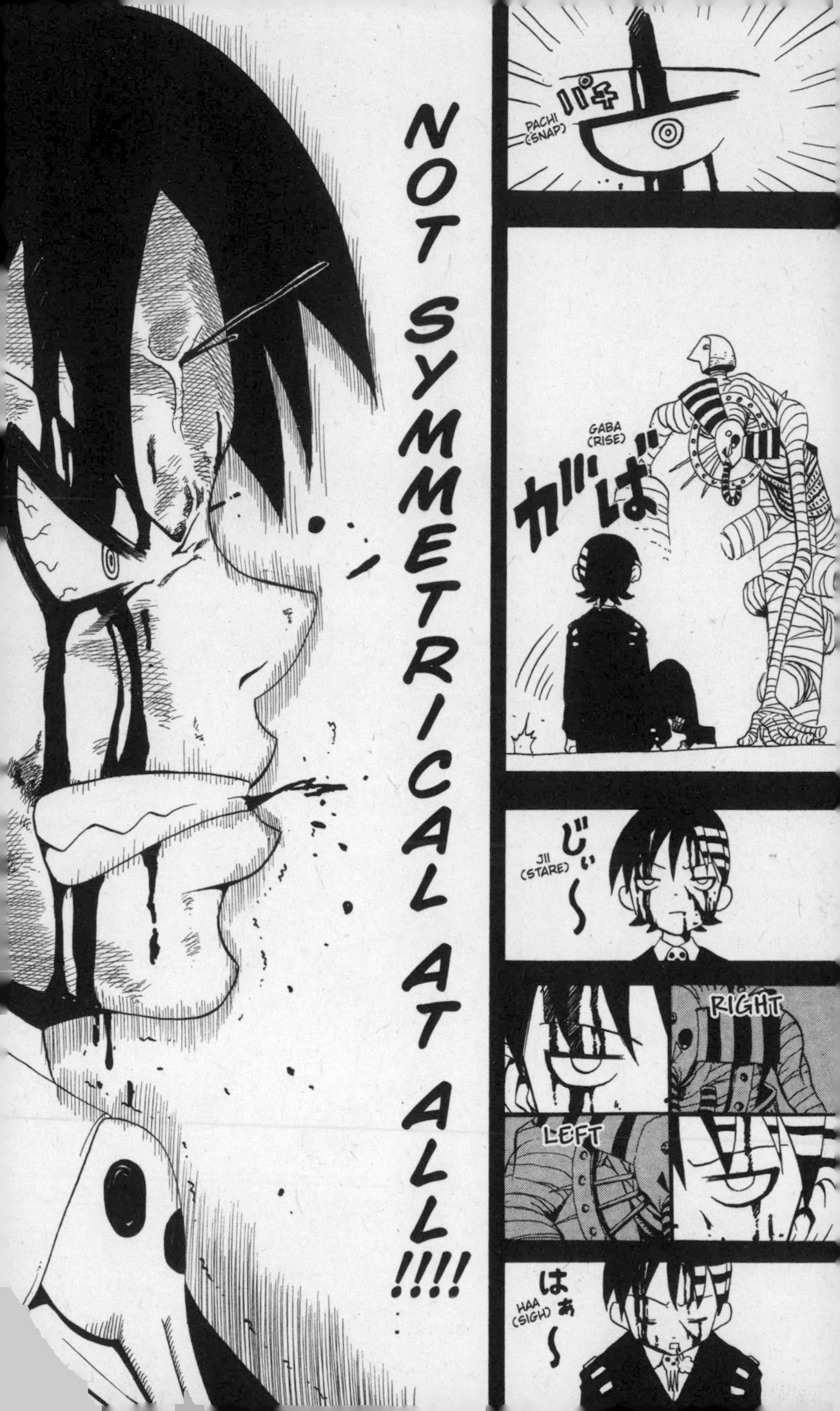
パチ
PACHI (SNAP)
ガば
GABA (RISE)
じぃ~
JII (STARE)
RIGHT
LEFT
はぁ~
HAA (SIGH)
NOT SYMMETRICAL AT ALL!!!!

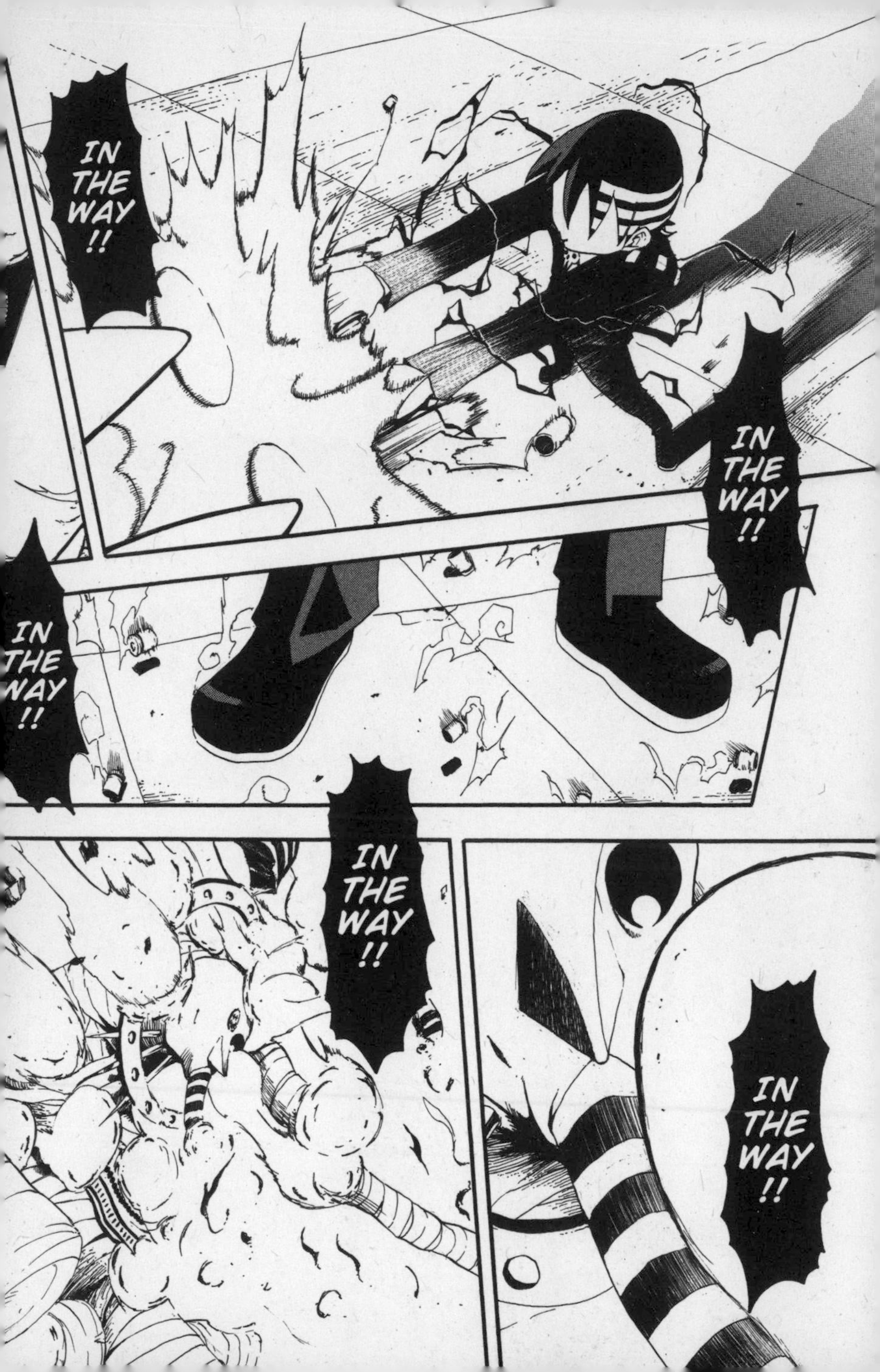
IN THE WAY!!
IN THE WAY!!
IN THE WAY!!
IN THE WAY!!
IN THE WAY!!

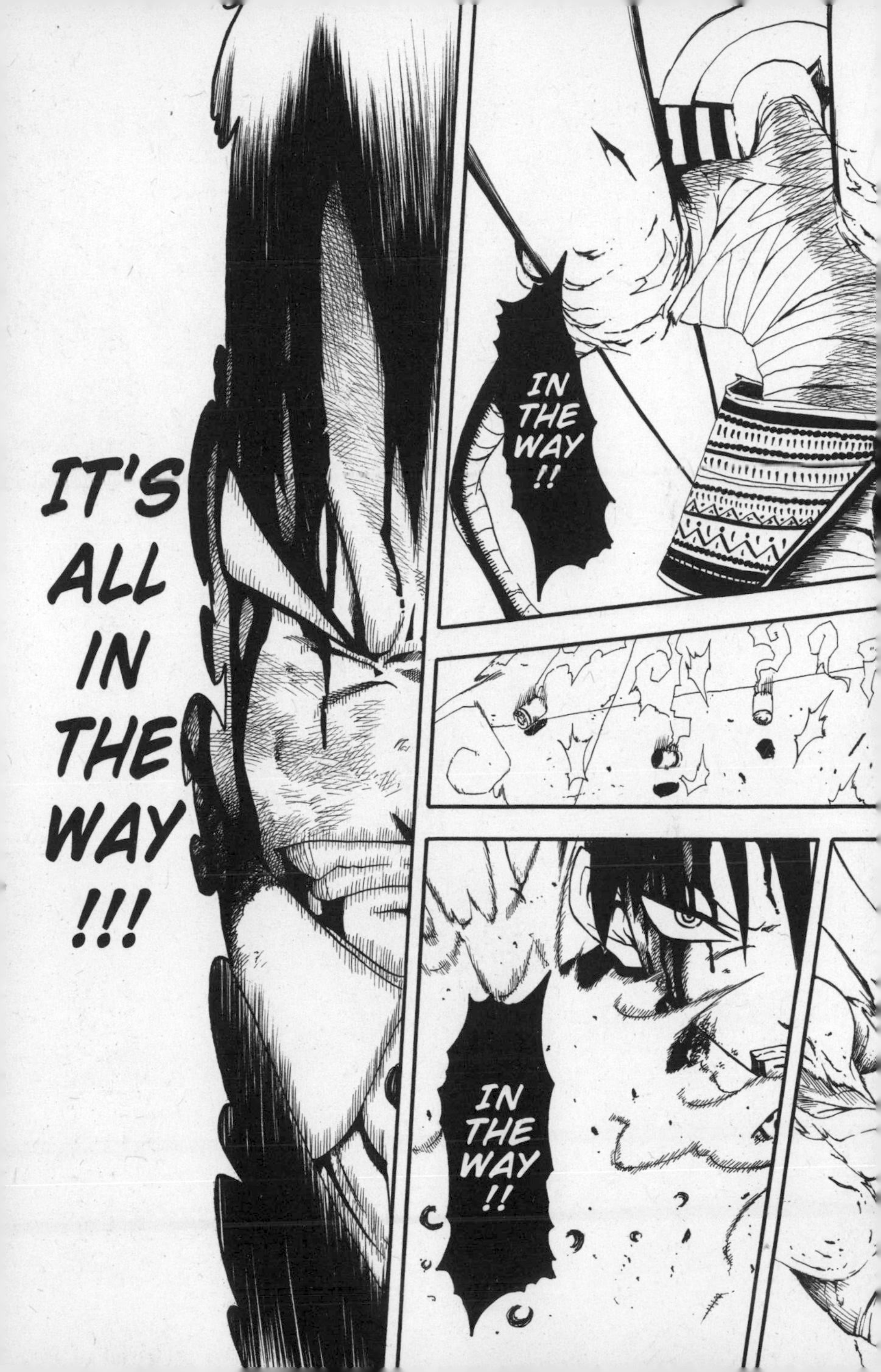
IN THE WAY!!
IN THE WAY!!
IT'S ALL IN THE WAY!!!

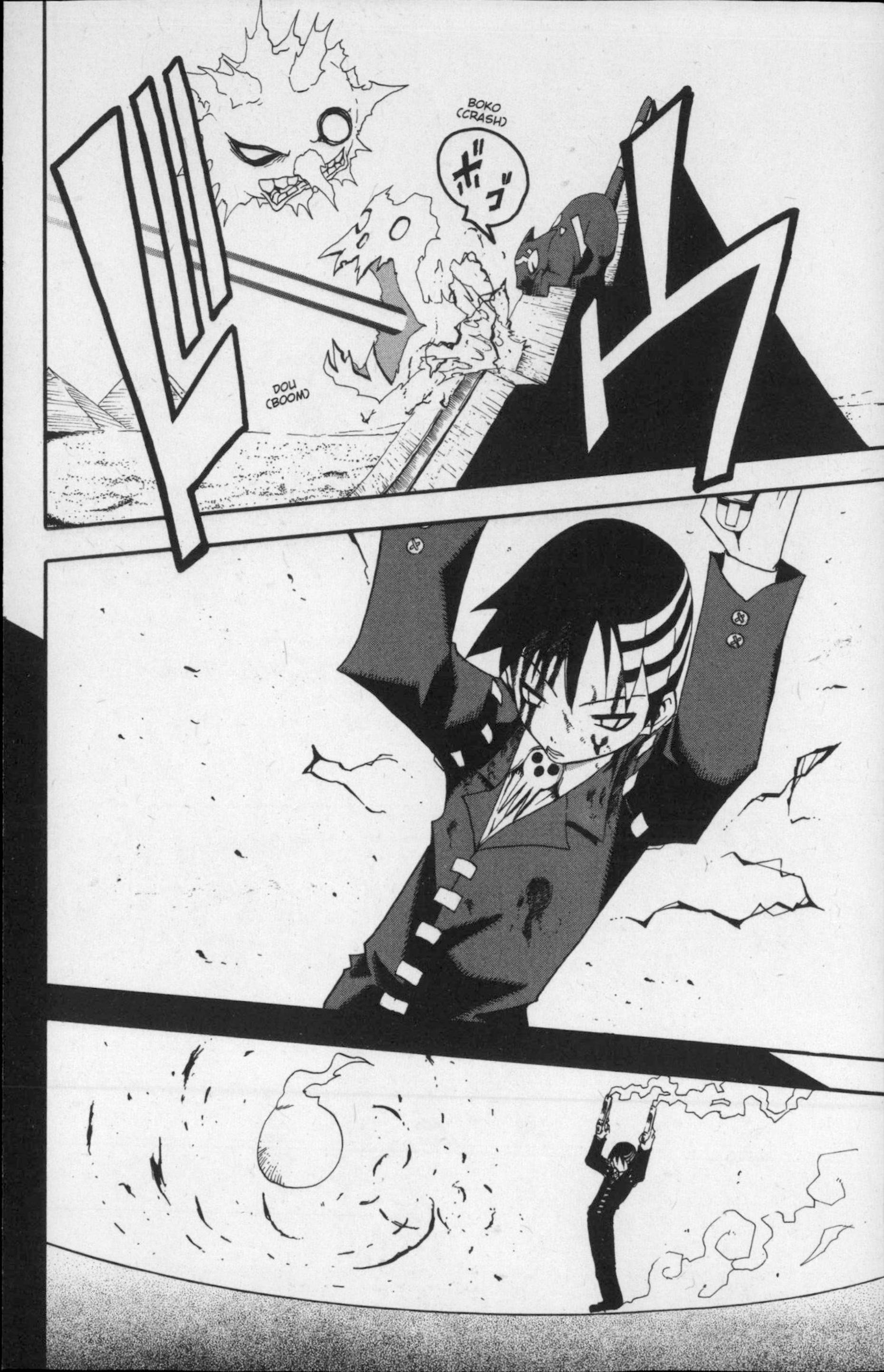
BOKO (CRASH)
ボゴ
DOU (BOOM)

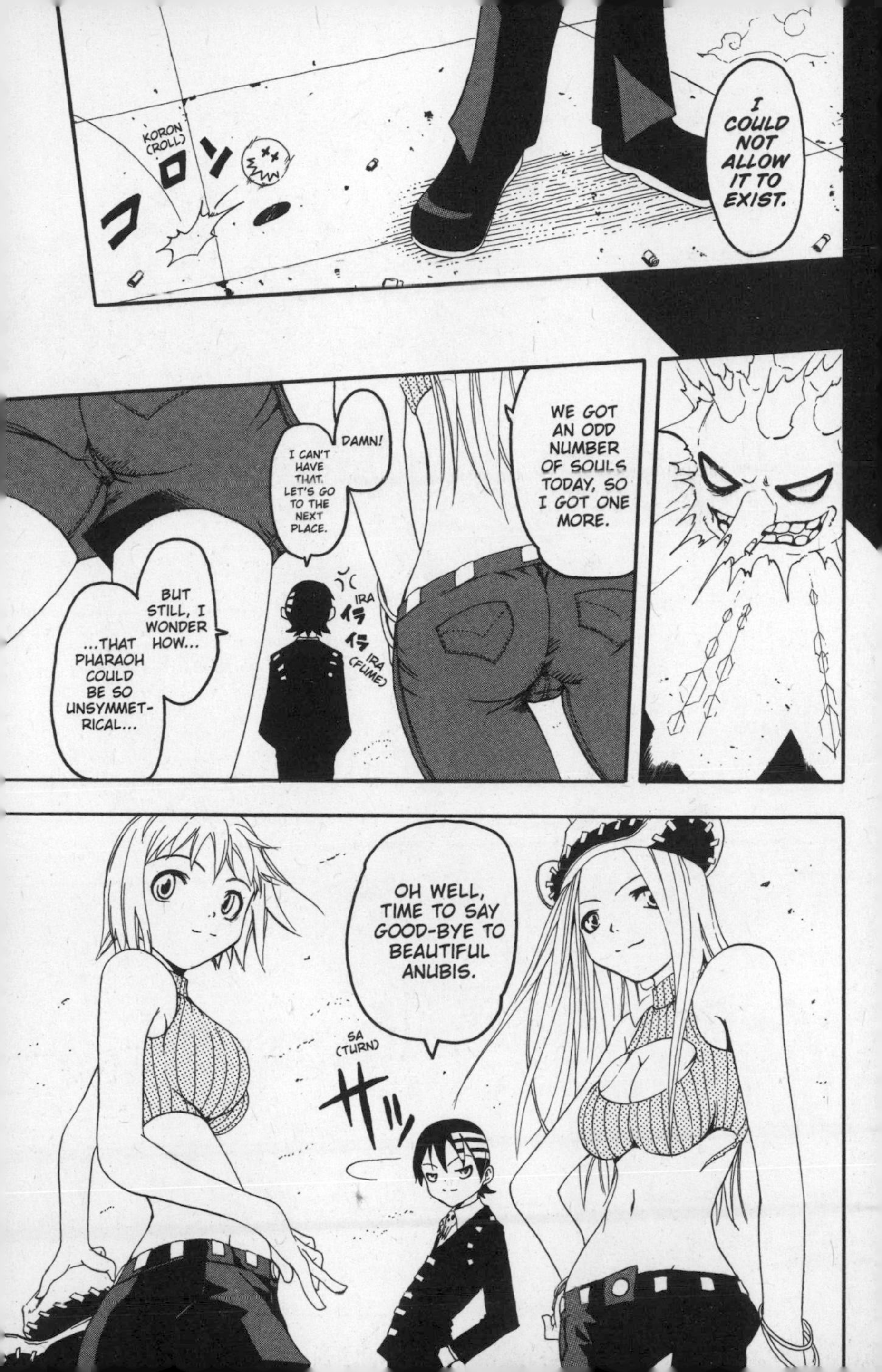
I COULD NOT ALLOW IT TO EXIST.
KORON (ROLL)
コロン
WE GOT AN ODD NUMBER OF SOULS TODAY, SO I GOT ONE MORE.
DAMN!
I CAN'T HAVE THAT. LET'S GO TO THE NEXT PLACE.
IRA イラ
イラ IRA (FUME)
BUT STILL, I WONDER HOW...
...THAT PHARAOH COULD BE SO UNSYMMET-RICAL...
OH WELL, TIME TO SAY GOOD-BYE TO BEAUTIFUL ANUBIS.
SA (TURN)
サッ

BON
(CRUMBLE)

WELL, WE DID GO PRETTY WILD IN THERE... YOU KNOW...

GO

HOW DID THIS...

GO

GO

GO
(CRASH)

KYA-HA-HA! IT FELL APART!

YOU GUYS...

CHEER UP! ♪

DON'T BE SO DOWN ON YOURSELF!! EVERYBODY DESTROYS A PYRAMID OR TWO. ♪

DAMN!

I'M SO SAD!

I WANT TO DIE!

I'M A STINKING PIG! NOTHING BUT GARBAGE. SO I ENDED UP TURNING ANUBIS INTO GARBAGE TOO...

DON

DON

DON
(WHAM)

DON

SOUL EATER

GASUN
(CRASH)

WALL: DEATH / CRIME / SUFFERING

WALL: DEATH

LET'S GO, SOUL EATER!

I'M GOING TO TAKE YOUR SOUL!

PHANTOM MONK RASPUTIN!

BEBON
(BABOOM)

MUKURI
(RISE)

DON'T WASTE YOUR TIME!! NOT EVEN BULLETS HAVE ANY EFFECT ON ME!!

TA
(GTMP)

TA

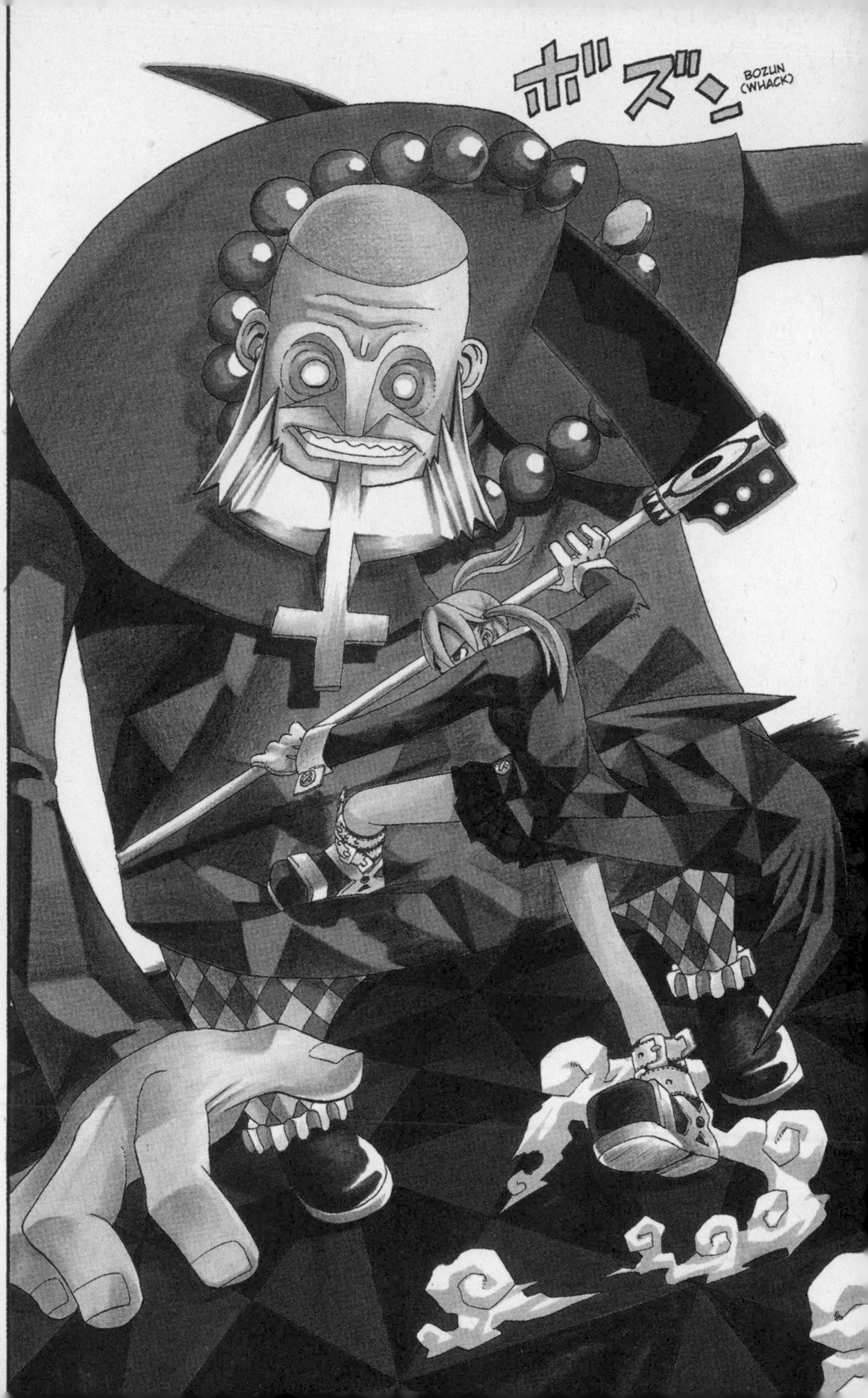
ボズン
BOZUN
(WHACK)

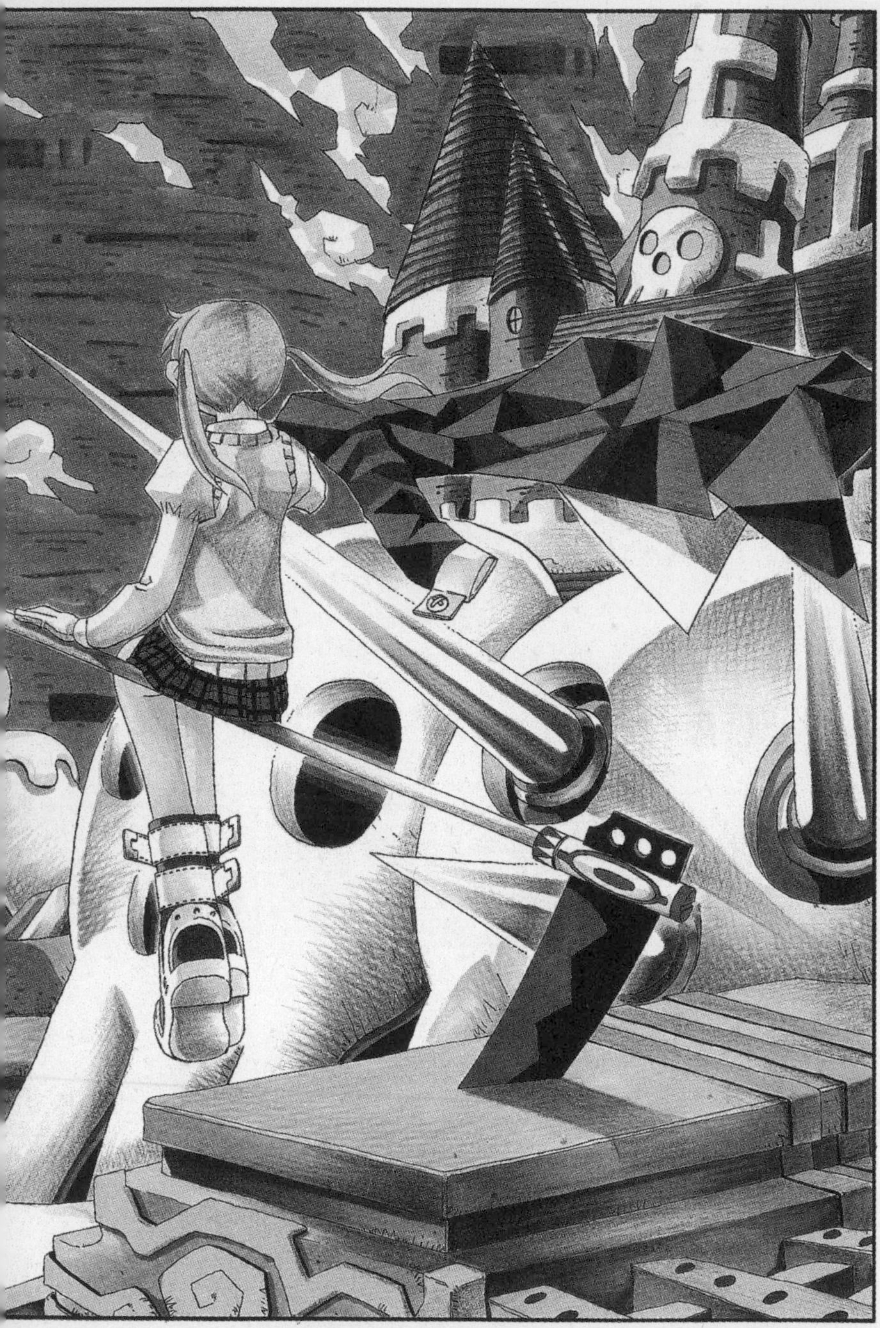

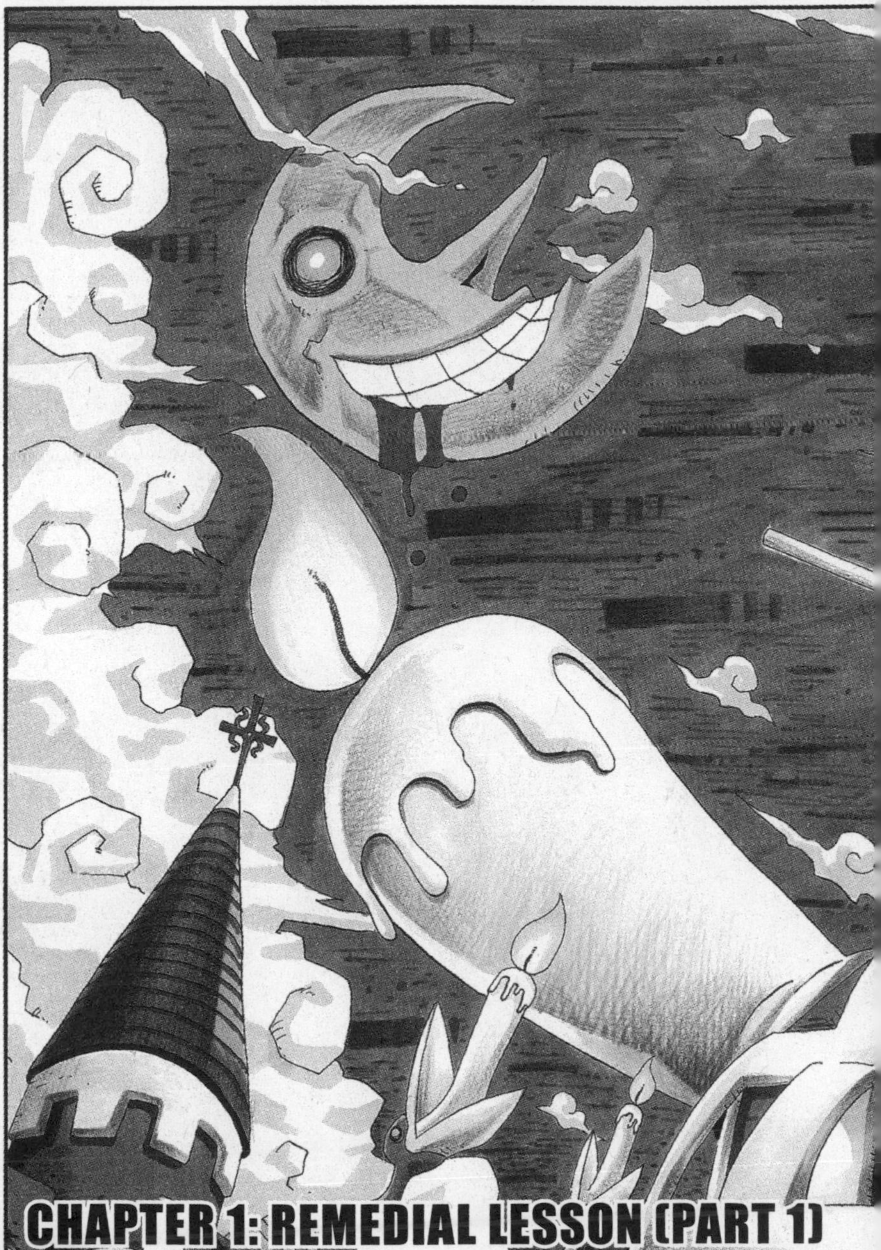
CHAPTER 1: REMEDIAL LESSON (PART 1)

SOUL EATER

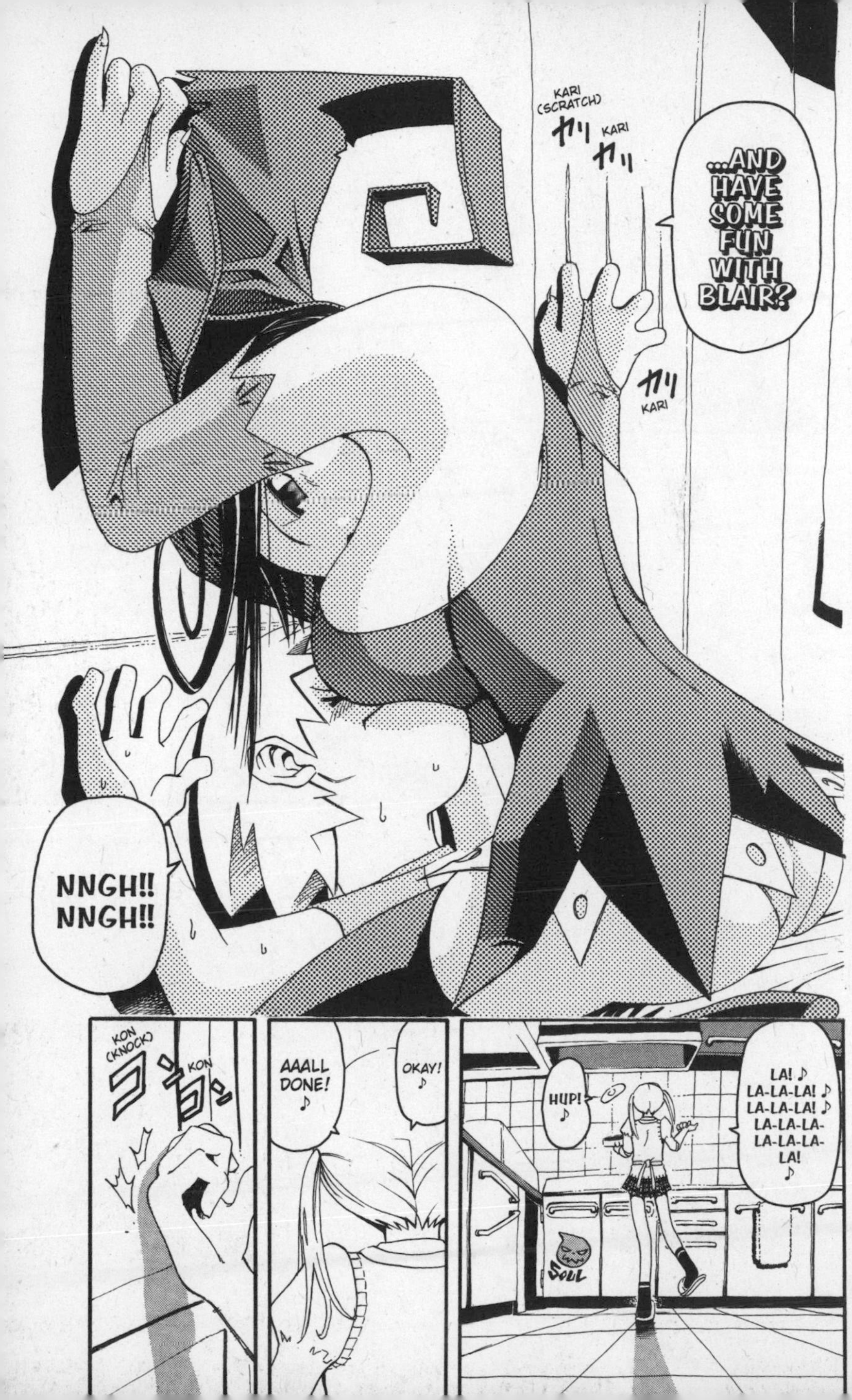
...AND HAVE SOME FUN WITH BLAIR?
カリ KARI (SCRATCH)
カリ KARI
カリ KARI
NNGH!! NNGH!!
LA! ♪ LA-LA-LA! ♪ LA-LA-LA! ♪ LA-LA-LA-LA-LA-LA-LA! ♪
HUP! ♪
OKAY! ♪
AAALL DONE! ♪
KON (KNOCK)
KON

DEATH WEAPON MEISTER ACADEMY (DWMA FOR SHORT)

WALL: DEATH WEAPON MEISTER ACADEMY

≈CHATTER≈
≈CHATTER≈

CLASS CRESCENT MOON

≈BUZZ≈
≈BUZZ≈

......
......

WHAT ARE YOU SO ANGRY ABOUT? BOOKWORM.

QUIET. I'M READING.

DON'T INTERRUPT ME.

HEY, MAKA?

......

TWELVE! WHAT ABOUT YOU?

HOW MANY SOULS HAVE YOU GOTTEN?

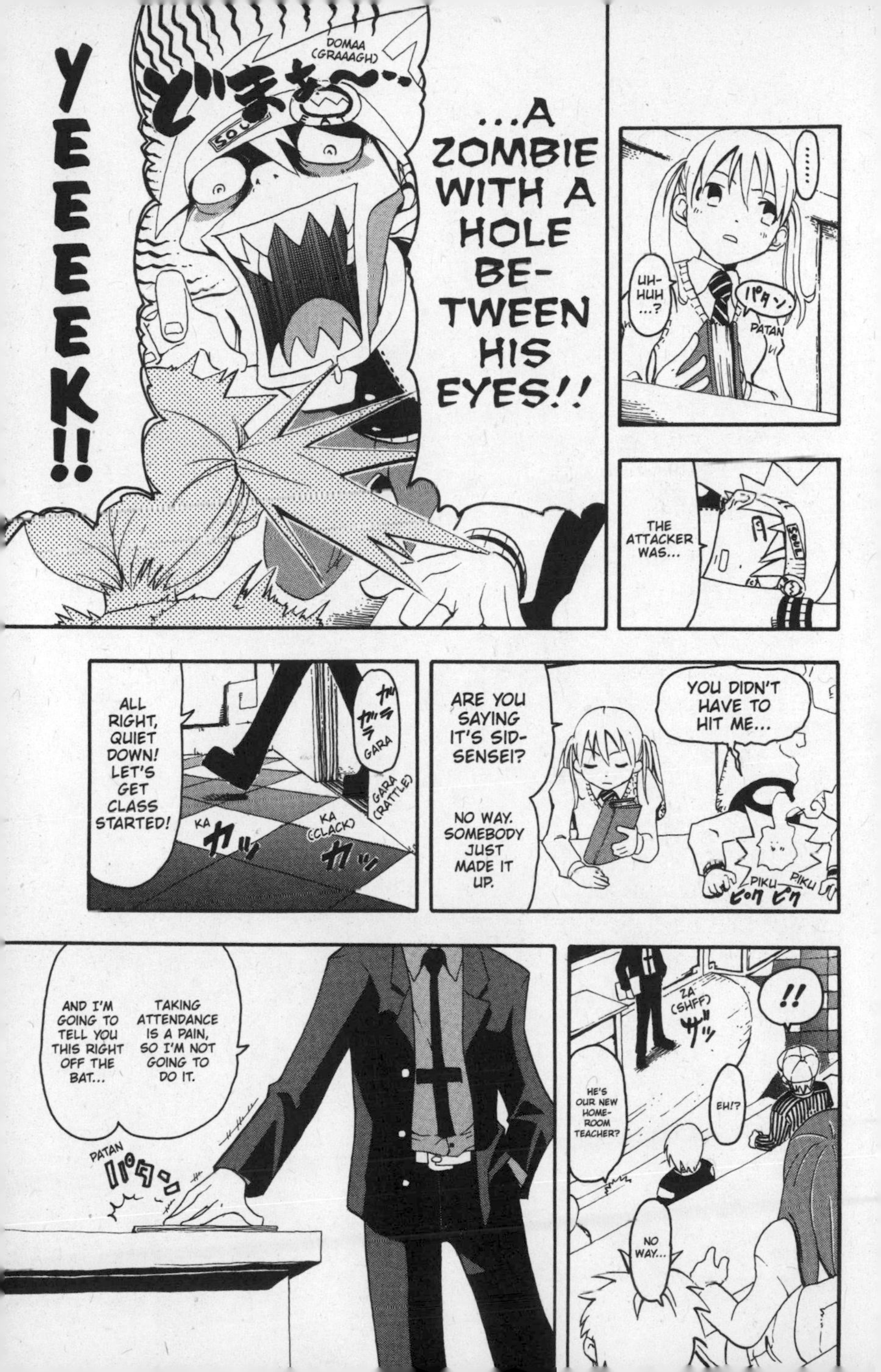
......
UH-HUH ...?
パタン
PATAN
THE ATTACKER WAS...
...A ZOMBIE WITH A HOLE BE-TWEEN HIS EYES!!
DOMAA (GRAAAGH)
YEEEEK!!
YOU DIDN'T HAVE TO HIT ME...
PIKU PIKU
ARE YOU SAYING IT'S SID-SENSEI?
NO WAY. SOMEBODY JUST MADE IT UP.
GARA
GARA (RATTLE)
ALL RIGHT, QUIET DOWN! LET'S GET CLASS STARTED!
KA
KA (CLACK)
!!
ZA (SHFF)
EH!?
HE'S OUR NEW HOME-ROOM TEACHER?
NO WAY...
TAKING ATTENDANCE IS A PAIN, SO I'M NOT GOING TO DO IT.
AND I'M GOING TO TELL YOU THIS RIGHT OFF THE BAT...
PATAN

AND CALL ME DEATH SCYTHE-SENSEI, GOT IT? DON'T FORGET THE "SENSEI," IDIOT!!

HUH!? IT'S JUST TEMPORARY UNTIL THEY DECIDE ON WHO WILL REPLACE THE TEACHER WHO DIED.

HEY!! DEATH SCYTHE!! ARE YOU GOING TO BE OUR HOMEROOM TEACHER FROM NOW ON?

PUI CHMPH)

HE'S NOT MY DADDY ANYWAY!!

BUT I WILL TAKE ATTEN-DANCE FOR THE LADIES. ♡

I SAID I WASN'T GONNA TAKE ATTEN-DANCE FOR THE GUYS.

BUT YOU JUST SAID YOU WEREN'T GONNA TAKE IT, DIDN'T YA?

NOW I'LL TAKE ATTEN-DANCE.

HEY!! YOU BASTARD!! WHAT DID YOU JUST WRITE DOWN!!?

NOW THEN, LET'S GET CLASS STARTED. ♪

PAN (CLAP)

PAN

LET'S SEE, SOUL EATER

SOUL EATER

BOOK: ASSESSMENT

評価 ASSESS-MENT...

E EVIL.

SCUM-BAG.

WHAT A LOAD OF CRAP, YOU PERVY OLD MAN!!

BE QUIET, YOU...

きゅっ KYU (SQUEAK)

149

150

YEP!

BUT DO YOU KNOW HOW MANY SOULS YOU'VE COLLECTED SO FAR!?

...MAKING IT INTO THE DEATH SCYTHE—SHINIGAMI-SAMA'S WEAPON!

TO HAVE THE WEAPON EAT THE SOULS OF NINETY-NINE HUMANS AND ONE WITCH...

DESU (DEATH)

ZERO!♪

I'M VERY SORRY.

PEKO (BOW) PEKO

HYA HA HA!

......

......

Y-YEAH.

BUT WHY? HE WAS A PRETTY GOOD TEACHER...

SEE! I TOLD YOU! WHAT I TOLD YOU WAS TRUE!

THEY SAY HE'S TURNED INTO A ZOMBIE AND IS ATTACKING STUDENTS.

NOW ...ABOUT ... THIS REMEDIAL LESSON...

THE ONES ABOUT SID-SENSEI, WHO WAS A TEACHER AT DWMA...

I ASSUME YOU'VE ALREADY HEARD THE RUMORS?

...HE'S BEEN TURNED INTO A ZOMBIE, AND NOW THAT HE'S BEEN FREED FROM THE FEAR OF DEATH, HE WANTS THE STUDENTS TO HAVE THE SAME EXPERIENCE HE DID. HIS ATTACKS ON THE STUDENTS AREN'T JUST ANNOYING, HE KEEPS DOING IT AS A SORT OF LESSON.

HE GETS SELF-SATISFACTION OUT OF IT.

← SID-SENSEI

YES, HE WAS A GOOD TEACHER BEFORE HE DIED, BUT...

HEADBAND: HOLE

NOT ONLY THAT, BUT THE PERSON WHO TURNED SID-SENSEI INTO A ZOMBIE MUST BE PULLING HIS STRINGS BEHIND THE SCENES.

HE DOESN'T POSE ANY PARTICULAR THREAT. HOWEVER...

YES. THAT'S EXACTLY RIGHT.

BASICALLY, WE JUST HAVE TO TAKE HIS SOUL, RIGHT?

OKAY! JUST LEAVE IT TO US, SIR!

EX-EX-

...WILL BE EXPELLED. ♪

...IF YOU FAIL THIS REMEDIAL LESSON...

I'LL BE CHEERING YOU ON. GOOD LUCK! ♪

EX-EX-

WHAAAT!!?

...ALL OF YOU...

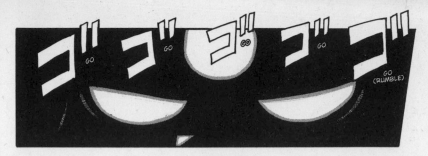

GO
GO
GO
GO
GO
(RUMBLE)

WOULD YOU WORRY JUST A LITTLE BIT, BLACK☆STAR? ...PLEASE?

WHAT'S WITH HER?

I THOUGHT I WAS GOING TO BE A FINE SCYTHE-MEISTER LIKE MY MOTHER...

...SINCE WHEN DID I... F-F-F-FALL BEHIND...

ZURU (SLUMP)
ZURU

HAS SOUL-KUN... SNAPPED ...?

GET OUT HERE, BASTARD!! I NEVER PAID THAT MUCH ATTENTION TO YOUR CLASSES ANYWAY. GYA-HA-HA-HA!!

LIKE HELL I'M GONNA GET EX-PELLED!!

KON— (KNOCK)
KON

IT'S JUST A NORMAL GRAVE.

GO
GO
GO
GO
GO

SOME-BODY STOP THEM...

...I WONDER... IF I CAN RISE TO THE CHALLENGE... y-YEAH. I CAN...I CAN STILL...MAKE IT... BUT I CAN'T EVEN STAND UP...

YEAH!! YEAH!! LET'S DO IT!!! LET'S POOP ON IT TOO WHILE WE'RE AT IT!!

IT'LL BE COOL.

HEY, SOUL, LET'S PISS ON SID'S GRAVE. ♪ HYA-HA-HA-HA!

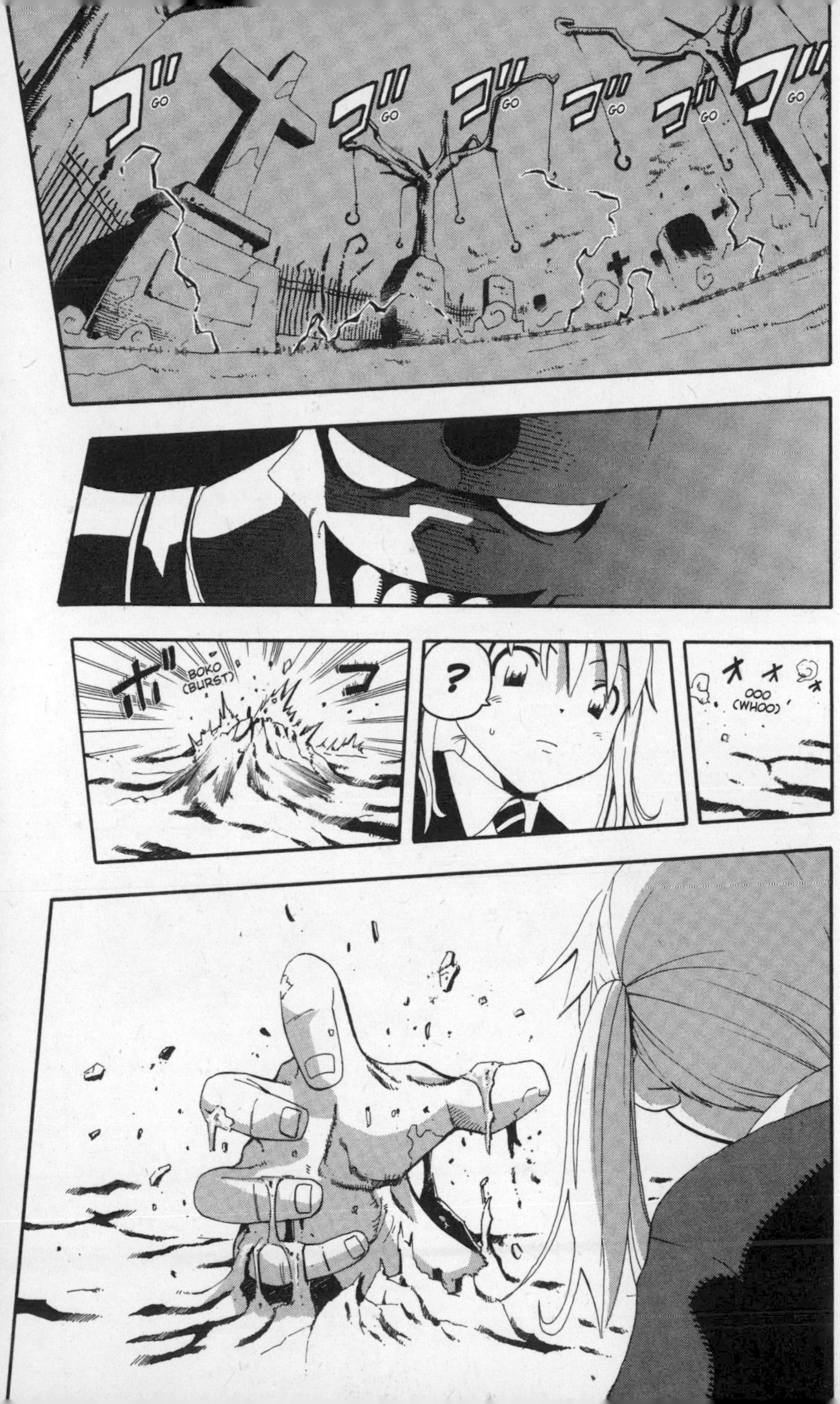
GO
GO
GO
GO
GO
GO
OOO (WHOO)
?
BOKO (BURST)

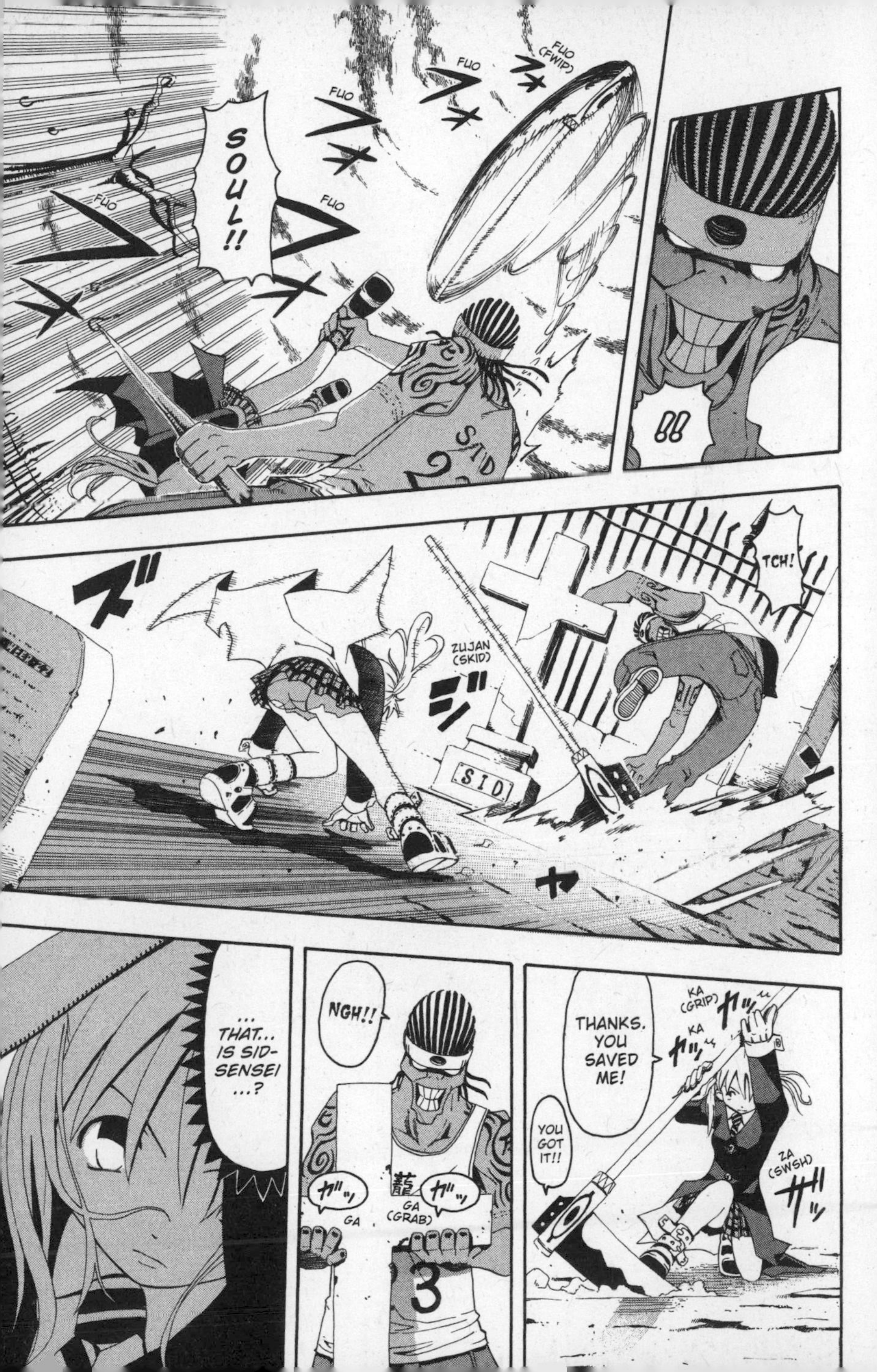
!!
FUO (FWIP)
FUO
FUO
SOUL!!
FUO
FUO
SID
TCH!
ZUJAN (SKID)
SID
THANKS. YOU SAVED ME!
YOU GOT IT!!
KA (GRIP)
KA
ZA (SWSH)
NGH!!
GA (GRAB)
GA
3
... THAT... IS SID-SENSEI ...?

...BUT IF HE KEEPS SWINGING A GRAVESTONE AROUND LIKE THAT, HE'LL GET PUNISHED AND DIE A SECOND TIME.

HE MUST BE PRETTY GOOD, THEN...

WE'RE ONLY ONE-STAR MEISTERS...

I CAN DO WHAT I WANT WITH IT.

IT'S MY OWN GRAVE-STONE.

...BUT BEFORE HE DIED, SID-SENSEI WAS THE HIGHEST RANK, A THREE-STAR MEISTER.

HEADBAND: HOLE / SHOULDERS: DEATH

NOW THEN... TIME FOR SECOND PERIOD.

DING DONG! ♪ DEAD DONG! ♪

I WANT TO FINISH THIS UP FAST AND GO TAKE A BATH...

THIS NEW SEMESTER JUST ISN'T STARTING OUT VERY WELL FOR ME...

WHEN THIS PERIOD ENDS, YOU GUYS WILL BE DEAD.

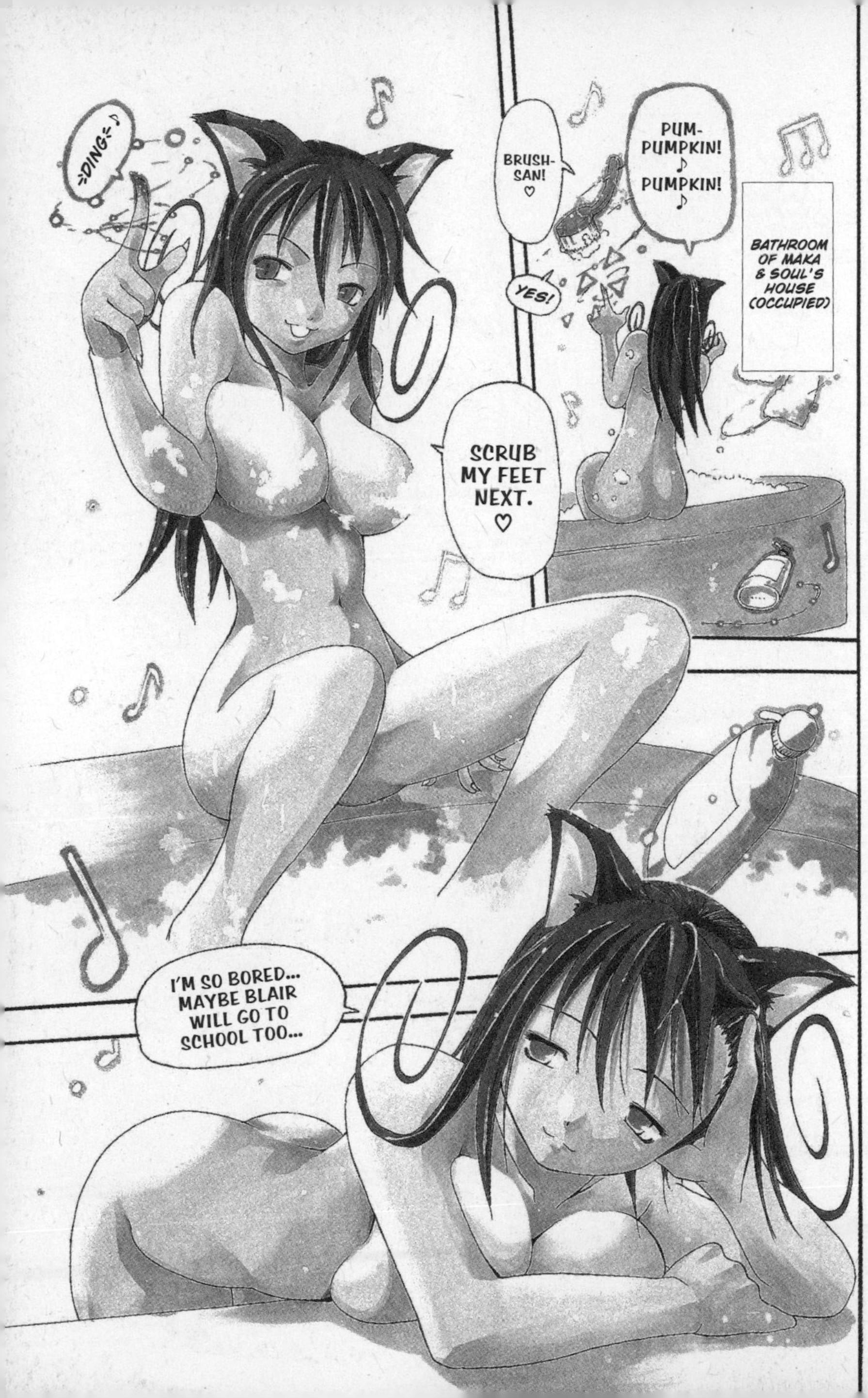
BATHROOM OF MAKA & SOUL'S HOUSE (OCCUPIED)
PUM-PUMPKIN! ♪ PUMPKIN! ♪
BRUSH-SAN! ♡
YES!
DING ♪
SCRUB MY FEET NEXT. ♡
I'M SO BORED... MAYBE BLAIR WILL GO TO SCHOOL TOO...

LIVING
END!!

WHA
!!?

I'M
GOING
TO PUT A
GRAVE-
STONE
ON YOUR
LIFE!!

TAKE
THIS!!

ZAN
(BAM)

...BUT HE CAN
FIGHT THIS WELL
WITH JUST ONE
GRAVESTONE,
WITHOUT EVEN
USING A DEMON
WEAPON...?

SID-SENSEI
WAS A
KNIFE
MEISTER...

BLACK
☆STAR!!

BLACK☆STAR!!!

...ONE OF THE VITAL POINTS ALONG THE BODY'S CENTERLINE.

HE LANDED A DIRECT HIT TO MY SOLAR PLEXUS...

I'M NOT LETTING YOU CATCH YOUR BREATH!!

TSUBAKI!! SHADOW WEAPON MODE: SHURIKEN!!

YES, SIR!

THAT WAS A GOOD ATTACK, AND QUITE FITTING FOR SOMEONE WHO EXCELS AT THE ART OF ASSAS-SINATION LIKE BLACK☆STAR.

OOH!♪

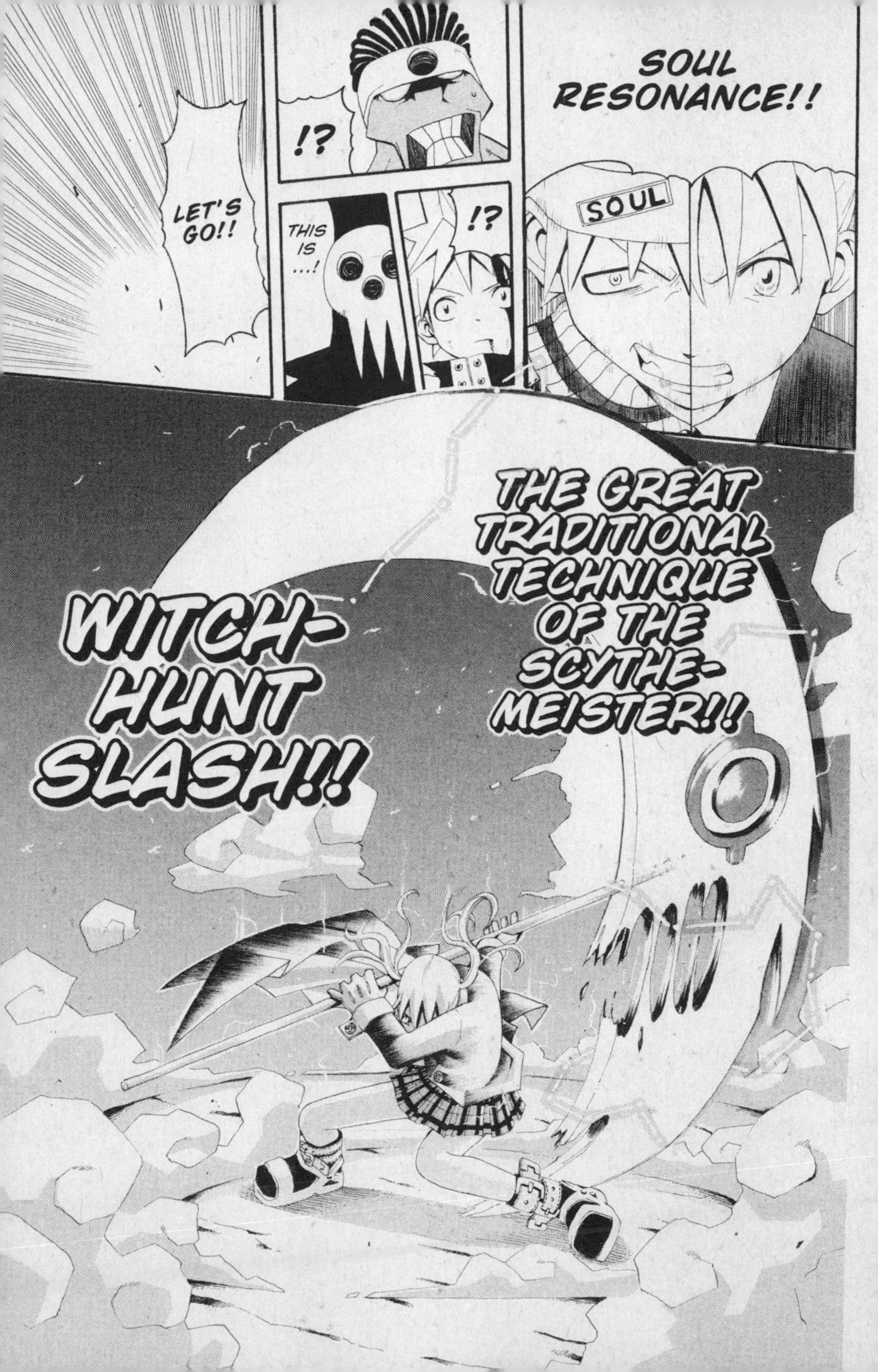
SOUL RESONANCE!!
SOUL
!?
!?
THIS IS ...!
LET'S GO!!
THE GREAT TRADITIONAL TECHNIQUE OF THE SCYTHE-MEISTER!!
WITCH-HUNT SLASH!!

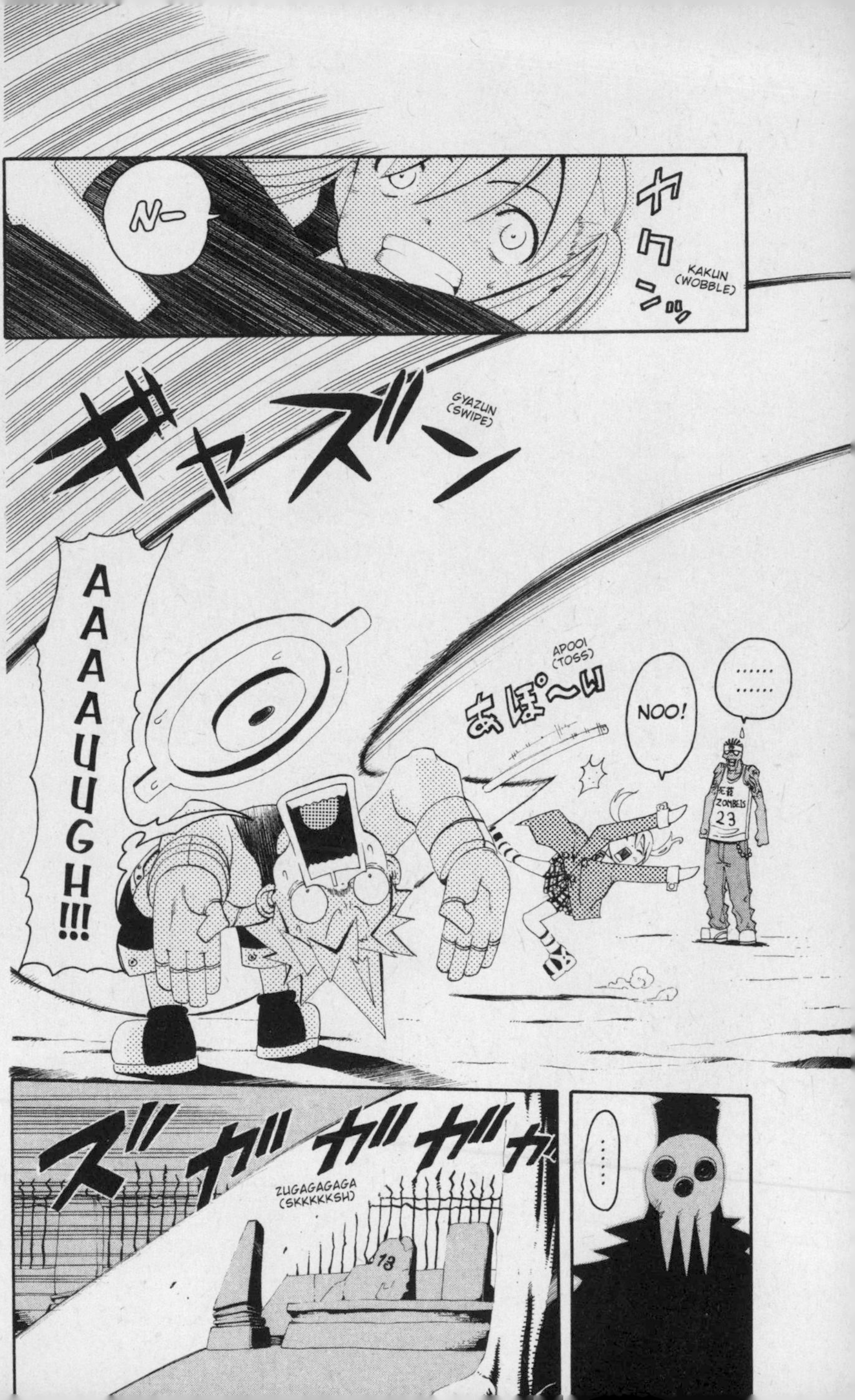

N-
KAKUN (WOBBLE)
ギャズン
GYAZUN (SWIPE)
......
......
NOO!
あぽ〜い
APOOI (TOSS)
AAAAUUUGH!!!
......
ズガガガガ
ZUGAGAGAGA (SKKKKKSH)

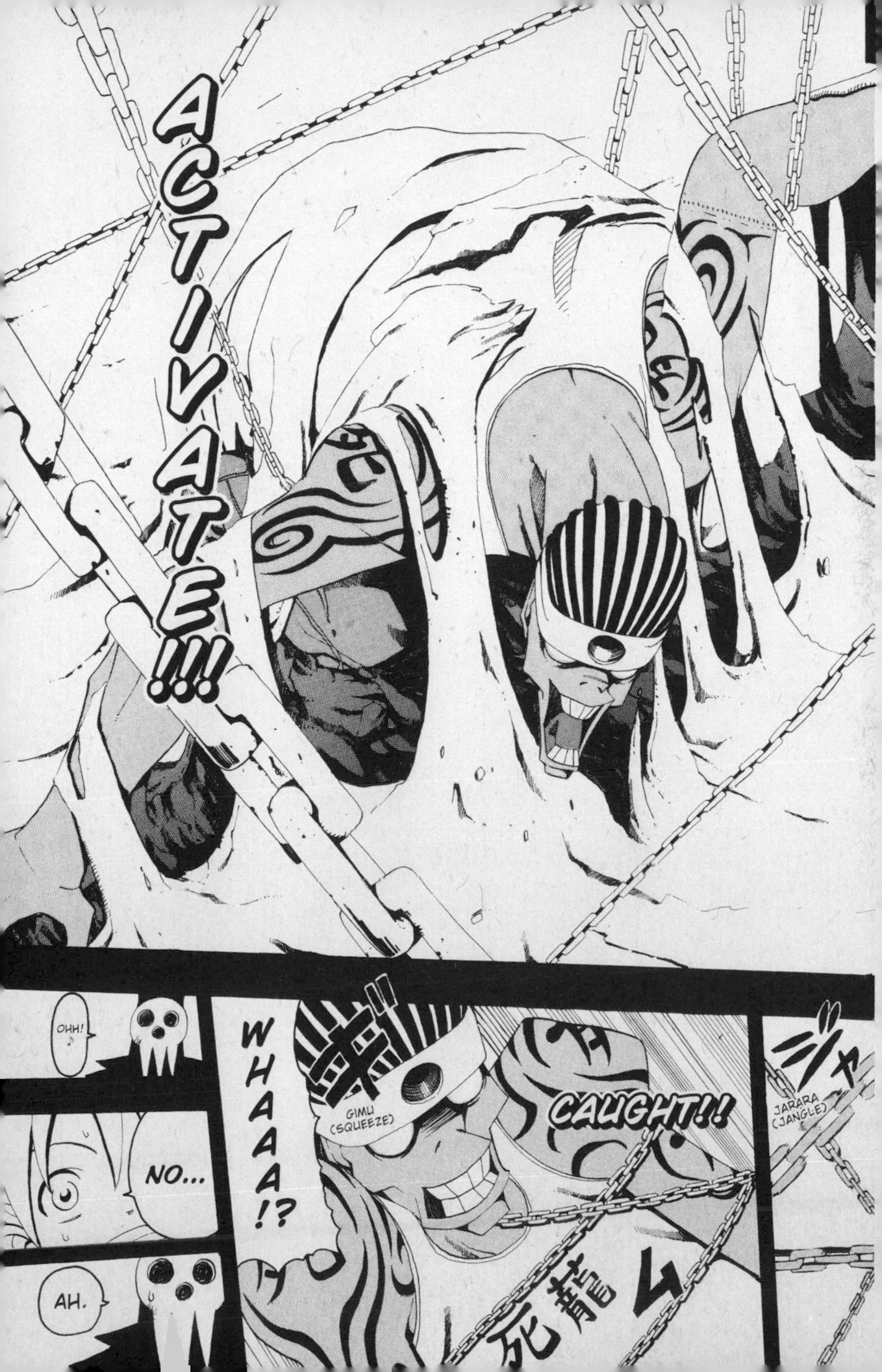
ACTIVATE!!!
ジャ
JARARA (JANGLE)
CAUGHT!!
ギ
GIMU (SQUEEZE)
WHAAAA!?
OHH! ♪
NO...
AH.

URI URI (FIDGET) HEY... STAY STILL.

HM?

BATA BATA (FLAP)

BATA

WHO IS IT...

...FA-THER?

DEMON TWIN GUNS
PATTY & LIZ
(YOUNGER) (ELDER)

SHINIGAMI-SAMA'S SON
DEATH THE KID

HE CAN'T BE JUST ANYBODY, RIGHT?

!!

!!

...

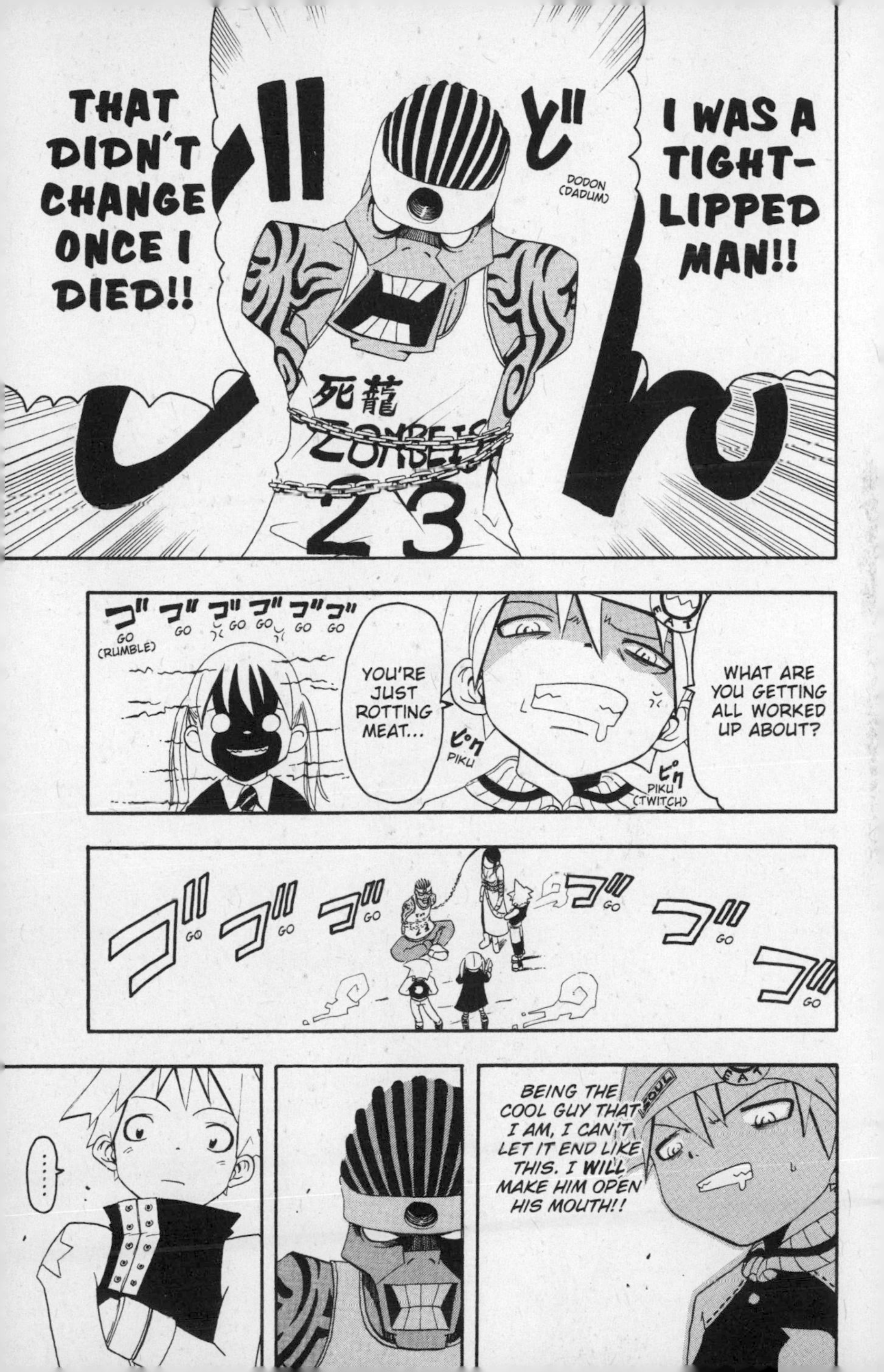
I WAS A TIGHT-LIPPED MAN!!
DODON (DADUM)
THAT DIDN'T CHANGE ONCE I DIED!!
死龍 ZOMBEIS 23
WHAT ARE YOU GETTING ALL WORKED UP ABOUT?
PIKU (TWITCH)
PIKU
YOU'RE JUST ROTTING MEAT...
GO GO GO GO GO GO (RUMBLE)
GO GO GO GO GO GO
BEING THE COOL GUY THAT I AM, I CAN'T LET IT END LIKE THIS. I WILL MAKE HIM OPEN HIS MOUTH!!
......

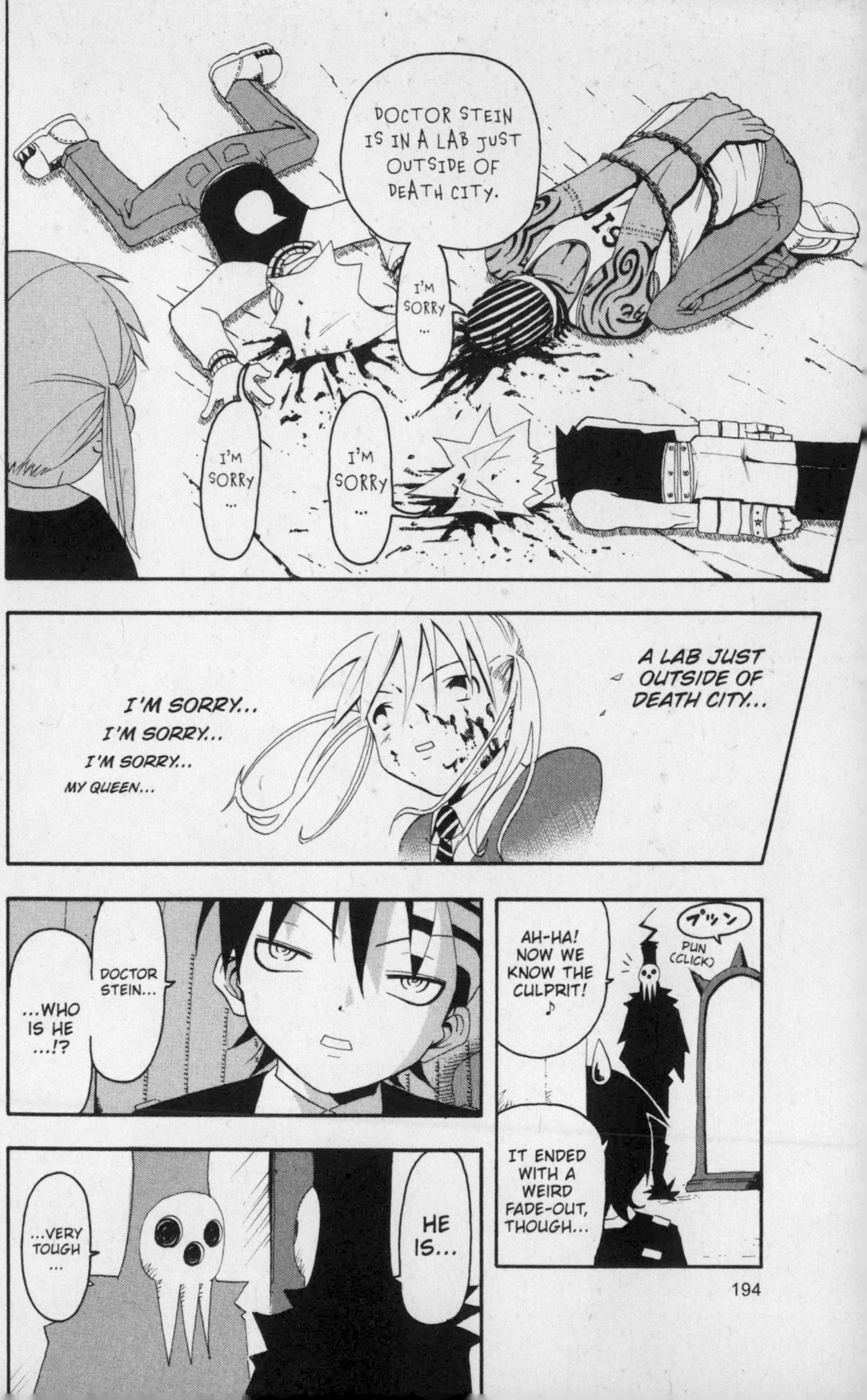
DOCTOR STEIN IS IN A LAB JUST OUTSIDE OF DEATH CITY.
I'M SORRY ...
I'M SORRY ...
I'M SORRY ...
A LAB JUST OUTSIDE OF DEATH CITY...
I'M SORRY... I'M SORRY... I'M SORRY... MY QUEEN...
プツン
PUN (CLICK)
AH-HA! NOW WE KNOW THE CULPRIT! ♪
IT ENDED WITH A WEIRD FADE-OUT, THOUGH...
DOCTOR STEIN...
...WHO IS HE ...!?
HE IS...
...VERY TOUGH ...

OUTSIDE DEATH CITY, PATCHWORK LAB

TAN

TAN (TAP)

GIKO
GIKO (CREAK)

HM...
GIKO
GIKO

MY HEAD JUST ISN'T CLEAR...

HMM...

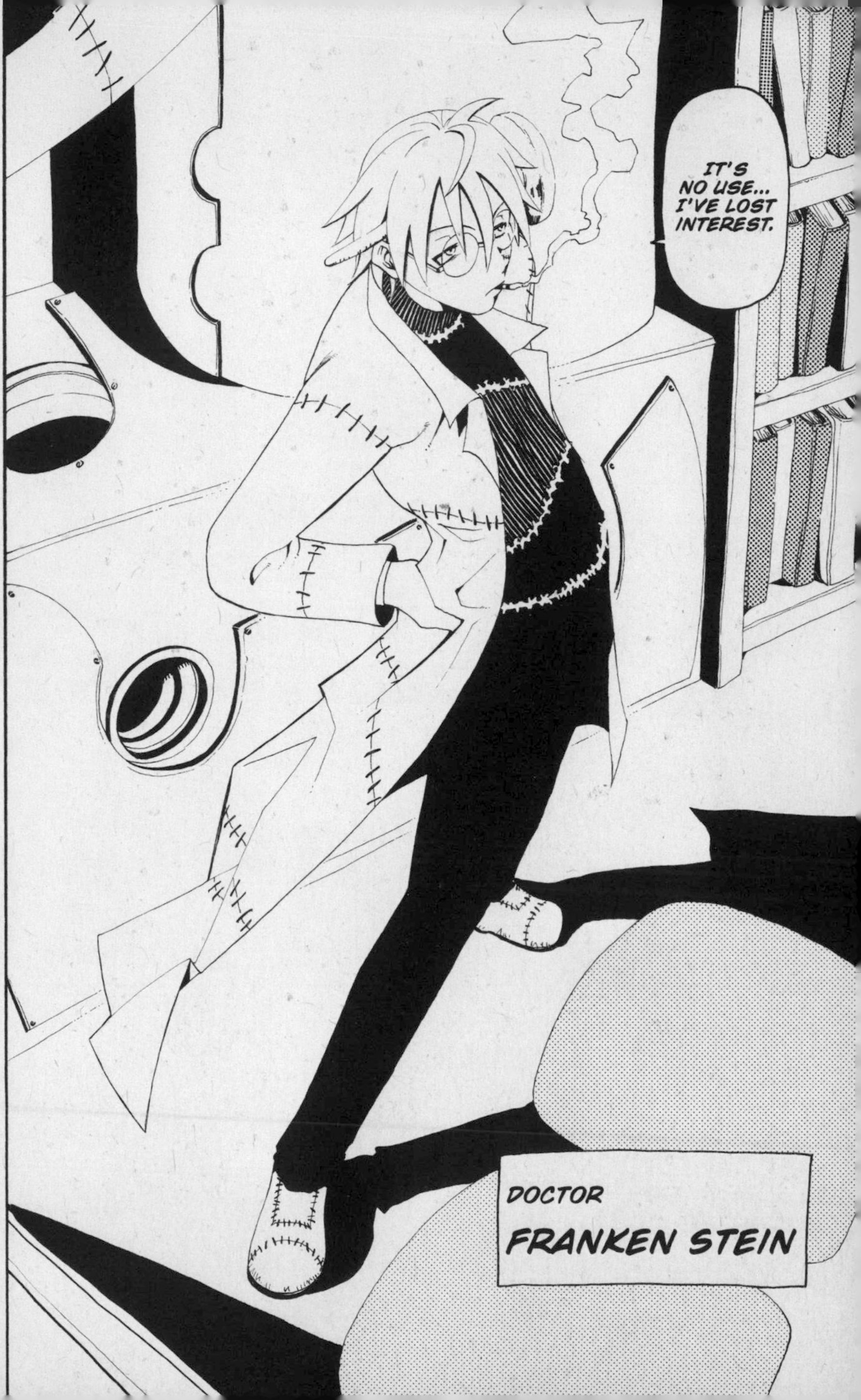
IT'S NO USE... I'VE LOST INTEREST.
DOCTOR
FRANKEN STEIN

DO YOU KNOW WHO THE MEISTER WAS WHO FORGED DEATH SCYTHE-KUN...

...MY MOST POWERFUL WEAPON RIGHT NOW?

HEY?

KID?

HE! HE!

WHAT?

WHAT ABOUT IT?

?

BIG SIS! BIG SIS!

YEAH.

MAKA'S MOTHER, RIGHT?

SFX: PATA (FLAP) PATA

...!!

...MAKA-CHAN'S MOTHER WAS DEATH SCYTHE-KUN'S SECOND PARTNER.

THE TRUTH IS...

YES ...

...WAIT, DO YOU MEAN... HIS FIRST PARTNER WAS...?

197

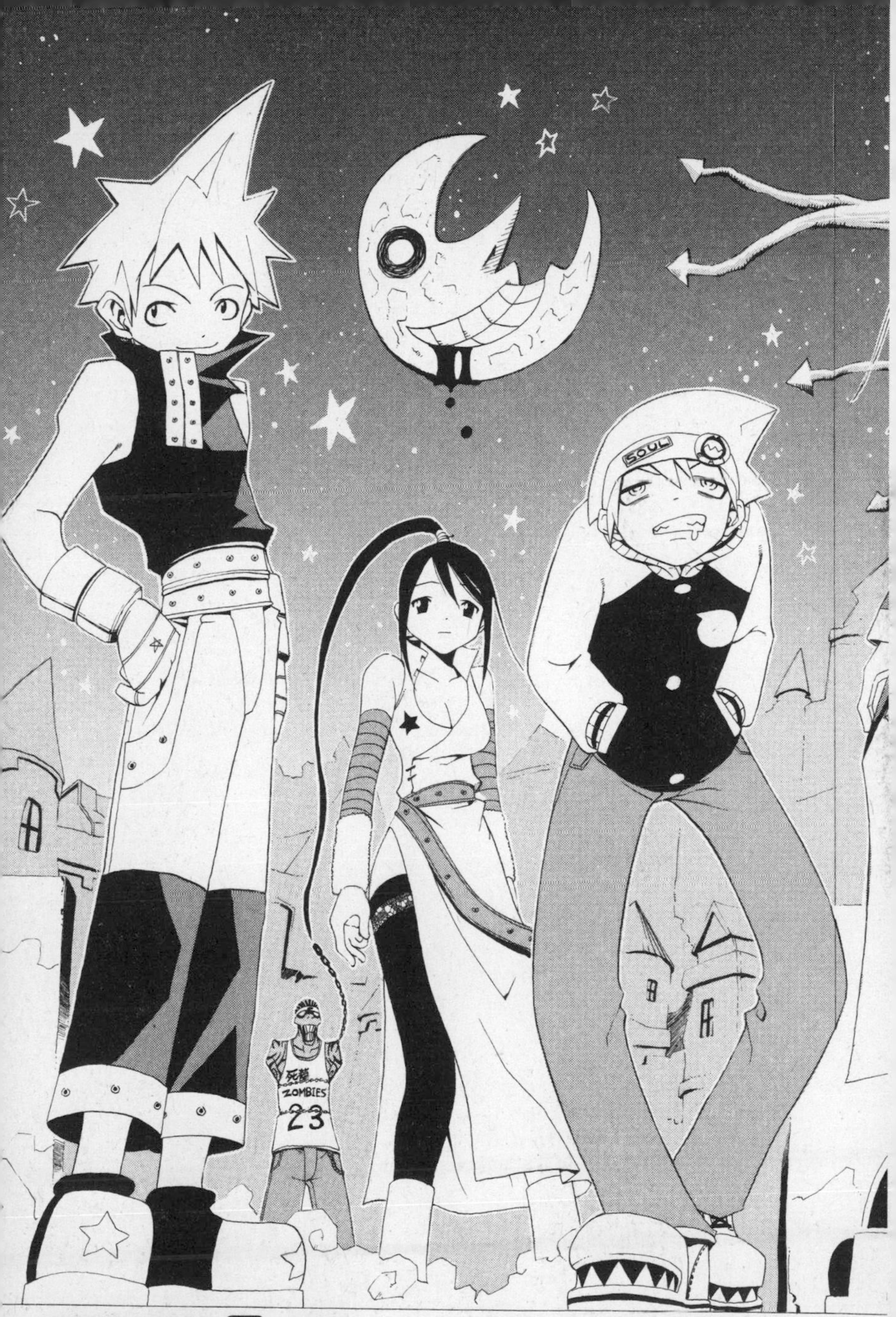
SOUL
ZOMBIES
23

SOUL EATER 1 END

I'M THE MANAGER OF ATSUSHI-YA, USHER. NICE TO MEET YOU.

YO! WELCOME! ♪

TIRED OF THE CRAZY WORLD, THEY COME HERE TO SLUMP IN A CHAIR AND LISTEN TO THE BLUES.

THIS IS ATSUSHI-YA, A BAR THAT'S A GATHERING PLACE FOR ALL MANNER OF STRANGE BASTARDS WHO HAVE A FEW SCREWS LOOSE.

SIGN: KAETTE KITA, ATSUSHI-YA

AT ANY RATE, I'M GLAD TO SEE YOU!! THE FACT THAT YOU WALKED INTO THIS BAR MUST MEAN OUR SOUL WAVELENGTHS ARE IN TUNE!!

IT'S NOT A GREAT DATE SPOT, BUT IT'S A NICE PLACE! MAKE YOURSELF AT HOME.

HE'S EATING THIS LOLLIPOP TO TRY TO LOOK COOL.

THAT'S MY INVINCIBLE BARTENDER AND BODYGUARD!! YOU-SAN!! ALL SHE EVER SAYS IS "MM-HMM♡," BUT SHE'S DASHING HER WAY ALONG THE PATH OF INVINCIBILITY!!

Mm-hmm. ♡

AS YOU CAN SEE, I AM RAT!! DO YOU KNOW WHAT THAT MEANS!?

THE RAT INDUSTRY HAS A LOT OF BIG RIVALS!! THERE'S THE MICE AND ALL THE REST!!

KEH-KEH-KEH. ME? WOULD YOU LIKE TO HEAR MY "AMBITION"? DO YOU REALLY WANT TO HEAR IT!?

NO!! WE'RE NOT AT THAT STAGE YET!! START WITH YOUR NAME!!

WHAT THE HECK ARE YOU!!?

ビクン (JUMP)

KEH-KEH-KEH-KEH-KEH!

I DON'T KNOW ABOUT THAT!!

IF PEOPLE SEE A FILTHY RAT HANGING AROUND MY BAR, IT'LL RUIN ITS REPUTATION!!

SPREAD...

DOKA (PUNT)

MY AMBITION IS TO REIGN ABOVE ALL OF THEM!!! I'M GOING TO START BY TAKING OVER THIS BAR!!!

GOOOO (ROOOAR)

C-C-CAN THIS GUY...USE ZARAKI!!?

PESTI- LENCE = LIKE POWERFUL VIRUSES THAT COME FROM RATS!!

WHAT!?

GUSUN (SNIFFLE)

PON (POP)

I'LL SPREAD PESTILENCE.

HUH!?

WHEN HE TAKES OFF HIS GLASSES, HE TURNS INTO A BIRD.

ALMOST IMMEDIATELY AFTER IT OPENED, ATSUSHI-YA WAS PLAGUED BY DISEASE. IF YOU ARE CONFIDENT YOU HAVE A STRONG IMMUNE SYSTEM, PLEASE STOP BY WHEN IT OPENS AGAIN!

YOU ONLY SAVED YOURSELF? THAT'S DIRTY!!

SHUKO (SHAKE)

SHUKO

MM-HMM...

AT TIMES LIKE THIS, I NEED MY INVINCIBLE BODYGUARD!! YOU-SAN!! DO SOMETHING ABOUT THAT GUY!!

TOTE (STRUT)

TOTE

203

Translation Notes

Page 11
A **shinigami** (literally "death god") is Japan's rough equivalent to the Grim Reaper in Western culture.

When spoken aloud in Japanese, Shinigami-sama's mirror number, **42-42-564**, becomes shini shini koroshi, which translates to "death, death, murder."

Page 18
"But your nose is gushing blood." When a guy gets a nosebleed in manga, it's an indication of sexual excitement.

Page 22
Chupa Cabra's is a reference to the Chupacabra, the legendary monster reportedly seen in Puerto Rico, Mexico, and parts of the United States. It supposedly attacks livestock (especially goats) and sucks their blood.

Page 24
Maka's Blair Witch Project is parodying The Blair Witch Project, a low-budget American horror film released in 1999.

Page 48
Al Capone was an infamous organized-crime boss most active during the 1920s. He was often seen wearing a hat like the one shown and smoking a cigar. He was involved in smuggling and the bootlegging of liquor and was also in control of a prostitution ring. He was eventually convicted of tax evasion.

Page 50
One of the major activities of Al Capone's gang was the bootlegging and sale of alcohol, which is why "**alcohol**" is written on his hat. At the time, America was in the midst of Prohibition, which meant the production and sale of alcohol was banned.

Page 52
"I'm going to start jumping at shadows instead of blending into them." In the original Japanese, Tsubaki uses the term gishinanki, which means to be suspicious of everything, to be paranoid — to jump at shadows. This is a play on anki (literally "dark tool"), which is what Tsubaki is.

Page 53
"Stop with the weird jokes, you bloke!!" In the original Japanese, he says "Hen na share wa yamen shai" (Stop the weird jokes). The "joke" here is that he slurs "yamenasai" (please stop) into "yamen shai," in order to make the end part, "shai," sound kind of like "share" (joke).

Page 56
The name **Mifune** is a reference to Toshiro Mifune, a famous Japanese actor who often played samurai characters. He appeared in many of legendary director Akira Kurosawa's films, including *Yojimbo* ("The Bodyguard").

Page 57
In Japanese, the "cinder" in **Demon Cinder Castle** is written *shinderu*, which can also mean "dead." In this case, the word *shinderu* is written in katakana (a form of Japanese writing often used for transliterating words from non-Japanese languages), so it could also be a a reference to Cinderella, the shortened, transliterated version of which is also *Shinderu* (from *Shinderura*).

Page 93
Lupin is a reference to Arsène Lupin, the gentleman thief who appears in a series of detective/crime novels by French author Maurice LeBlanc. He was also the inspiration for the manga and anime character Lupin the Third.

Page 105
You'll notice that when Liz gets licked by the mummy, she crosses her fingers. This is supposed to be a way to ward off "dirt."

Page 146
Sid-sensei's name is written "Sid" in English, but in Japanese it's written "Shido," spelled with the characters meaning "dead" and "person." Quite an appropriate name for this particular character.

Page 158
Sid-Sensei is saying "***Ohisashiburi-desu***," a common phrase in Japanese that is roughly translated into "long time, no see." However, to make the term polite (as he insists he is), he adds -*desu* at the end, which sounds like "death" in English. He is using a pun by saying "*death*" where he should say "*desu*."

Page 162
Ding dong, DEAD dong. In the original Japanese, Sid-sensei says "*KILL (kiru) koon kaan koon*." "*Kiin koon kaan koon*" is a fairly standard way to represent the sound of school bells in Japanese. But Sid-sensei replaced "*kiin*" with "*kiru*" (kill).

Page 169
Sid-sensei calls his attack **"Living End,"** but written next to the words "Living End" is the phrase "*juuji otoshi*," which means "cross slam."

Page 202
Kaette Kita, which means "Returned" in Japanese, is a reference to *Kaette Kita Ultraman* ("The Return of Ultraman"), a short live-action film made by Daicon Films — a company that would eventually develop into Gainax, a major anime production company.

Usher
When written in Japanese, "Usher" is *Asshaa*, which contains the same letters as Atsushi-ya.

Page 203
Zaraki is the name of an attack spell in the *Dragon Quest* game series.

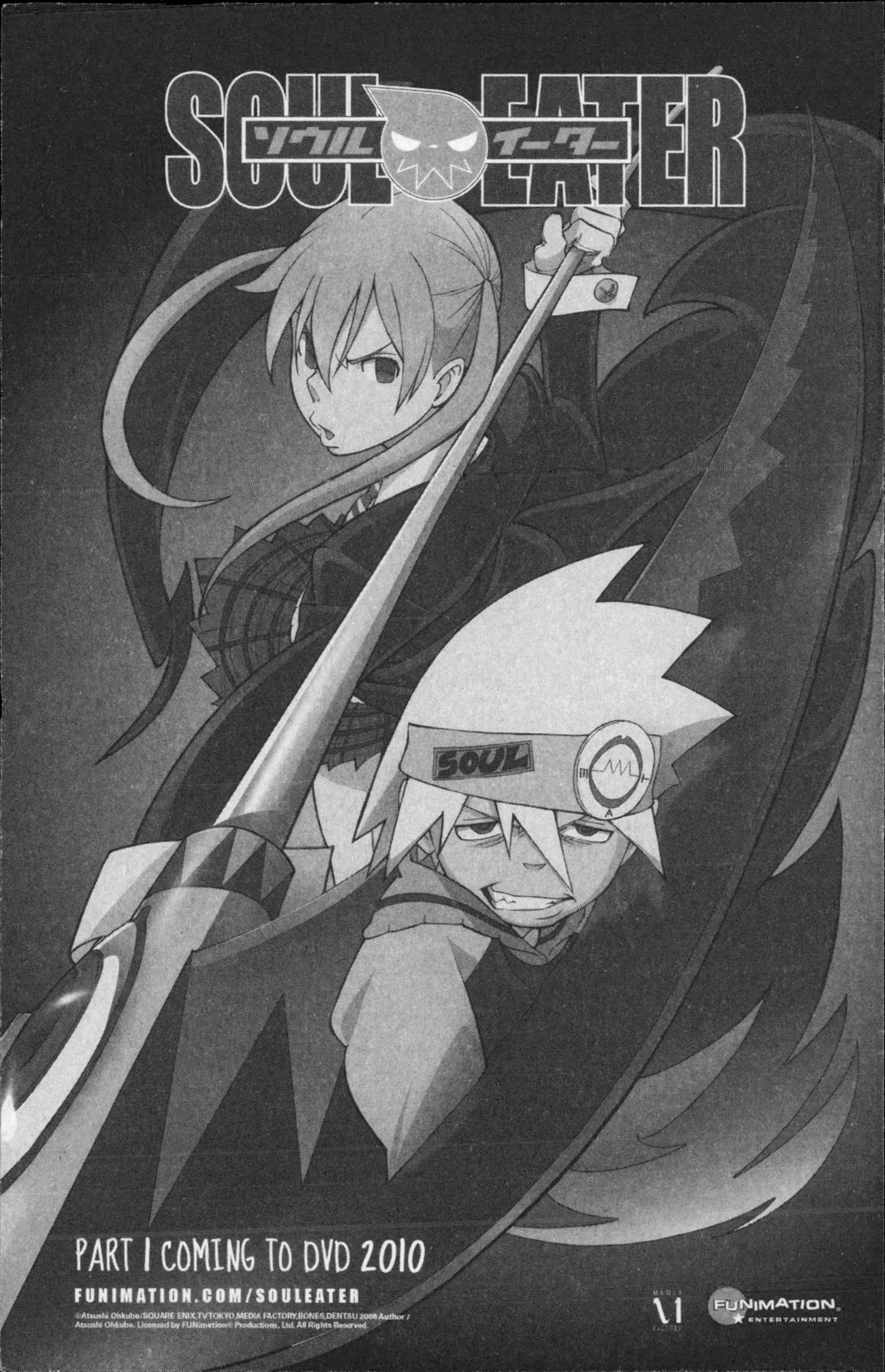
SOUL EATER
ソウルイーター
SOUL
PART I COMING TO DVD 2010
FUNIMATION.COM/SOULEATER
©Atsushi Ohkubo/SQUARE ENIX,TV TOKYO,MEDIA FACTORY,BONES,DENTSU 2008 Author / Atsushi Ohkubo. Licensed by FUNimation® Productions, Ltd. All Rights Reserved.
FUNIMATION ENTERTAINMENT

SOUL EATER ①

ATSUSHI OHKUBO

Translation: Amy Forsyth

Lettering: Alexis Eckerman

SOUL EATER Vol. 1 © 2004 Atsushi Ohkubo / SQUARE ENIX. All rights reserved. First published in Japan in 2004 by SQUARE ENIX CO., LTD. English translation rights arranged with SQUARE ENIX CO., LTD. and Hachette Book Group through Tuttle-Mori Agency, Inc.

Translation © 2009 by SQUARE ENIX CO., LTD.

Yen Press
Hachette Book Group
237 Park Avenue, New York, NY 10017

Visit our websites at www.HachetteBookGroup.com and www.YenPress.com.

Yen Press is an imprint of Hachette Book Group, Inc. The Yen Press name and logo are trademarks of Hachette Book Group, Inc.

First Yen Press Edition: October 2009

ISBN: 978-0-7595-3001-0

10 9 8

BVG

Printed in the United States of America